Contents

Preface

The familiar shapes and forms of our flowers and vegetables differ from those of their ancestors due to man's practice of 'artificial selection' whereby he has tailored the products of nature more closely to his own needs. Over many hundreds of plant generations, this process has been responsible for changing lettuce from a 'dandelion' type of plant into the many hearted forms which we grow today. Similarly, the various cabbage, cauliflower, Brussels sprout etc. have their origins in the large-leaved rosettes which can still be found on the coasts of France and England, cohabiting with the wild radish, parsnip and carrot. Though flowers have been subjected to fewer changes, the results of selection for bloom sizes and colour, length of flowering season etc. have been dramatic.

Within the past 60 years, progress in producing new forms has accelerated greatly due largely to the need for higher yields, quality and disease-resistance, coupled with increasingly sophisticated cultural techniques. The knowledge and experience to produce these advanced types has been gained in many ways; from approved university courses in plant breeding and genetics, from the maintenance of growers' own cultivars by astute observation and selection, through the enthusiasm of amateurs for a particular species of crop and, not least, the desire to obtain financial benefit through the award of plant patents.

The intention of this publication is to enlarge the interest of the A level and Horticultural college student, the enthusiastic amateur gardener or grower etc. by leading them – if they wish – towards the more complex genetic/plant breeding text books. While the basis genetic functions are described, the degree of detail is limited to that which is considered necessary for the satisfactory running and comprehension of a plant-breeding progamme. The essential parts of every programme – selection, breeding system, inbreeding, mass-pollination and seed multiplication – are covered in depth, while the possible approaches to improvement of all flower and vegetable families are considered in detail. Pollination and seed-collection is described, mainly from personal experience, since many pitfalls exist before the operator can be certain that genetically unique seed seed is being formed upon his chosen material.

Because of their wide and increasing use, male sterility, self-incompatibility, and the production of F_1 hybrids are given special mention while, to complete the evaluation of new types, systems of field trialling and analysis are described.

Introduction

The task of meeting the world's increasing demand for food is a continuous one which involves contributions from specialists in many disciplines. Perhaps few contributions are greater, however, than those of the plant and animal breeders whose aim is to introduce and improve types which will grow and flourish more abundantly than their predecessors.

We acknowledge with gratitude, the steady increase in cereal yields of about three per cent per annum over the past 20 years, so that an average yield of 25 cwts per acre has now become 2½ to 3 tons. It is not generally realised, however, that vegetable crops such as Brussels sprout have, over the same period, shown increases from a former 1½ tons per acre to their present 10 tons, autumn cauliflowers from 250 to 1000 crates per acre (not because of smaller crates!), while onions can now be grown overwinter to give yields of up to 20 tons per acre the following August. Less easily definable, but just as positive, are the advances made through the introduction of disease resistance into crops such as dwarf beans, lettuce, peas and tomatoes, or the benefits of preventing crops like beetroot from bolting.

These are measurable advances in crops which have a known value, yet if the virtues of vegetables are left unsung compared with cereals, how much more neglected are the breeders of flowers? Just as an industrial society needs its art forms, so too does the aesthetic side of plant breeding warrant attention – and progress with flower crops has probably matched that of the vegetables.

If we could recall the appearance of park and garden flower beds 25 years ago, the difference between then and now would be very obvious. Our parks are now patterned by flowers which fit ideally the situation in which they have been planted. Every border is full of uniform colour, uniform height, predictable design etc. for the sole reason that flower breeders, having chosen to specialise in particular crops, have made improvements by using precisely the same techniques as those of the vegetable breeders. So we now have undreamed of shades and forms – dwarf hollyhocks and delphiniums, completely uniform perfumed cyclamen, red marigolds, blue roses (but so far no yellow sweet peas), busy lizzie as a colourful border plant – and so on.

While most of these improvements have been brought about by the efforts of professionals, the enthusiastic amateur has also made a large contribution, most often as a result of close observation accompanied by intelligent selection. In spite of limited genetic knowledge (which this monograph hopes to expand), the amateur has had a greater effect than is generally realised on the content of seedsmen's catalogues, through developing plant material in such a way that it eventually reaches the status of a cultivar which can be offered for sale. Many catalogued sweet peas and gladioli have been synthesised by amateurs, new cultivars of chrysanthemums (usually bud sports) and daffodils have been produced privately for years, while one of the most recent examples of successful commercialisation is the colour breakthrough in potentilla, Red Ace.

Today there is even greater encouragement for the breeder through the operation of patents – Plant Breeders Rights.

There is at present, much talk of the need to preserve old cultivars, and to guard or save seed of wild species and ancestral forms for 'gene banks' which could provide genetic variation for the future. If it is possible to encourage more people to develop an interest in plants with a view to producing new genetic types, this in itself will help to create and maintain the hoped-for diversity.

In this sense the 'horticultural' crops have much to offer – they are commonly known and widely grown, while their ancestral forms – wild cabbage, radish, parsnips, beet – are on hand whenever one takes a holiday at the coast. Each species rewards patient research into its breeding system; whether it is capable of setting seed on its own, whether the flowers are attractive to, or are pollinated by, insects; whether the male and female parts of the flower are together or separate, which part matures first, how soon can the seed be harvested and resown, etc. Following this research one must investigate the best ways of commercialising the result – as pure lines, mass-pollinated cultivars or F_1 hybrids.

So many facets present themselves in the production of new plant forms, but the crowning feature is that the result has been produced by one's own decisions and the end product is unique.

PART 1: THE BASIS OF PLANT BREEDING

Pollination and Fertilisation

No matter whether one is interested in breeding flowers or vegetables, all breeding work must start with the flower and must result in the formation of a seed, the fore-runner of a new race or variety of plants.

Seed is produced by the female cells of a plant (the ovules) after they have been fertilised by pollen which is shed in great quantities by the same or different plants. While pollen is only visible to the naked eye when coating the backs of insects, or in occasional dense clouds as from sweetcorn, the ovules are contained in a larger ovary.

At first, the size of the ovary is relative to that of the flower, but after fertilisation it enlarges into a characteristic shape to give pods (peas and beans), *capitulae* (aster, cornflower, lettuce, globe artichoke), capsules (*cyclamen* and poppy), berries etc. Some ovules are relatively unprotected and after fertilisation may be seen upon the flower heads as clusters of single seeds such as candytuft, carrots and parsnips.

Pollination and fertilisation are not the same as one another. Pollination of one plant by another, or with its own pollen, may be carried out by insects or artificially. Unless the pollen is able to germinate on the stigma (the apex of the style), however, fertilisation will not occur.

Under natural conditions, pollination between plants of the same species is usually followed by fertilisation. In those circumstances when pollen is transferred artificially by brush, however, the ovules will be fertilised only if the stigmatic surface is mature and sufficiently receptive to allow penetration. In some species (e.g. *cyclamen*) pollen applied to the stigma in the bud is less likely to produce satisfactory fertilisation than a later application when the flower is fully mature.

On the other hand, flowers of Godetia may appear ready for fertilisation with fully open petals, but until the stigma splits into three segments at the apex, fertilisation cannot take place.

Flower Form

Not all flowers are attractive to insects, yet many which are may not need insects for their pollination. Generally speaking, however, the more involved flower forms are adapted to insect pollination, their unusual shapes having been produced by many generations of evolution. Primitive flowers were much more simple in construction than present types but in the course of evolution slight variations arose. Because some of these were more attractive to insects than others only the 'newer' types were satisfactorily pollinated. In consequence these produced more seed than the others and showed a proportional increase in the population. In subsequent generations more variations would arise, some to be favoured and others neglected, thus setting up an evolving pattern. As the size of plant populations increased so their area of colonisation would spread, new climatic factors would be encountered, and possibly new insect forms which would favour a different flower form.

In this way many diverse flower forms would develop, each proving to be the best adapted to its local environment until another, better adapted, type appeared. Today we can recognise a range of adapted forms from the umbels of carrot and parsnip to the *capitulae* of cineraria and sunflower, the former pollinated by flies and ants, the latter by bees and butterflies while yet other forms such as foxgloves, *antirrhinum* and broad bean are most adapted to bumble bee pollination.

Plant breeders must be aware of the natural system of pollination in the species with which they are working so that they may either encourage the pollinators or copy their system of pollination as closely as possible.

The Reproductive Cycle

A complete life cycle begins with seed germination and ends with the production of seed by the now mature plant. This cycle may range from a few weeks (ephemeral types such as groundsel, *Senecio vulgaris*, which has a number of generations in a year) to a number of years in the case of fruit trees, or a shorter period for herbaceous perennials. Biennial crops such as wallflowers, sweet williams, cabbages and beetroot produce vegetative growth in one season and flowers and seeds in the next. Life cycles may be dramatically altered by certain types of treatment however, and these are discussed in Part II.

As all reproductive cycles in plants have proved themselves by continuing to exist alongside one another, an ideal system is hard to define. In the evolutionary sense, the best system could be regarded as one which allows great variation amongst a large population of individuals – thus giving scope for immediate response to changing environments. The annual or ephemeral forms would best fit this requirement. There is also a case for stability however, so that the species does not respond too rapidly to short periods of change and consequently suffer by abandoning a satisfactory evolutionary niche.

The ideal life cycles, as they affect the plant or the plant breeder and cultivator often differ considerably. The main advantages and disadvantages of each type of reproductive cycle are shown in tables 1A and 1B.

TABLE 1A – THE EFFECT ON THE PLANT OF ITS OWN REPRODUCTIVE CYCLE

Reproductive cycle	Advantages	Disadvantages
Ephemeral	Rapid multiplication of population which allows colonisation of desirable locations and 'swamping' of competitors. Increased opportunity for producing variations in progeny and adaptation to seasonal conditions.	Usually little vegetative growth to smother competitors. Limited genetic stability.

Annual	Completely adapted to seasonal requirements. Seed dormant in adverse conditions. Flowering simultaneously with other plants of the same species.	Susceptible to poor germination or seed-setting conditions.
Biennial	Good vegetative growth and strong competitive ability. Potential for production of larger quantities of seed.	Less chance of genetic change unless long life cycle is compensated by high seed multiplication. Susceptible to destruction in long vegetative stage.
Perennial	Permanently situated in suitable environment. Consistent seed production.	Less opportunity for colonisation by progeny.

TABLE 1B – THE EFFECT OF REPRODUCTIVE CYCLE FROM CULTURAL STANDPOINT

Reproductive cycle	Advantages	Disadvantages
Ephemeral	Frequent crops, but not always easy or convenient to harvest.	Embarrassment as 'weeds'. Too short a period for volume harvest.
Annual	Regular, predictable cycle – allowing cultural preparation.	Resowing annually. Single seed-harvest entails some risk.
Biennial	Regular cropping sequence – earlier than annual types in year following sowing. Good weed competitor.	Present in ground for too long a period (vegetables). A blank first year (flowers).
Perennial	Continuous productivity. Allows long-term planning of cropping system. Ease of vegetative (clonal) multiplication.	Long period before initiation of cropping. Wasteful crops if frequent replacement is required due to disease etc. effects. Labour saving and predictable (flowers).

From the genetical point of view each form of reproductive cycle has a particular advantage, and the numbers of seeds produced under each system are probably similar. The plant breeder of annual crops may make no faster progress than the breeder of perennials since his material must 'settle down' genetically after a few generations of seed production and testing. The breeder of perennials may succeed in producing the right types with his first cross and then can propagate the exact form continuously by vegetative means.

Basic Genetics

The Control of Heredity

All living matter is composed of cells – either singly, in clusters or in highly developed groups which, in plants, form tissues such as leaves, flowers, stems, roots, fruit etc. Simple cells have evolved over many years and, grouped with others, have become specialised in such a way that those in the underground part of a plant for example, develop roots to absorb water, while others produce leaves to trap and use sunlight.

If we consider a complete, though relatively simple, organism such as a Puffball (with no apparent roots, stems or flowers), it is just as important that its offspring should be puffballs as it is that an Oak or an onion should give rise only to further oaks or onions. The factors which determine the form taken by any living creature are contained within the cell, in an organising body known as the nucleus.

One nucleus is present in every cell, with minor exceptions such as leaf hairs, and even though they may be working to produce different end-products in different parts of the organism, each possesses the same information for total plant growth. For this reason, a leaf of Begonia will produce roots when forced to do so, and from these a number of young, identical, plantlets can be derived. Other, more common, methods of vegetative propagation encourage leafy cuttings (which may have been formed far above ground level) to produce roots; this they are able to do since they contain the appropriate genetic information. Alternatively, roots and tubers have access to the genetic information which allows them to form stems, flowers and fruit.

If the transmitted genetic information is not accurate plants will probably develop erratically and fail to flourish – such accuracy is the responsibility of the contents of the nucleus, the chromosomes and genes.

Chromosomes and Genes

In any plant or animal the number of chromosomes in a cell nucleus is characteristic of that organism and of the group or species to which it belongs. Every cell nucleus, with the exception of the reproductive cells and some others as already mentioned, comprises the same number – and within the chromosomes lie the genes. These are the real controllers, working together to dictate activities within the cell (and therefore the whole organism), even giving instructions which influence the immediate behaviour of the chromosomes on which they are borne.

4

The total content of genes in an organism is unknown, mainly because they exist in large numbers, their activities overlap and inter-relate, and they cannot be observed microscopically. On the other hand, the chromosomes are countable and have a characteristic number and shape for each species. The nucleus of potato cells for example has 48 chromosomes, that of a cabbage 18, globe artichoke 34, primrose and runner bean 22, strawberry 56 and wallflower 14. It will be noticed that all chromosomes are present in even numbers – a fact which is basic to the process of sexual reproduction.

Cell Duplication (Mitosis)

Complete plants, with their diversity of structures but constancy of chromosome numbers, are built up in a cellular fashion by the process of mitosis. Chromosomes occupy the centre of a 'mitotic' cell and each begins to split in half longitudinally. The last part to split, the centromere, remains in the central part of the cell while the 'arms' of its split chromosome move away in opposite directions from one another. Eventually (and almost simultaneously) each centromere too splits in half, the two groups of chromosomes move to opposite ends of the cell and coalesce independently to form a pair of nuclei where there was previously only one. The wall of the large cell becomes constricted while the nuclear movements are in progress until it physically separates the identical nuclei from one another. As mitosis occurs at the same time in many other cells, there is a continual increase in genetic material; growth of the plant follows during development of the newly formed cells.

Formation of Reproductive Cells (Meiosis)

At the reproductive or flowering stage in the life cycle a new type of cell division occurs, leading to the formation of pollen grains and ovules. The new plant which will result from the fusion of the ovule and pollen grain (via the seed) comprises cells with the same number of chromosomes as its parents. It therefore follows that the chromosome number of both pollen and ovules must be reduced by half in some way. This is achieved during the process of 'meiosis' in the flowering organs when reproductive cells are formed.

Each chromosome in a normal cell has an identical partner and, instead of splitting longitudinally as in mitosis, the partners pair together, exchange genetic material and ultimately move away from each other to the opposite end of the cell. After separation of all paired chromosomes within the cell, the two new chromosome groups are divided by a cell wall. One further, *mitotic*-type division follows immediately so that the original cell and its nucleus has now become four, each containing half the normal chromosome number.

Cytoplasm

As well as chromosomes and their genes, cells also contain a further substance known as cytoplasm. When chromosomes are released from their nuclear envelope into the body of the cell (during either mitosis or meiosis) they come into direct contact with the surrounding cytoplasm and are accompanied by it when the new cell wall is formed. Although the effect of the cytoplasm is negligible compared with that of the genes it nevertheless comprises some genetic material (plasmagenes) and can modify, in some degree, the effect normally produced by the nuclear material. This effect may be observed in some (though by no means all) cross-pollinations because of a difference in the two progenies when a plant is used separately as a female and then as a male for the same cross. While pollen grains contain only minute quantities of cytoplasm, ovules have considerably more because they are attached to the maternal tissue, and the mother plant may thus have an extra influence on the expression of characters in the cross-fertilised offspring.

Genetic Inheritance

If there are no marked cytoplasmic influences, the behaviour of genes is quite predictable – especially if they are the types known as major genes, i.e. those having a major effect upon the expression of a character.

The gene is formed as two parts, each of which is present in the same position on each of a pair of chromosomes. The two parts (or alleles) may produce the same or different responses in the visual expression of a character according to their individual 'strengths'. Thus a gene for 'flower colour' in *Brassicas* will be present as two alleles. If a plant produced yellow flowers, each allele could be shown by experiment to be identical. If on the other hand, the *Brassica* flowers were white we could establish either that one 'white' and one 'yellow' allele were present in combination, or that both alleles were 'white'. The extra strength of the 'white' allele means that it is DOMINANT, while the 'yellow' allele cannot express itself in the presence of its 'white' partner and is known as the RECESSIVE gene.

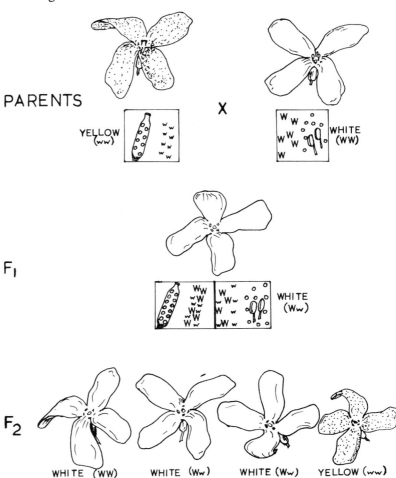

Fig 1. Inheritance of flower colour, controlled by a single major gene. (Monogenic inheritance. White dominant. Yellow recessive).

This form of behaviour, the control of a single characteristic by a single gene, is the simplest example of genetic inheritance – from which all other forms of inheritance follow. Using flower colour in *Brassicas* (Cabbage, Cauliflower, Brussels sprout etc.) as an example, genetic symbols *WW* may be given to the dominant 'white' gene (comprising two alleles i.e., 2 W's) while the yellow recessive gene is denoted not as '*y*' but as *ww* – thus implying recessivity to the *W* gene. The system of inheritance of flower colour is illustrated in Figure 1. The principle in this example shows that genes segregate independently of one another, in this case to give a 3:1 ratio of white to yellow flowered plants in the F_2 generation.

The Exchange of Genetic Material; (crossing-over)

Results such as those outlined above are possible only if the chromosomes which pair together at meiosis exchange some of their gene material. By doing this, the reproductive tissues ensure that all ovules or pollen grains (the gametes), will differ genetically from one another as well as having half the chromosome number of the mother plant, Figure 2 gives a diagrammatic example of pairing and crossing-over between 'sister' chromosomes A and B, each having split into two *chromatids*, in readiness for the increase of two cells to four, as described previously. At the point where the cross-over takes place the adjacent chromatids break and exchange partners with one another; in this way new combinations of genes are formed.

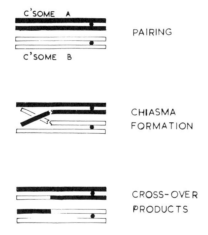

C'SOME A
C'SOME B
PAIRING

CHIASMA
FORMATION

CROSS-OVER
PRODUCTS

Fig 2. Chromosome pairing, with chromatid breakage and crossing-over at meiosis.

The same process is followed by every pair of chromosomes within the nucleus simultaneously until eventually the chromosomes move towards opposite ends of the cell, separating last of all at the *chiasma*, or crossover point. The second division to take place resembles that of mitosis when the chromosome splits lengthwise into two chromatids. Thus, of the four cells now formed, two will contain a chromosome with its original genetic constitution while the other two cells will contain the recombined forms.

Due to the number of chromosomes involved, and the reshuffling of genes at meiosis, it is almost impossible that any pollen grains or ovules should have identical genetic constitutions – unless dictated by the breeding system as discussed later.

To illustrate the effects of crossing-over, Figure 3 makes the assumption that five genes control easily identifiable qualitative characters in a flower species. From a cross-pollination of two true-breeding parents an F_1 *hybrid* (the *heterozygote*) has been produced with coloured flowers, coloured stem, long seed pods, smooth-edged, hairy leaves and hairy stem. For the purpose of this example it is assumed that all dominant alleles are present on one chromosome and all recessive on its partner. It is also assumed that seed of the next generation has been formed by the fusion of identical gametes – most improbable situations in nature. Crossovers will be less likely to occur near the centromere – the attachment of the chromatids.

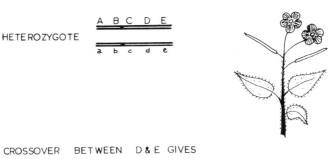

HETEROZYGOTE

A B C D E

a b c d e

CROSSOVER BETWEEN D & E GIVES
4 GAMETES WHICH, WE WILL ASSUME,
FERTILISE GENETICALLY IDENTICAL OVULES

ABCDE   ABCDe   abcdE   abcde

Fig 3. The effect of crossing-over between genes D and E (example 1) and C and D (example 2) on the phenotype of a plant where:
A = Coloured flowers
a = white flowers
B = Long seed pods
b = short seed pods
C = Entire leaves
c = 'ragged' leaves
D = Hairy leaves & stem
d = hairless leaves & stem
E = Coloured stem
e = green stem
For these examples it is assumed that each gamete (pollen grain or ovule) fuses with one which is genetically identical.

CROSSOVER BETWEEN C & D GIVES :

ABCDE   ABCde   abcDE   abcde

AS ABOVE   AS ABOVE

Depending upon the position of the crossover (or chiasma), the re-assortment of genes will result in the production of predictable new plant forms in the F_2 generation. In this example we should never expect to find progeny with long seed pods and 'ragged' leaves or short seed pods and smooth-edged leaves, however, since the genes controlling these characters lie either side of and close to, the centromere and will not be subject to cross over.

The segregation of characters controlled by major genes can be further studied in the chequer-board below using as our example the original pea experiment of Mendel from which the genetic theory of plant-breeding was derived. Plate 1 shows the within-pod segregation of round and wrinkled seed. It can be seen from the chequer board that, when character expression is controlled by two major genes, the crossing together of two distinct plant types can lead to the production of an additional two forms in the F_2 or segregating generation. If round-seeded dwarf plants (RRtt) had been used initially to cross with tall wrinkled-seeded types (rrTT) the F_1 generation (RrTt) round-seeded tall plants would be different from either parent since each differed by a dominant gene.

Plate 1. within-pod segregation for round and wrinkled seed of peas. Round seeded dominant, wrinkled seeded recessive.

PEAS. ROUND SEEDED TALL PLANTS (RRTT) X WRINKLED SEEDED DWARF PLANTS (rrtt)

F_1 RrTt

F_2 MALE (♂) GAMETES

		RT	Rt	rT	rt
	RT	RRTT	RRTt	RrTT	RrTt
FEMALE (♀) GAMETES	Rt	RRTt	RRtt	RrTt	Rrtt
	rT	RrTT	RrTt	rrTT	rrTt
	rt	RrTt	Rrtt	rrTt	rrtt

9 ROUND TALL: 3 ROUND DWF: 3 WRINKLED TALL: 1 WRINKLED DWF

In the F_2 generation in our example nine plants resemble the dominant carrying parent in external features. Six plants, in two groups of three, are different from parental forms and only one plant (bearing both recessive genes) resembles the recessive parent. Only the *homozygous* plants will reproduce their kind in the next generation, the *heterozygotes* will undergo further segregation to give either a similar 9:3:3:1 ratio or, if one of the two major genes is *homozygous* (e.g. rrTt), no segregation will occur for one character but a 3:1 ratio will be produced for the other. Homozygotes reproduce themselves exactly, heterozygotes inevitably produce an assortment in the next generation. Further ratios (knowledge of which is vital to the plant breeder when studying variability) may be produced by major genes and these are explained, together with more complicated practical genetics, in Appendix 2.

It becomes progressively more difficult to identify the effects of major genes   9 when more than three are involved in character expression, especially when some may be more subject to environmental modifications than others. The list of known major genes in plants runs into thousands and their particular value lies in producing disease resistance in F_1 hybrids, in identification by marker genes, and other practical effects which are discussed later.

Various examples of major genes (and their corresponding recessives) in horticultural crops are given in Table 2.

TABLE 2 – EXAMPLES OF MAJOR GENES IN HORTICULTURAL CROPS

S = Identified in seedling stage (most useful forms)
M = Identified in mature plant only (least useful 'markers')

| | | Character | |
	Dominant	Recessive	Stage of Identification
Vegetables			
Beans	Climbing habit	Dwarf	S
Broad Beans	Coloured flowers		M
	stipules	No colour	M
	stem		S
Brassicas	White flowers	Yellow flowers	M
	Waxy foliage	Glossy foliage	S
Celery	Green leaf stalks	Yellow leaf stalks	S
Tomatoes	Normal leaf	'Potato' leaf	S
	Purple stem	Green stem	S
	Tall habit	Dwarf	M
	Red fruit	Yellow fruit	M
Flowers			
Alyssum	Green leaves	Variegated leaves	S
Antirrhinum	Red leaves	Green leaves	S
	Double flowers	Single flowers	M
Cyclamen	Perfume	No perfume	M
	Silver leaves	Green leaves	S
Salvia	Red flowers	White flowers	M
Stock	Dark cotyledons	Light cotyledons	S

Polygenes

The plant characters which are the concern of modern plant breeders are, generally, not under the control of major genes but of genes which, by themselves, have only a small effect. When aggregated together in one plant these minor, or POLYGENES, are able, nevertheless, to produce a very marked response upon the character in question. The effects of these genes are *quantitative* as opposed to the *qualitative* major genes and they commonly control those characters which vary continuously such as yield, height, shape, or flowering period.

Instead of gene W as used to illustrate single-gene segregation in Figure 1 a large number of minor or polygenes affecting the same character could together produce the same degree of dominance as the original W. These polygenes, however, would be located in numerous positions on any number of the chromosomes and their reassortment during meiosis and subsequent divisions would inevitably reduce the overall degree of dominance.

If white and yellow flower colours were under polygenic rather than major gene control, the sharp distinction between the two colours would disappear and a form of 'blended' inheritance would be evident. Although a large number of genes would be involved in producing a single characteristic (in this instance, flower colour) they would, nevertheless still be subject to the same laws of inheritance as elaborated in Appendix 3.

The reason that segregation of polygenes (or multiple factors) would be less easily defined than that for major genes can be illustrated by the following comparative examples.

Flower colour
Major gene inheritance (W = white; w = yellow)
Parents: ww x WW (yellow x white)
F_1 : Ww (white)
F_2 : WW Ww Ww ww (3 white : 1 yellow)

Polygenic inheritance
(A to J produce whiteness in differing strengths
 A = 10 units, B = 9 units ... J = 1 unit

 a to j produce yellowness in differing strengths
 a = 10 units, b = 9 units ... j = 1 unit)

Parents: aabbccddeeffgghhiijj x AABBCCDDEEFFGGHHIIJJ (yellow x white)
F_1: AaBbCcDdEeFfGgHhIiJj (white)
F_2: (Many alternatives according to segregation)
eg. (a) AAbbbccDdEEFfggHHiiJj   = 32 unitsfor whiteness
                                   23 units for yellowness

  (b) AabbCCddEEFfGgHhIIjj   = 38 units for whiteness
                               17 units for yellowness

  (c) aaBBccddEeFfGgHhIiJJ   = 30 units for whiteness
                               25 units for yellowness

Because dominance and recessiveness are as applicable to a polygenic system as to one controlled by major genes, the 'yellowness' effect can be produced by recessive genes only when homozygous. The most common method of illustrating polygenic inheritance is to draw a graph where the number of individuals (or their products) in a hybrid population is plotted against the characteristic being measured. Thus 617 fruits of an F_1 hybrid tomato cultivar were weighed to give the distribution of sizes shown in Plate 2.

By comparing the superimposed graph (frequency distribution) with that for the parents a visual assessment of the dominance of a character can be obtained. The hybrid graph and the mean (or average) of its components will show greater resemblance to the 'dominant' parent than the 'recessive' if the measured characteristic is controlled by largely dominant genes.

Although the smaller-fruited parent is missing from the photograph because it matured too late, slightly greater dominance was shown by the heavier-fruited parent as can be surmised from the two real means and the postulated mean (derived from the harvest taken later).

11

Plate 2. The effect of poly enic inheritance on fruit size in tomato. Size grading of F_1 hybrid (foreground) compared with that of the heavier parent (top right). Lighter fruited parent matured too late, but its size distribution is postulated top left.

Genotype and Phenotype

Whether characters are controlled by major genes or polygenes, the genetic constitution of an individual cannot be determined directly by observation. Because of modifications imposed by the environment, the external appearance, or *phenotype*, does not completely reflect its genetic constitution or *genotype*. While the judgement of a crop is based upon what we see, the real value of plants as parents or as future breeding material can only be studied objectively through their *genotypes*; and this requires the raising of progeny – the essence of any breeding programme.

Breeding Systems

Practical Applications of Genetic Theory

In horticultural as with agricultural species, crops are raised both sexually (seed) and asexually (cuttings or plants). The proportion of species propagated vegetatively for horticulture is considerably higher than that for agriculture, however, (despite the large acreage of potatoes) because of the popularity of herbaceous and bulb species. Whether propagated sexually or asexually, however, improvement by plant breeding can be accomplished only by sexual means.

Improvement of asexual types can be achieved in one generation, since the form which will eventually be commercialised can be propagated directly, as soon as a successful fertilisation is recognised. Improvement of the sexual forms continues through a number of generations, however, during which period the best types are selected from segregating material. (Exceptions to this generalised rule are mentioned in Appendix 1.)

Whatever the technique, the ultimate product will take about the same time to reach a commercial stage because of the need to raise sufficient material for sale.

TABLE 3

Period needed to breed and commercialise new cultivars which are normally propagated vegetatively or by seed.

Examples: Roses and Salvia

	Roses – vegetatively propagated	*Salvia – sexually propagated*
Year 1	Cross made	Cross made
Year 2	F_1 plant selected on basis of seedling performance.	F_1 progeny seeded (no selection).
Year 3	Three buds propagated to root stocks.	F_2 Progeny grown, selections made and seeded.
Year 4	Further propagation to 100 ? root stocks.	F_3 Single F_2 plant gives approx. 200-400 seeds.
Year 5	Quality acceptance trials and further budding.	F_4 Further selection from 200-400 plants.
Year 6	Acceptance, budding accelerated on commercial scale.	F_5 Selections seeded together but some segregation still occurring.
Year 7	Acceptance, budding accelerated on commercial scale.	F_6 Multiplication of desired type, small percentage of offtypes discarded before flowering.

Year 8	Acceptance, budding accelerated on commercial scale.	F_7	Commercial multiplication of homozygous material.
Year 9	First commercial release on three year old bushes.	F_8	Release this year in small quantities or year 10 in large.

Variations to this timetable can of course be made, depending upon the degree of urgency for release of the variety to the trade, the need for purity, the need to produce large, good growing vegetative plants etc. Some sexually propagated crops may reach the cultivar stage more quickly by shortening the generation time through the use of glasshouses and added illumination, but selection standards are correspondingly less efficient.

Inbreeding and Outbreeding

To give satisfactory conditions for fertilisation, numerous pollen grains should be present on the stigma regardless of the number of ovules within the ovary. Whatever the breeding system, it does not alter the fact that each seed is produced as a result of fertilisation by a single pollen grain only.

The breeding systems of plants fall mainly into two classes – those which are normally self-pollinated (i.e. inbreeding types) and those which produce seed only after cross-pollination (outbreeders). Many species have an intermediate breeding system with varying proportions of crossing and selfing, however, although the tendency is usually towards one or other of the extremes. Species which normally reproduce themselves by inbreeding may, with a change of environment, resort to some degree of cross-fertilisation.

Under normal flowering conditions, cross-fertilisation in lettuce rarely exccceds one per cent, but up to ten per cent hybrids may be produced (because of the presence of higher numbers of pollinating insects) when flowers are open in late Summer. Conversely, some outbreeders may resort to self-fertilisation under circumstances which do not favour cross-pollination. Cornflower and winter cauliflower are normally insect-pollinated but fertilise themselves when insects are absent. One of the easiest ways to determine whether or not a species normally inbreeds is to cover the inflorescence with a porous cellophane bag. As long as the inflorescence has remained healthy, the plant will be shown to be capable of some inbreeding if the flower heads ultimately set seed while still protected from insects.

Categories known as 'obligate' and 'facultative' pollinators can be recognised. Obligate inbreeders are rarely cross-fertilised, while obligate outbreeders are normally cross-fertilised because of the presence of a built-in system preventing self-pollination. Within the obligate systems most plants conform to the general pattern of pollination and fertilisation behaviour. Crops, plants or types with a facultative breeding system, however, tend to reproduce either as inbreeders or outbreeders but are quite capable of adopting the characteristics of the opposite system according to the need at the specific time of pollination. Thus, in the large and versatile *Brassica oleracea* species, Brussels sprout and sprouting broccoli cultivars tend to be facultative outbreeders (with some obligate) while early summer cauliflowers are very strongly orientated towards inbreeding, though this is not obligatory. Within the two former *Brassicas*, single plants can be found which are as highly self-fertile as the summer cauliflowers, while the summer cauliflowers themselves comprise cultivars and plants which may be preferentially cross-fertilised.

Although Table 4 classifies species on their general breeding systems the genetic variation within most species or crops is such that the generalisations

14

should not be taken for granted and tests should be made on a sample of the selected population before designing a comprehensive programme.

TABLE 4
GENERALISED BREEDING SYSTEMS, SHOWING ALTERNATIVE TRENDS (ARROWED)

Inbreeder	Preferentially an inbreeder	Preferentially an outbreeder		Outbreeder
Impatiens	Antirrhinum	Ageratum	←	Alyssum
Sweet Pea	Aster	Anemone	←	Aquilegia
Dwarf Bean	Dahlia	Cornflower		Begonia
Garden Pea	Salpiglossis	Cyclamen	←	Cineraria
Lettuce	Salvia →	Delphinium		Petunia
Tomato	Wallflower	Marigold	←	Polyanthus
	Broad Bean →	Verbena	←	Primula
	Spring Cabbage →	Brussels Sprout	←	Asparagus
	Summer Cauliflower	Summer Cabbage		Spinach
	Leek	Winter Cabbage		Sweet Corn
	Swede	Carrot		
		Autumn Cauliflower		
		Winter Cauliflower		
		Celery		
		Cucumber		
		Curly Kale		
		Kohl Rabi		
		Marrow		
		Onion		
		Parsnip		
		Radish		
		Runner Bean		
		Sprouting Broccoli		
		Turnip		

Although this table comprises only a small proportion of plant species, the majority tend to be facultative outbreeders, probably reflecting the situation over a wider range in nature. The tendency towards outcrossing is present (and preserves the genetic variation which is essential for a species to evolve) but, when pollinating insects are absent, such species may still produce seed by selfing.

The Inbreeding System

In spite of the fact that their floral morphology may be adapted for insect pollination numerous species are, nevertheless, obligate or semi-obligate inbreeders. Dwarf beans, peas, sweet peas and Salvia each have flowers which have obviously been derived from cross-fertilising ancestors, yet self-fertilisation is the conventional mode of reproduction.

It is generally considered that natural inbreeding species have been derived from outbreeding ancestors which were able to survive, proliferate and colonise when isolated individually. Being then adapted to the environment, further change by outbreeding may have become unnecessary. Horticulturally, inbreeding types have been favoured because of man's search for uniformity, while an associated benefit is that inbreeders tend also to be annuals, thus giving regular crops. Cultivars of inbreeding species are usually recognisable by their extremely uniform phenotype, are known as pure lines and are genetically homozygous.

In spite of the fact that progeny of an inbreeding line will closely resemble the parental type, however, not all inbred cultivars are uniform. If a cultivar is composed of a mixture of pure lines the positioning of plant types in the field will be random, and the cultivar will appear to have the variability associated with that of a true *genetic* admixture. If seed is harvested separately from single plants and sown as individual progenies in rows, there should be extreme uniformity within lines but dissimilarity between them. Thus, heterogeneity or lack of uniformity on a field scale cannot be attributed solely to cross-pollination.

Obligate Inbreeders

Obligate inbreeders are reliable as field crops because their performance is usually predictable. Variation is likely to occur only through seed admixture as described above, mutation or, even for obligate inbreeders, a small percentage of cross-fertilisation. Because of the normal uniformity, any offtypes within the crop can be readily identified and removed. Species adapted to inbreeding retain their vigour through successive generations. Inbreeding produces genetic homozygosity – and this, over many years, will have revealed many gene combinations which, in the heterozygous recessive state, would be masked by their better adapted dominant alleles. Any plants carrying undesirable homozygous genes would be removed from the general population in the build-up towards a cultivar.

Facultative Inbreeders

These tend to show slightly less uniformity (homogeneity) on a field scale because of the tendency towards some outcrossing between neighbouring plants according to seasonal and environmental influences. Crops of Broad beans for example, appear uniform but, when compared with a crop of dwarf beans, the uniformity is less apparent. Up to 30 per cent outcrossing occurs regularly in Broad beans and, in the variety Triple White in particular, off-types from crosses with coloured beans can occasionally be identified. Since this contamination would probably have occurred through crossing between two isolated crops, the degree of crossing *within* the Broad bean crop can be appreciated. If occasional rogues are not quickly removed from a 'contaminated' Triple White crop being grown for seed, introgression (or infiltration) of 'foreign' genes will occur and their removal in later generations will be almost impossible.

The loss of vigour associated with inbreeding has been overcome in obligate inbreeders, but facultative inbreeders are subject to some inbreeding depression although the degree is difficult to determine. Since inbreeders can show hybrid vigour when crossed together to produce an F_1, the yield or abundance of flowers of most facultative inbreeders probably benefit by the presence of a small proportion of hybrids. However, when selfed, the progenies of these hybrids will suffer inbreeding depression. In each generation therefore, a cultivar will be in a state of balance – the majority of plants will be inbred while a minority will be hybrid. The net effect on yield will probably be unnoticed and crop stability will be maintained year after year.

Cleistogamy – the guaranteed inbreeding system

16 A very restricted number of species (none of which is used horticulturally in

Britain), have developed the inbreeding facility to such a degree that self-pollination occurs before the flower opens – thus thwarting any subsequent efforts at cross-pollination by insects. Because the system evolved in the distant past, progenies are genetically identical to their parents – all variation having disappeared.

Apomixis

Found in some blackberries and in many citrus species, is a rare reproductive system. It occurs as a form of inbreeding where seed formation takes place in the absence of pollen grains or due to the stimulating presence of pollen grains which do not actually fertilise the ovule. It is thought to occur occasionally in some *compositae* such as marigolds, but unless the plants in which it takes place are genetically *heterozygous* the apomictic behaviour is undetectable and may be confused with normal self-fertilisation.

The Outbreeding System

Obligate outbreeders are rare in horticultural crops since most cross-pollinated cultivars contain a small proportion of selfed seed. Crops which may be regarded as obligate outbreeders are those in which the two sexes are on separate plants (dioecious) while monoecious plants, with male and female flowers borne separately upon the same plant, are also more likely to be cross – than self-fertilised. Dioecy is the general breeding system in spinach and asparagus while marrow, cucumber and begonia are monoecious. In spite of such sexual differentiation, hermaphrodite plants can be found in most crops of asparagus and spinach, thus increasing the chance of some self-fertilisation. In the monoecious forms there is no inhibitory mechanism to prevent self-pollen from fertilising ovules in a female flower of the same plant. Nevertheless, difference in flower maturity (time of pollen production i.e. anthesis, and of female receptivity) tend to encourage cross-pollination and fertilisation between different plants.

In spite of the separation of the sexes, obligate outbreeding may be harder to achieve than in some hermaphrodite flower forms. Petunia plants, for example, are commonly unable to set seed if pollinated with their own pollen because of the presence of a self-incompatibility system which favours pollen from other plants. Other species, mainly *Umbelliferae* such as carrots and parsnips, are completely self-fertile but individual flowers shed their pollen before the stigmas are receptive (protandry), thus encouraging outcrossing. Here also the cross-breeding system tends to break down, however, as flowers on a single umbel mature over an extended period while other umbels of the same plant prolong the total maturity period still further. Thus, the isolation of stigmas of umbelliferous flowers from pollen of other flowers on the same plant is never totally achieved. A further example of species forced to cross-pollinate may be found in the Primula. Here 'pin' plants with long style and short anthers cannot be self-fertilised but must be cross-fertilised by pollen from the long anthers of short-styled 'thrum' plants. These plants in turn must be fertilised by 'pins'.

Although outbreeders tend to possess floral modifications which encourage cross-pollination, self-fertilisation is unlikely to be prevented unless the flower forms are associated with an incompatibility system such as that of Petunia. Pollinating insects tend to concentrate upon flower heads of individual plants

17

Plate 3. Separate plants of
spinach showing Dioecy:
Female plant left, Male plant
right.

before moving to neighbouring plants and it is therefore axiomatic that self-pollen is more likely to be deposited on the stigmas than 'foreign' pollen.

While species or crops may be classed as outbreeders it is apparent that circumstances seldom arise which completely and continually prohibit self-fertilisation. In this respect, inbreeding systems are more able to achieve their extreme expression than outbreeding systems.

The value of outbreeding in maintaining variability is probably more beneficial when coupled with a small degree of inbreeding since some of the inherent defects can then be exhibited and, to some extent, eliminated. Under natural conditions the population would tend to attain a steady level of competence, fully adapted to the environment, with built-in-variability to mould itself to any new requirements.

Self-incompatibility

Self-incompatibility is a major factor in the preservation of any outbreeding system and must therefore be described in detail under the general heading of outbreeders. Plants which exhibit self-incompatibility do so because of their inability to set seed when mature flowers are pollinated with pollen from the same plant. Self-incompatibility may be complete or may be modified to some degree (often by differing environments) when a small proportion of self seed is set, but the general term 'incompatibility' is still considered applicable. The reaction in plants is in direct contrast to that of foreign tissue rejection in animals, since antagonism occurs between the style and pollen grains of the same individual.

The two main forms of self-incompatibility are gametophytic and sporophytic, each having the same result of restricting or prohibiting selfed-seed-set although the mode of action differs, both physically and genetically, for each type. Self-incompatibility is under the control of a *multiple allelic system*. An 'S' (sterility or self-incompatibility) gene is composed of a number of alleles, only two of which comprise the whole gene within any one organism. Thus the S gene may be either homozygous e.g. S1S1, or S2S2, or heterozygous S1S2. Other alleles S3, S4 – Sx may of course be involved.

Because ovules and pollen grains are the sex cells which will eventually combine, only one of the S alleles is represented in each. Thus, heterozygous plants S1S2 produce both S1 and S2 gametes. However, the tissues of the whole plant (the sporophyte) – which includes the ovary, style and stigma – contain both alleles and can activate an antibody-type reaction against its own pollen.

Gametophytic Self-incompatibility

The gametophytic incompatibility system, (with independent action in both pollen and style) operates in the wild Tomato and Petunias and retards the growth of pollen which bears either of the two S alleles present in the maternal (female plant) tissue. Pollen tubes are retarded within the style before the ovules are reached. Pollen from other plants is also inhibited if it has the same S alleles.

If, in the gametophytic incompatibility system, a plant of S1S2 constitution is pollinated by S2 and S3 pollen from another plant the S2 pollen will be inhibited. Since S3 is not present in the style, however, the S3 pollen grains will be able to fertilise both S1 and S2 ovules, thus producing progeny of S1S3 and S2S3 constitution.

Sporophytic Self-incompatibility

In the sporophytic incompatibility system (found in *Brassicas* and *Compositae*) the pollen grain bears only a single S allele as in the gametophytic system, but the whole pollen grain behaves exactly as if it possessed both S alleles of the plant from which it was derived. Inhibition of fertilisation in the sporophytic system occurs immediately after germination of the pollen grains upon the stigma – and the stigma is rarely penetrated. If the pollen tube succeeds in reaching the style, after passing through the stigmatic region, however, subsequent growth is unrestricted, and fertilisation can occur just as easily as it would with a 'compatible' pollen-grain tube.

If the same self-incompatibility alleles (S1S2) as those used to illustrate the gametophytic system were present in the female plant with a sporophytic incompatibility system and this was pollinated by an S2S3 male, a different situation could apply. Because the pollen grains are able to act as the parent (diploid) plant the S allele components can interact together or show dominance or recessiveness. If we assume that in the pollen, the effect of S2 was dominant to S3 there could be no fertilisation of ovules since S2 in the female parent would inhibit pollen growth. If S3 was dominant to S2, however, both S3 and S2 pollen would be able to fertilise all ovules within the female – to give S1S2, S1S3, S2S3 and S2S2. Thus, sporophytic incompatibility is a more complicated and less predictable system which allows the production of S allele homozygosity, yet nevertheless works adequately to preserve outcrossing.

It will be shown later that self-incompatibility in both sporophytic and gametophytic systems can be regularly overcome by the use of certain techniques which do not rely upon genetic interactions, thus making the production of homozygotes quite practicable.

Heteromorphic Self-incompatibility

The third type of self-incompatibility system is typical of *Primula* species where 19 pollen from 'pin' flowers can only pollinate 'thrums' and vice versa. Here, the system has been overcome naturally through the appearance of 'homostyles' where stigma and anthers are on the same level and self-fertilisation is not prevented by either morphological or physical barriers. In general *Primula obconica*, *P. denticulata* and *P. vulgaris* show a pin-thrum relationship (thrum Dd, pin dd) while *Primula sinensis* is totally pin and *Primula malacoides* is thrum.

Clonal Reproduction

While it cannot be legitimately included under genetic breeding systems the importance of clonal (or vegetative) propagation for the raising of crops or plants cannot be ignored since many species are reproduced in this way and are never (or very seldom) grown from seed. Instead, cultivars of crops such as garlic, shallots, globe artichokes, rhubarb, chrysanthemum, dahlias and daffodils are consistently raised by the vegetative splitting-off of mother tissue. New cultivars may be produced by hybridisation in all these crops although commercial exploitation is seldom through direct use of seed.

The main characteristic of a vegetatively propagated variety is the extreme uniformity between plants, which is to be expected since all are genetically identical. If we exclude the chance 'mutation' – see next section – and there is no effect of virus disease, new cultivars in use today which have been produced as clones will be identical in appearance to their 'ancestors' of a number of decades ago.

Improvements to cultivars cannot be made by vegetative propagation unless this has been preceded by sexual reproduction. 'Seed' of seed potatoes and 'stools' of chrysanthemum will produce crops with the same characteristics year after year. Clonal propagation has an immense value (and potential) as a commercial technique and this is explained and elaborated in Appendix 1.

Chimaeras or 'Sports'

'Sports' or bud mutations arise – usually from the bud position – on the vegetative portions of plants; they differ in some observable feature from the plant on which they are growing, and can be propagated to give rise to a completely new plant type. This may ultimately be produced as a cultivar following large-scale propagation.

Because sports arise spontaneously but irregularly, the greater the dispersion of a cultivar through vegetative cuttings, the greater the chance that a sport will arise, be noticed and commercialised. For this reason it may be argued that clonal propagation is a direct cause of sport production.

Somatic Mutations

Bud sports often arise because of breakdowns in mitosis when normal developmental (somatic) cells are altered in constitution relative to their neighbouring cells. Multiplication of these 'new' (or mutant) cells during tissue development gives rise to a patch of tissue which differs from that which surrounds it. If the mutant area includes the reproductive region the gametes (ovules and pollen grains) produced later will bear the genetic constitution appropriate to the new tissue type. Because somatic mutations are noticed most frequently where cells are rapidly dividing, the newly formed buds or side shoots (particularly of roses) are most commonly affected.

Somatic mutations are, generally, only of value for the production of new varieties when clonal propagation is the normal method of varietal multiplication. On crops raised from seed, however, spontaneously arising somatic mutations may be found – such as chlorotic yellow patches upon leaves of sweet corn and the leafy vegetables such as lettuce and *Brassicas*. These are recognisable as mutations because of their geometrical margins – often along leaf veins. Chlorosis (the lack of ability to form chlorophyll in the leaf cells) is the most common somatic mutation but flower mutations such as doubleness, Penstemon-type flower in Antirrhinum and frilled edges in Petunia also occur quite frequently.

The somatic mutations have contributed greatly to variability of form in the plant kingdom but to make a full contribution they must be re-assorted genetically by sexual crossing – thus spreading the mutant genes widely through all compatible species.

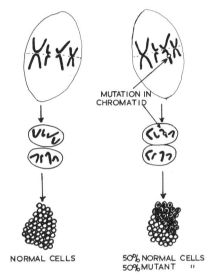

MUTATION IN CHROMATID

NORMAL CELLS

50% NORMAL CELLS
50% MUTANT "

Fig 4. The development of a somatic mutation. Normal cells (left) Mutated cells (right).

Chimaeras

Many plants are normally variegated in tissue colour (chimaeras) – while some may be chimaeras without showing any external signs. This is because cells are laid down in layers which may be genetically and phenotypically different from one another. The formative tissue or growing point of dicotyledons consists of three layers of tissue, the epidermal layer forms the surface, that immediately beneath gives rise to internal leaf cells (pelisade layer) and, importantly, reproductive cells, while the third layer forms the inner leaf and stem tissues.

Leaf variegation as in *euonymus*, holly and privet, is a very common form of chimaera; the epidermal layer always lacks chlorophyll but when the internal tissues also show chlorosis (lack of chlorophyll), – often because epidermal cells have displaced inner cells in particular regions – the result is a patchy green. In vegetatively propagated plants variegated forms are usually stable and, of course, valued for their decorative effect. Variegated plants may breed true from seed (sweet corn, decorative dwarf kale), while other normal types may have a tendency to develop chlorotic patchiness in a certain proportion of their progeny.

Many hybrid tea roses and pelargoniums which may not exhibit recognisable

21

symptoms must, nevertheless, be regarded as chimaeras since plants produced from their root cuttings often differ in morphology from cuttings taken from the above-ground vegetative material. This is due to the fact that shoots from portions of roots arise from what are effectively the internal layers of the stem.

Polyploidy

Although not a breeding *system* in the same way as outbreeding or inbreeding, polyploidy may nevertheless be regarded as a basic change which sets one group of plants apart from another and therefore involves a different breeding process.

Plant species possess a characteristic number of chromosomes – the 'haploid' number – consisting of all the basic chromosomes which bear the complement of genes for that species. To enable the plant to function properly, however, these must be present in multiples of two. The majority of plant species have twice the haploid number of chromosomes and are *diploid*, referred to as 2x. Certain modifications to the number have occurred during evolution or can be made by using suitable techniques, with the consequence that the basic diploid chromosome number becomes duplicated. The most common form of duplication is from diploid (2x) to tetraploid (4x).

Potato, *cyclamen persicum*, *salpiglossis* and catmint are natural tetraploids while tetraploids have been artificially induced in antirrhinum, *dimorphotheca*, lettuce, tomato and many other species. Hexaploids (chrysanthemum) and octoploids (dahlia) also prove valuable in horticulture but the number of species with a high degree of ploidy is very restricted. Plants with any number of chromosomes above the diploid value are classed as polyploids but the only ones with any chance of producing viable, adapted, progenies are those with even numbers of chromosomes. This is because reduction division to form gametes can only be successful when the paired chromosomes divide equally to form balanced cells. The greater the duplication in chromosome numbers, however, the higher the chance that mishaps will occur at meiosis and fertilisation – sometimes resulting in the production of unfit progeny.

In addition to differences in chromosome number, polyploids are usually recognisable by their more fleshy leaves, larger stomates, larger flowers and pollen grains and, generally, slower maturity. They are cross-compatible with diploid forms from which they were derived and often bear characteristics which can be capitalised. Their commercial and technical advantages will be dealt with in Appendix 4.

Technical Applications of Breeding Systems

Selection

Until recent years, any attempt at plant breeding has been made by adapting the natural breeding system of the chosen species. The natural breeding system favours those characteristics which are more useful under natural conditions, however, and rigid control must be maintained to prevent the commercial aspects of cultivars from deteriorating. The process of choosing plants with the desired characters, and of combining these together in such a way that the next generation shows improvement for the appropriate character, is known as selection.

Selection is basic to plant breeding and is the corner-stone upon which the whole edifice of plant improvement rests. It is generally correct to say that plant types adapted for eating or decorative purposes tend to be the opposite of those which are most successful in nature. Improvement of a species is therefore an abandonment of the easy routine since high quality and yield can be maintained only by applying rigid standards. There are no hard and fast rules for successful selection – merely guidelines – but in order to produce a satisfactory result in as short a time as possible the selection technique must be followed consistently.

Selection in one direction over a number of generations can ultimately change the breeding system of a species – partly by accident or partly by the observation and retention of new types. The tomato, *Lycopersicon esculentum*, has changed its natural outbreeding system by becoming a complete inbreeder. In the cauliflowers the original types are presumed to have resembled sprouting broccoli with numerous small heads and a perennial or biennial life cycle; selection of the earlier heading types has led to the annual forms of early summer cauliflowers showing marked varietal uniformity together with high self-fertility. The ancestral types were (and still are) unable to flower without being overwintered and are mainly self-incompatible. Thus, selection at one level has produced changes in various other characteristics, known genetically as a *correlated response*.

Many other examples may be given to emphasise the directive force of selection; dwarf beans and peas are self-fertilised but their flower structures indicate an origin as outcrossers. In other species, double flower types have often been produced by selection, causing transformation of the stamens into petals and thus selecting directly away from the pollination and seed-setting characters which would be of advantage in nature. Species such as marigolds and antirrhinum possessed smaller, less colourful, flowers until selection processes were put into operation.

23

Selection is very easily practised for qualitative characters (i.e. those which are mainly controlled by major genes) but quantitative characters such as plant height, yield, leaf number etc., can only be altered gradually by continued selection in the same direction. If, for example, a programme is started in the hope of producing a blue carnation, only those plants (collected from far and wide) containing some degree of blueness should be allowed to set seed to produce the next generation. Gradually, by selecting and seeding together the bluest plants, each successive generation should approach more closely the desired objective. Now and again, however, odd plants with red, pink or white flowers could still appear and it is vital that they should be removed. If the 'odd' flowers appeared valuable in their own right they could be dealt with separately in another breeding programme – but for the blue carnation programme the selector must be single-minded and not allow himself to become diverted.

Selection in Inbreeding Systems

Selection must be applied in different ways according to the breeding system. In an inbreeding system the amount of genetic variation is very restricted and advances by selection are likely to be marginal at best. If a small degree of outcrossing is common, however, the chance of selecting different genotypes will be extremely high since a uniform crop (brought about by inbreeding) will clearly show any unusual plant. These can usually be classed as hybrids although admixture of seed cannot be ruled out initially.

Selection in inbreeders is most usefully applied (a) to identify and propagate *accidental* hybrids on the off-chance that the new characteristics will respond to selection with further inbreeding to produce a more desirable inbred line; (b) in the late segregating generations when a cultivar needs to be 'trued-up' before attaining complete homozygosity or (c) in the F_2 and subsequent generations of a deliberate cross. If the variation in an inbred line is due to environmental rather than genetic effects the next generation from the selected plant will still be completely uniform and the time involved in selection would have been wasted.

When building up an inbred cultivar from a heterozygous ancestor, the breeder must save seed from single plant selections for at least five generations (to I_5 or S_5) before he can be certain that the new line will be reasonably pure genetically. Although segregation for minor characters will still occur, the phenotypic appearance should be stable, and subsequent generations can probably be produced by mixing the seed of all selected plants. Without continued close selection, segregation for unselected characters could occur ad infinitum. Thus, in dwarf beans, selection for bean length, shape and colour may achieve relative stability by the fourth generation from a cross, but seed colour – for which no selection has been applied – would probably remain variable.

In the initial stages of inbreeding, individual plants are becoming genetically more uniform (homozygous) within themselves, so causing them to appear more distinct from one another. In every successive generation, progenies from separate self-pollinated selections should be grown alongside (but never mixed with) one another. The similarity of plants within one line and the differences between the separate lines will become apparent as early as I_2 (or S_2) and will become even more pronounced as inbreeding progresses. At this stage, the plant breeder has his greatest opportunity for selecting the most desirable types since most of the variability provided by the original cross will still be present, while plant or crop potential can be assessed by the performance within progeny rows.

It cannot be repeated too often, that selection towards a particular characteristic must always be consistent – otherwise the chances of reaching the ultimate objective will be greatly reduced.

When selecting in inbreeders, one must beware the dangers of being over-ambitious; in short one must aim for overall improvements by degrees. If one is swayed by the swede, for example, a target for improvement could be a slight decrease in size, a true globe shape, orange flesh, white skin, a high 'solids' content, and the ability to stand for a long time without becoming pithy. If all these characters were essential in a single selected plant, there would be very long odds against the selection of any plant at all. In such a case, progress would best be made by selecting plants showing the greatest resemblance to the ideal form, while other plants would then be selected for the other desirable characters. Thus, we could end up with a heavy, globe swede with a non-pithy flesh, while another line, mediocre for these features, would have the exact colour required. Further crossing, using these two types as parents, coupled with well-directed selection should ultimately provide a cultivar very close to that which we originally had in mind. While over-ambition must be avoided, so too must the impossible. Some characters respond more slowly to selection than others while others such as earliness and large size, cannot be expected to accompany one another (a negative correlation).

Selection in Outbreeders

For cross-pollinating crops the process of selection is subject to a greater number of limitations.

When plants of an outbreeding crop are self-fertilised, their progeny often suffer a loss of vigour and it is therefore impracticable to select only single or a small number of plants. In general it would be genetically safe to select a minimum of five or six plants and these should, of course, resemble one another as closely as possible in all the chosen characters. All selected plants would be dug and potted or replanted so that they would be inter-pollinated by insects when the flowering stage is reached. The resulting seed should be vigorous and should give progeny which resemble the five or six parents more closely than the general population from which they were derived. If the number of plants selected is too small there may be some breakdown in uniformity because the effect of close mating will be almost as marked as inbreeding; there will be genetic segregation as well as a general loss of vigour.

On the other hand, choosing too many plants, even if they all look alike and are equally desirable, will produce progeny which are different from the parent population and there will have been no advantage in making selections.

Because cross-pollination is rarely absolute (the hermaphrodite flowers in the majority of species invariably receive some of their own pollen) some inbreeding is inevitable amongst a selected group of plants, however large, but the inbreds will be unthrifty and almost certainly ignored for selection purposes.

Selection in outbreeders should preferably be associated with progeny testing, as described later.

Since, faced with a large population, it may be difficult to decide which are the best plants to select, various scoring systems can be devised to cover all the desired aspects. For example, if selecting cornflower plants for garden border decoration, the selection decisions can be based upon an overall classification similar to the following (Table 5). For each candidate plant a maximum of five points is awarded for excellence in the chosen character while fewer points are given (down to one) for lower qualities.

TABLE 5
SELECTION INDEX TO AID THE CHOICE OF PARENTS IN A CROSS-BREEDING PROGRAMME

Species	Purpose	Required Characteristics	Evaluation	
Cornflower	Garden border decoration	Bright colours which do not fade	1 = dull	5 = bright
		Large flowers	1 = small	5 = large
		Long flowering period	1 = short	5 = long
		Growth to conceal old flowers	1 = poor	5 = good
		Flower cover	1 = top only	5 = all round
		Colour of foliage	1 = light green	5 = deep green
		'Bushiness'	1 = sparse	5 = bushy
		Seed germination	1 = slow	5 = rapid

Cornflower with scores nearest to 40 should be retained for inter-pollination.

If the object was to grow cornflowers for cutting and floral arrangement, some characteristics such as 'bushiness' and colour of leaf would probably have less significance while 'life of single flower' would need to be recorded.

Mass Selection

Until recent years this was the normal method for cultivar formation or improvement and though better systems are now known and used, some reference should be made to its particular merits. It has its main effects in outcrossing species.

Plants which have been selected must either be dug up and removed to an isolated area in pots or replanted in the soil – or the original crop must be cleared and the selected plants left in position. Cross-pollination by insects will take place between all plants as they flower together.

The level of selection is subject to no hard and fast rules but is related to the degree of outcrossing normal to the population. For a complete outcrosser the number of plants selected should be higher than for an equivalent population of facultative inbreeders. As a subjective guide, the number of plants of high quality selected in an outcrossing type of population should be approximately one per cent, as long as this does not reduce the number of plants to less than 20. Selected plants are seeded together and the seed harvested in bulk – thus combining numerous genotypes. Mass selection has proved successful with numbers of plants either side of one per cent of the total population and the ultimate test of the efficiency of selection can be found only in the response of the next generation. The population mean or average for the selected character will probably be moved quite noticeably in the direction of selection and although the proportion of genotypes will be altered, mass selection is another direction (but using the same principles) in the following generation can again change the population mean.

Because of the continued outcrossing, heterozygosity will still be of a high order though less pronounced than before selection, and it will not be possible to make improvements beyond a certain level. As the amount of seed raised from a small number of selected plants will be inadequate for commercial use, a further seed crop will be required (from their progeny) and selection will inevitably become less stringent.

Single Plant Selection and Progeny Testing

As with mass-selection, the principle involved in single plant selection is that individual plants should be chosen on their merits. In this case, however, there is less emphasis on directional selection because it is not intended that the seed of selected plants will be mixed together. Depending upon the crop, the single plant selections.may, or may not, have been removed to be seeded in isolation. In a crop of cabbages grown for market, any plants selected for seeding purposes would need to be removed. In a crop of cabbages grown for seed, however, selected individuals could be left to flower with the rest of the crop. Pollination at flowering time will be random in either instance and the identity of the male (pollen) plants will be unknown. The genetic contribution of each female parent will nevertheless be capable of assessment since all seed in a sample will be from that parent only. The value of the female contribution will be judged by sowing a portion of each seed sample separately to observe inherited differences, a procedure known as progeny testing.

The one-per-cent rule for selection can be relaxed in this instance, provided that each selection satisfies the plant breeder, since the object is to look for quality in separate progenies rather than a general directed improvement. Many of the progenies will probably be poor or atypical in spite of the fact that only the best phenotypes were chosen, while others will exhibit few defects. The seed which remains of the poor lines should now be discarded – it will contribute nothing of value to the next generation if retained. Seed of the good single-plant-lines will either be bulked or, if progenies show marked differences, the seed from each will be retained and only the more desirable progenies resown to multiply seed quantities for commercial use.

Selection should not be relaxed after this improvement – recombination of genes in the outcrossing population will still take place and, because of the unpredictability of pollen dispersion, poor genotypes will remain and may even be favoured in the population. In cauliflower, for example, 'riceyness' and 'looseness' of curd (both undesirable characteristics) may be proliferated because plants with this type of curd 'break' more easily to produce more flowering branches and set more seed than plants which bear perfect curds.

As an example of the effect of progeny testing we can momentarily consider the animal kingdom. In a population of 101 Dalmations it would be impossible to sort out the separate families because of the confusion of spots. When each mother collected her own puppies around her, however, the family resemblances would become much more apparent – as would differences between one family and another.

Progeny Testing to Control Transfer of Characters

Occasionally, attempts are made to improve outcrossers or partial outcrossers by interplanting small numbers of plants of two different cultivars in pots or in the field and allowing them to intercross naturally. This is a rather casual system, and is not recommended, but can nevertheless be made to work. The red Brussels sprout variety 'Rubin' is reported to have been produced in this way – diligent selection proving reasonably effective in the progeny from the original cross – green Brussels sprout x Red Cabbage.

27

The transfer of single gene characters may seem uncomplicated but, unless followed by single-plant progeny testing at some stage, problems will arise in purifying the material so that it performs as a consistent cultivar. If we take as an example a cross between red and white flowered Salvias where it is intended to produce a red flowered type with foliage characters from the white, an F_2 population will give ratios of three reds to every white flowered plant. The white-flowered type would be discarded and we would be left with reds only, one in three being homozygous (RR) while the others would be heterozygous (Rr).

Selection and pollination can now be carried out in three different ways with, as will be seen, three markedly different results.

A. Red-flowered plants mass-pollinated and seed harvested in bulk

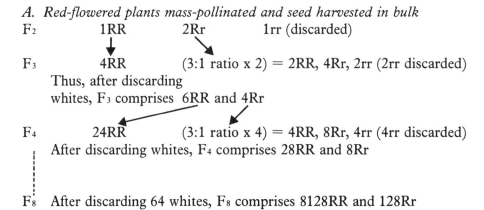

F_2 1RR   2Rr   1rr (discarded)

F_3 4RR   (3:1 ratio x 2) = 2RR, 4Rr, 2rr (2rr discarded)
Thus, after discarding
whites, F_3 comprises 6RR and 4Rr

F_4 24RR   (3:1 ratio x 4) = 4RR, 8Rr, 4rr (4rr discarded)
After discarding whites, F_4 comprises 28RR and 8Rr

F_8 After discarding 64 whites, F_8 comprises 8128RR and 128Rr

The removal of white-flowered plants at each successive seed multiplication leads to a reduction in the relative number of whites so that from F_2 to F_8 the proportion of whites will comprise respectively, ¼ (F_2), 1/6 (F_3), 1/10 (F_4), 1/18 (F_5), 1/34 (F_6), 1/66 (F_7), 1/130 (F_8), and so on, doubling the differences between successive denominators in the fraction at each generation.

While the proportion of plants heterozygous for red declines in each generation, with this system of seed multiplication there will *always* be a proportion of unwanted white-flowered plants.

B. Red-flowered plants pollinated individually (self-pollinated)
Homozygous parent plants would be identified by their production of progeny of uniform colour. Further selection should be continued only within these lines. If selection was continued amongst red plants from heterozygous parents, there would be a 2:1 chance that heterozygous plants would again be chosen.

C. Red-flowered plants mass-pollinated, but each plant harvested separately
Here we have a situation intermediate between A and B – progeny testing from a group of chosen parents whose true genetic make-up is unknown. Since all plants are red-flowered they will be either RR or Rr and pollination can be expected to be at random between them. The only single-plant progenies which will breed true for red flower-colour will be those whose parent was homozygous RR and plants within these lines should be the only ones chosen for further seed production. The possibility remains that some of the plants within the chosen lines could be heterozygous because they were the result of fertilisation with an 'r' allele and a number of selections should therefore be made within each progeny. Repetition of this process in successive generations should hasten the production of a new cultivar, compared with the progress to be expected under selection method A.

Hybridisation

Hybridisation is the cross-fertilisation of one genetically unique individual by another – usually after mechanical removal of anthers to avoid *self*-fertilisation. Plant breeders are frequently referred to (particularly by the layman or novice) as *hybridisers*, with the implication that all improvements in plants result from cross-pollination. While hybridisation is almost inevitable sometime during the course of a breeding programme it is used with effect at different stages, and with different ends in mind depending upon the type of project. Hybridisation is a normal part of the reproductive process in outcrossing species or cultivars, – without it the species can no longer exist as a balanced system – but it is nevertheless random, with unknown proportions of parental genetypes contributing to each successive generation.

Hybridisation is essential for major advances in lines which are normally inbred. As a generalisation, the best method for improving inbreeders is to make cross-fertilisations (hybridisation) while outbreeders are most likely to be improved by an initial programme of inbreeding – in short, to adopt the system directly opposite to that which is natural for the species or crop.

Genetically, hybridisation has two main virtues – one is to increase the genetic variation of plants and their progenies and to keep the population stable, while the other is to increase plant vigour and thus make the plants or cultivar more able to compete with others. Not all hybrid combinations result in above average vigour (heterosis) but commercially desirable types can be isolated by experiment.

It must be emphasised that hybrid vigour which results from interaction between different sets of genes (and there are tests which determine this – see Appendix 3) can be reproduced only by repeating the same or very similar sets of crosses.

In general the greatest heterosis is found when the least similar genotypes are crossed together – crosses between cultivars tend to produce better hybrids than crosses between plants of the same cultivar because of the greater genotypic differences.

Hybrid vigour can be preserved where the subject can be vegetatively propagated. F_1 hybrid Carefree geraniums for example are more vigorous and uniform when grown on from cuttings than are F_2 plants obtained from their seed.

Backcrossing

After hybridisation between two plant types it may be desirable in certain circumstances to retain only a limited number of characters from one of the parents. Examples are the incorporation of resistance to disease into an otherwise desirable form – mosaic resistance into Dark Skinned Perfection Pea, for example, or colours other than blue into the dwarf cornflower 'Little Boy Blue'.

In some cases – particularly where major genes are involved in inheritance it is possible to recover something approaching the desired type in segregating progenies. If this is impossible, however, backcrossing ('crossing-back') the progeny to the chosen – or recurrent – parent will be continued for as many generations as are necessary to produce the desired result. In each successive generation, only those plants which possess the 'introduced' character will be selected for further backcrossing to the recurrent parent. It is immaterial whether the hybrid or the parent is used as female in successive crosses.

29

Backcrossing can begin with the F_1 hybrid or with suitable F_2 segregants. It may be continued for only a single cycle or for three or four generations, but little further genetic advance is made beyond a series of three backcrosses.

TABLE 6
BACKCROSSING AND THE RECOVERY OF PARENTAL TYPES

Genetic constitution of each plant

	100% A x 100% B		
F_1	50% A 50% B		
Backcross to A	(recurrent parent)	Backcross to B	(recurrent parent)
1st backcross generation (BC1)	75% A 25% B	1st backcross generation (BC1)	25% A 75% B
Backcross to A (BC2)	87.5% A 12.5% B	Backcross to B (BC2)	12.5% A 87.5% B
Backcross to A (BC3)	93.75% A 6.25% B	Backcross to B (BC3)	6.25% A 93.75% B
	etc.		etc.

The products of backcrossing need not be subjected to field selection if the introduced character can be easily identified, and the process can be accelerated by growing crops entirely under artificial conditions.

Whether or not backcrossing is desirable must be the decision of the breeder in the face of his particular problem. Backcrossing is an invaluable technique for proven cereal cultivars where new disease resistance is often needed quickly. For the majority of horticultural crops it is probably of less importance, except in the case of unusual flower colours or where rapid transfer of disease resistance from a wild species could have considerable commercial benefits.

TABLE 7

List of characters incorporated into some horticultural cultivars from wild species by using the backcrossing technique.

Crop	– *Character and wild species*
Tomato	– *Didymella, cladosporium, tobacco-mosaic* resistances from L. hirsutum, L. peruvianum, L. pimpinellifolium respectively.
Pea	– Frost and root rot resistance from Pisum arvense.
Dwarf Bean	– Anthracnose resistance from Phaseolus spp. ex Venezuela.
Beetroot	– Monogerm (single-seeded character) ex Sugarbeet.
Lettuce	– Mosaic and Downy mildew resistance from Lactuca scariola.
Rose	– Yellow colour from *Rosa foetida.*
Delphinium	– Red colour from D. Cardinale.
Spinach	– Downy mildew resistance from Iranian species.

Although backcrossing has an obvious value the improvements obtained are in the single selected character only. For many species and breeding programmes there is a better chance of obtaining improved or unique forms by allowing segregation, coupled with selection, from the single cross or after only one cycle of backcrossing. By selecting types which resemble the chosen plant as segregation occurs in successive generations, it should be possible to produce a form with most of the desired characters, plus useful gene combinations from the other parent.

Pair-crossing

Crosses between plants can be made at random as in the case of mass-pollination, between groups of individuals or, in the most refined cases, between a pair of plants only. The pair-crossing technique is commonly applied where individual plants possess unique characteristics which tend to isolate them phenotypically from the rest of the population. By virtue of the fact that the phenotype is a direct reflection of genotype, pair-crossing concentrates the desirable characters into a restricted genetic population and should accelerate the response to selection.

Each plant involved in a pair-cross can be used in other pair-crosses thus producing a series of F_1 progenies which will be directly comparable, by relationships or through linked relationships, with one another. Crosses between inbred populations where homozygosity is complete (or almost) need never be made on a pair-cross basis since all plants of one cultivar are genetically identical.

Diallel Cross

An extension of the pair-cross principle allows every plant to be used in pair-crosses with every other plant in the selected group. Reciprocal crosses can be excluded from this scheme since many years of experiment have seldom produced evidence of major differences between the progeny of a cross or the progeny of its reciprocal cross. Although much has been written about the application and analysis of the diallel cross it is intended here only to illustrate its usefulness to practical plant breeding in simple terms. The statistical analysis is elaborated in Appendix 3 'plant breeding mathematics'.

The importance of the diallel cross technique lies in its thorough assessment of parental contributions as they relate to F_1 and later generations. For genetical reasons, the diallel cross technique can be applied satisfactorily only to homozygous diploid populations where genes are distributed *independently* among the parents. This latter point is difficult to satisfy, particularly as plant breeders deliberately choose parents for their phenotypic characters and the genes are not, therefore, representative of the population as a whole. In practice, however, the diallel analysis still has a value for genetic determination – as it has also where the individuals chosen are from an outcrossing population and are, therefore, not homozygous.

The diallel cross may be made using individual plants or small groups of plants as parents to represent the whole cultivar or population. If small groups of plants are chosen they should be used at random as parents since no individual should make a greater genetic contribution to crosses than others within its group.

The main limitation of diallel crosses is the practical one of making enough crosses to give sufficient progeny for analysis. Providing that seed germination does not deteriorate rapidly, however, it is often possible to make the necessary crosses over a period of two years and thus increase the size of the population under test.

The number of crosses to be made is, of course, related to the number of parents (n) and is calculated as $\frac{n(n-1)}{2}$. Thus, for eight parents there should be 28 crosses, expressed most practically when the programme is in operation according to the following chequer board.

Diallel crosses involving 8 parents and parental types

Parents	A	B	C	D	E	F	G	H
Parents A	S	A x B	A x C	A x D	A x E	A x F	A x G	A x H
B		S	B x C	B x D	B x E	B x F	B x G	B x H
C			S	C x D	C x E	C x F	C x G	C x H
D				S	D x E	D x F	D x G	D x H
E					S	E x F	E x G	E x H
F						S	F x G	F x H
G							S	G x H
H								S

In addition to the 28 crosses it is advisable to self-pollinate each parent or parental group since the selfed progeny are used in one form of diallel analysis (that of Jinks) though not in some others (Griffing, Kempthorne). On the assumption that there will be no reciprocal differences it is not compulsory to use parent plants as male or female according to the above diallel chart but it is easier to confine results to one half of the table. It can be appreciated from the table that any increase in the number of parents will entail considerable extra work in the crossing programme in addition to the practical difficulties of matching flowering dates, etc.

From the diallel analysis (or even an observation of the mean values for each F_1 hybrid and parent in the above table) it is possible to assess whether the inheritance of a character such as intensity of flower colour is due entirely to (a) polygenes which produce an additive effect (i.e. increased genic content – increased character expression), or (b) major genes (those having large effects) which exhibit dominance or recessivity, or (c) to interaction between groups of genes. If inheritance of characters can be attributed to either (a) or (b) the diallel analysis can identify those parents which are most capable of transmitting desirable characters to their progeny. Selection in their segregating progenies could then produce types which are better than either parent.

If the genetic result is shown to be gene interaction there will be no chance of finding high value types in segregating progenies. Nevertheless, the diallel cross will have indicated the right combination of parents which should be used for the production of a promising hybrid population.

Convergent Improvement

Improvement of crops may be carried out by crossing in such a manner that desirable genes from each species of cultivar *converge* upon one another. The system is practised mainly within inbreeding species with the objective of combining desirable characters from a number of cultivars in as rapid a manner as possible.

'Starting' cultivars may be of any number above two, and while the method can be adjusted to absorb new gene combinations, it carries a risk that all the desired characters may not be present in the final segregating population.

Using eight cultivars for our first example the system is as follows:

1st Crosses	A x B	C x D	E x F	G x H

2nd Crosses F_1's (no selection needed in this generation)
               AB x CD   EF x GH

3rd Cross   (Segregating F_1's)
                         ABCD x EFGH

ABCDEFGH segregates to give many different forms, each bearing some characters from the eight original parents.

The second example illustrates convergent improvement with five desirable parents; other combinations may obviously be preferred depending upon the starting material.

1st Crosses

A x B   C x D   E

                 x

   AB   CD   BE

2nd Crosses   AB x CD   CD x BE

3rd Cross   ABCD   x   CDBE

ABBCCDDE segregates to give many different forms which bear characters mainly from B, C and D.

As can be seen, A and E will have contributed only ⅛ each to the final product while B, C and D will each have contributed ¼ by the time the final segregating progeny is produced. Manipulation of crosses can be made in any way, however, and decisions can be based upon the qualities of each F_1 before the next stage of crossing takes place.

This form of improvement can be used with effect on partly outcrossing crops. Since the ultimate population will be highly heterozygous, however, undesirable recessive genes may be given a selective advantage, and very careful attention would be essential at selection time.

The Use of Polyploids in Breeding New Varietal Forms

Polyploids have occurred naturally in the past during the process of species formation and may appear spontaneously among plant material at any time. The establishment of the polyploid individual under natural conditions is unlikely, however, unless the new type can exhibit immediate advantages in growth habit, seed-setting, general vigour, etc. In cultural conditions where observation can be immediately followed by selection, however, the polyploid will be preserved and, if the progeny proves satisfactory, utilised.

Polyploid flowers which have arisen spontaneously and are now commercially recognised are *Primula Kewensis, Cyclamen Persicum, Pelargonium zonale* and *Dahlia* while Swede (*Brassica napo-campestris*) is the only polyploid vegetable, unless potatoes or a few herbs are allowed.

Polyploidy is most advantageous in the flower species since one of the effects of chromosome replication is an enlargement of the cell size – often expressed as the formation of large flowers. An adverse effect of polyploidy is a tendency for flower production to be later, although floriferousness is usually unaltered. Certain techniques can be utilised for the artificial production of polyploids, these are discussed in Appendix 4, but polyploids themselves can be involved in a whole set of breeding systems as follows.

Reproductive Efficiency of Polyploids

Polyploidy is a condition of chromosome duplication giving numbers of chromosomes within the cell nucleus over and above the basic diploid number. Unless the number of chromosomes is an exact multiple of the diploid, however, 33 the polyploid is unstable, gives rise to gametes with irregular numbers of chromosomes and cannot be reproduced by seed. Gametes of such an irregular polyploid (or aneuploid) may combine in a fortuitous manner, however, to give rise to a polyploid with even chromosome numbers – a multiple of the diploid – and plants from the newly formed seeds will probably then be fully fertile.

The success of the diploid type in natural evolution is marked by the fact that it is still the most common nuclear condition and, in general, its reproductive efficiency is higher than that of the polyploid forms. This is because pairing in meiosis is between identical chromosomes and the cell system is less liable to error when only two identical chromosomes pair together than when pairing is between four, six or eight.

TABLE 8
POLYPLOID SPECIES USED IN HORTICULTURE

Tetraploids (4x)	Hexaploids (6x)	Octoploids (8x)
Antirrhinum	Carnation	Strawberry
Cyclamen persicum	Delphinium	Chrysanthemum (5 to 7x)
Begonia	Siberian Wallflower	
Delphinium	Fuchsia	
Marrow	Rose	
	Michaelmas Daisy	
	Jerusalem artichoke	

Amphidiploidy

Certain situations can be found in which polyploids behave as diploids as far as reproductive efficiency is concerned, yet otherwise possess the phenotypic characteristics of polyploids. Plants which possess in their cells the *diploid* number of chromosomes of one species in addition to the diploid constitution of another are known as *Allo*polyploids of *Amphidiploids*, as distinct from *Auto* (or self) polyploids which have attained polyploidy by doubling the same chromosome set.

Allopolyploids (also known as alloploids or amphiploids) arise in a number of ways and can be formed deliberately by astute crossing. Their main advantage is through inducing fertility in what would normally be sterile interspecific hybrids. Crosses between diploid species, or sometimes genera, are frequently possible but the product of such crosses is likely to be sterile and unable to set seed because of the lack of similarity of the respective chromosome complements. If the cells become polyploid however, in the simplest (and most common) case there will now be two complete diploid sets of chromosomes within the same cell. Each set will carry out meiosis and mitosis independently of the other set, though simultaneously – and the whole polyploid combination will make a contribution to the cell and the plant. The cell enlargement of alloploids may not be as marked as in autopolyploids but the hybrid plant-form usually appears to be intermediate between both parents.

Practical Use of Polyploids

Polyploidy is a valuable tool for extending the variability of species. Chromosome duplication (as for Autotetraploids) does not increase a plant's genetic variability but can alter the effect of one gene upon another by intensifying dominance or interaction effects between alleles. This is particularly so where the diploid form shows a degree of self-incompatibility. The gametes (pollen grains and ovules) of polyploids are diploid and fail to induce the incompatibility reaction so that self-fertility results.

The production of polyploids from genetically sterile diploids may not always be commercially desirable. The sterility which is normally associated with interspecific crosses is often preferred to full fertility because many unique plant forms can be maintained vegetatively. If seed production was made possible by the induction of allo-ploidy the characteristics of the vegetative plant would probably disappear because of the subsequent genetic segregation.

Production of Triploids

The cross-pollination of diploid and tetraploid plants of the same species results in the production of a triploid – having three sets of chromosomes, one from one parent and two from the other.

Because of confused chromosome pairing at meiosis, such triploids produce very few gametes which are genetically viable. In a plant with 21 chromosomes (basic no. x = 7) for example, meiosis may result in the production of numerous gametes having 14 and 7 chromosomes. The 14 chromosomes do not necessarily form two complete sets, nor the seven another complete set, as chromosomes would be distributed to cells more or less at random. In practice, gametes from such a triploid would consist of any number of chromosomes within the range 7 to 14. To produce a functional seed, complementary male and female gametes must fuse with one another. Viable plants can be produced when the haploid gametes (x = 7) are fertilised by haploids to give a fertile diploid (2x = 14), when fertilised by a diploid gamete (2x = 14) to reproduce the triploid (3x = 21) form which is again sterile, or when a diploid gamete (2x = 14) is fertilised by another diploid gamete to form a fertile tetraploid. It will be appreciated that the chances against satisfactory fertilisation are much greater than those in favour, but as long as vast numbers of gametes are produced, adequate fertilisation may occur. This is so with some fruit trees (apples Baldwin, Ribston pippin, Blenheim orange and Bramley's seedling for example) of 3X constitution.

The infertility of triploids can have important economic consequences for plant breeding. Perhaps the best known use of triploidy is in a marginally horticultural crop confined to the tropics – the banana. Its infertility (it is a triploid) is marked by the failure of ovules to be fertilised. Fortunately for us the flowers are stimulated to form parthenocarpic fruits and are highly edible because they contain no annoying seeds. In general, the most useful triploids are those with fleshy fruit which may be formed without successful fertilisation of the ovules. Use has been made of this principle in melons and marrows – it is also possible with cucumbers though rarely practised commercially. Triploidy is of advantage also in decorative subjects such as marigolds (produced from male-sterile diploids crossed with tetraploids) – because seeds are not formed, flowers are retained for a longer period, and plants do not become covered in unwanted seed pods. Because of the fact that tetraploids tend to produce a higher proportion of abortive gametes than diploids it is better to use them as male parents – production of pollen grains being so great that numerous fertile ones will still be present in spite of the very large majority being non-functional. The presence of sterile female gametes on the other hand (if tetraploids are used as females) would result in drastic reductions in seed yield.

As triploids *can* be produced whichever way the cross is made, there can be no hard and fast rule, and final decisions must be left to the discretion of the plant

35

breeder. The tetraploid form may be easier to emasculate or, conversely, may produce more seeds per ovary to compensate for some degree of ovule sterility. To date, triploidy as a breeding tool has been used less than its potential deserves, but this is probably because of the need for the manual operations of emasculation and pollination.

Male Sterility

The commercial difficulties of making triploids are largely economic and would be overcome to a large extent by the use of male sterility. Male sterility is, by definition, the complete absence of pollen in a conventionally hermaphrodite flower. Male sterility may express itself as absence of the whole stamen structure, absence or abortion of anthers, infertility of pollen grains or inability of anthers (containing pollen grains) to dehisce (split) and release the pollen. While male-sterility is undesirable in nature and was considered an embarrassment by selectors and propagators in past years, it is now considered to be a very important tool for the modern technique of cultivar production. Male sterility may be due to genetic or environmental causes, or a combination of both.

Genetic male sterility, in fact, often breaks down under environmental 'stress' and to use it as a tool, therefore, it is important that it should be reliable under all conditions found in the field.

Male sterile plants often appear following the inbreeding of normally outcrossed species due to the increase in homozygosity of recessive genes. Where male sterility is not known to exist at present it is often revealed by carrying out inbreeding within large plant populations.

In addition to genetic male sterility the interaction between cytoplasm and nuclear genes can produce another form which, in the case of onion and carrot in particular, is highly adaptable for the production of commercial hybrids. Here again, however, environment tends to complicate the reliability of male sterility and not all seeds can be guaranteed to be hybrid.

The advantages of male sterility are (1) for F_1 hybrid production, (2) for the production of parthenocarpic fruits, (3) the non seed-setting of ornamentals thus giving long retention of flowers (as for triploidy) and (4) doubleness in flowers. Many plants are male-sterile because their anthers have been transformed into petals.

F₁ Hybrids, Their Value, Synthesis and Versatility

It is fitting that F_1 hybrids should be allotted a whole section, because of their immense usage throughout the world and because their production requires the knowledge and manipulation of a wide range of breeding techniques.

F_1 hybrids are now used so widely in horticulture that only asparagus, beetroot, celery, leek, lettuce, beans and peas of the more common vegetables are not represented.

Although interest in F_1's in the flower crops is increasing rapidly they have been less extensively developed and the proportion of F_1 hybrids to the total number of flower species is consequently much lower than for the vegetables.

The first flowers and vegetables to be used for F_1 hybrid production were those in which parental lines or cultivars were homozygous or could be easily inbred, and (most important) also gave large numbers of seeds from small numbers of hand pollinations. Thus tomatoes and petunias made the first genetical and commercial impact, while species used later required generations of inbreeding and selection to produce the right parents. Self-incompatibility also proved useful for F_1 hybrid production and led to the 'second stream' F_1 hybrids from the *Brassicas* in the vegetables to Ageratum, Primula and Pansies in the flowers.

Inbred lines and their F_1 combinations are derived from the obligate outbreeders only after a long period of preparation and investigation. In spite of the extra involvement in labour and expenditure, however, the advances made by the production of F_1 hybrids from a mass-pollinated population tend to be proportionately greater than those of F_1 hybrids between well adapted lines from inbreeding species.

Principles of F₁ Hybrid Production

(a) Inbreeding

An F_1 is the result of a cross between any two genetically distinct parent plants, irrespective of their state of homozygosity. Thus, in an outbred population, because self-pollination is unlikely to occur, all plants will be F_1 hybrids. In the modern connotation, however, an F_1 hybrid is the result of a cross between two homozygous (but genetically distinct) parents or lines, and all F_1 plants resemble one another exactly.

The importance of obtaining homozygous parent lines lies in the fact that the full effect of the genes can be observed only in this condition. Without homozygosity, recessive genes will be masked by their dominant alleles.

37

Continuous inbreeding, on the other hand, allows identification and selection (or removal) of particular gene combinations. The rate at which homozygosity is achieved depends upon the original level of heterozygosity in the selected plant. Inbreeding is generally practised on single plants and upon further single plants in their self progenies, and the amount of heterozygosity will decrease by half in each selfed generation unless certain gene linkages exist. In general, for most commercial requirements homozygosity is adequate by the S_5 generation.

While major genes can be sorted out within one or at most two, generations of inbreeding, polygenes (generally affecting yield characteristics) will continue to show segregation until very late generations of inbreeding. By S_5, however, their main effects will have become stabilised in the phenotype. In the unlikely event that a programme of inbreeding is started with only a single outbreeding plant it is quite possible that numerous distinctive inbred lines will be produced because of segregation for genes affecting phenotype. These should not be inter-crossed to form F_1 hybrids but should be used as separate inbreds in crosses with progenies from other, less closely related plants.

While the effect of inbreeding in cross-pollinating species is to increase homozygosity levels within lines, it also commonly leads to a reduction of vigour – or depression of yield. In the early generations, plants within lines vary in their level of inbreeding depression, but as the lines become genetically more uniform, plants within lines show similar responses to the effect of inbreeding. While some lines may remain almost as vigorous as the parent plant from which they were derived, other very closely-related lines may become so weakened that further seed production by inbreeding is impossible. The first characters to be affected by inbreeding are those having associations with fertility. Fecundity (the ability to produce off-spring in adequate numbers) is usually reduced for a number of reasons, ranging from ovule sterility and poor pollen-grain germination to paucity of flower production.

Over a wide range of species the most commonly observed result of inbreeding usually appears in the first inbred generation as a notable increase in the proportion of albino seedlings. These are usually recognisable for their yellowish-white first leaves. Albinos rarely grow beyond the seedling stage since the absence of chlorophyll in their tissues prevents photosynthesis. The allele controlling albinism is recessive and would be paired with its dominant chlorophyll allele in the normal outbred population. The double recessive condition would rarely occur and probably never be recognised because the germinated seedlings would die at a very juvenile stage. Inbreeding, however, increases the likelihood of pairing between recessive alleles and albinos occur in conspicuous numbers. In general, the greater the tendency of a cultivar towards cross-pollination the greater the chance that it will produce albinos in its first inbred (S_1) generation. In the cultivars which undergo some inbreeding as part of the normal system (facultative inbreeders) the recessive albino alleles will have paired together more frequently over a number of years and many will have been removed from the population.

Inbreeding is virtually unnecessary before hybridisation in homogenous cultivars except where the cultivar is thought to consist of a number of very similar *pure lines* which can only be satisfactorily 'sorted out' by saving progenies of single plants separately. In these circumstances one generation of inbreeding is adequate – and no inbreeding depression would be found even if inbreeding was continued over a number of years.

38

Plate 4. Albino seedlings (arrowed) in a 1st generation of inbreeding (S₁) in cyclamen. These seedlings will die because of lack of chlorophyll.

(b) Assessing Hybrid Combinations

It is impossible to generalise for all crops since their level of outcrossing determines the results of inbreeding, but it is a fairly safe rule that single plants may be selected almost at random from the population before raising the first inbred generation. There will be a natural bias towards plants which show most of the characteristics demanded by the breeding programme but more doubtful individuals may also produce desirable inbred progenies.

Inbred lines from cross-pollinated ancestors will be selected for specific qualities during the selfing programme. In many instances the characters selected will probably be only marginally acceptable and some may, in fact, appear to be worse than those of the parent. Selection, nevertheless, should be relative to all other lines and only the least desirable lines should be discarded in the early stages.

By the S_2 generation the level of homozygosity should be sufficient to show clear quality and yield differences between lines. Single plant selections in this and subsequent generations must be made from *the best lines only*. An outstanding plant in a mediocre line should be ignored since the phenotype is most probably a reflection of its local environment rather than its genetic potential.

If there is evidence of reasonable homozygosity by the S_3 (or even the previous generation), tentative assessment of F_1 hybrid potential can be made by crossing pairs of representative plants from different lines. Although uniformity is one of the features of an F_1, the lack of it must be allowed for in these early experimental crosses.

39

Plate 5. Most F₁ hybrids show advantages over the parental inbreds. Sometimes, however, as in this primula obconica cross, the combination of parents (single plants either side) produce an 'abortive' hybrid (4 central plants) due to undesirable gene associations.

The early assessment of F_1 hybrid combinations involves pair crosses between the most desirable parental types. It is unlikely that a single parental line will possess all of the characters required in the F_1 hybrid and it is common practice to choose parental types in which the required characters complement one another. Thus a light green Brussels sprout inbred with tight 'buttons' (for example) would be crossed with a dark green inbred to produce a desirable dark green F_1. Lines which apparently complement one another may react in a totally unexpected way when brought together in a hybrid, however, and for this reason all inbred lines of a series should be combined as pairs to produce hybrids.

While F_1 hybrids usually show increased vigour over conventional cultivars this is best expressed in an F_1 derived from a cross between inbred lines of different cultivars. Intra-varietal F_1's whose parents were derived from the same ancestor in previous generations will seldom yield as well as F_1's from lines with diverse ancestry. This is due to the fact that some of the expression of F_1 hybrid vigour is brought about by the combination of two groups of genes which have previously been spatially and physiologically isolated to some extent. An F_1 produced by crossing genotypes which originate from a single grandparent or great grandparent can be an improvement over the original type however, although it comprises groups of genes which previously existed together. This is due to the fact that ancestral deleterious recessive genes will have been largely removed by selection during inbreeding. Inbred lines which combine best in the early stages should be inbred further until complete visual homozygosity is obtained although there is little need to repeat the crossing programme until the S_5 or S_6 generations. By this time there should be complete phenotypic uniformity which the F_1 will echo, and production will be on a commercial basis.

The advantages of F_1's can be briefly stated:

a) Greater vigour expressed as yield, flower or seed production, earlier germination, disease resistance etc.

b) Greater adaptability to varying environmental conditions because all genes are present in the heterozygous state.

c) The expression of advantageous characters when these are controlled by dominant alleles e.g. disease resistance, tall habit.

d) Exclusivity of control by the breeder, since he alone retains the parents which together produce the commercial product.

Techniques for the Production of F₁ Hybrids

Before any detailed programme of F_1 hybrid production can get under way, a number of test crosses must be made, and the numerous F_1's evaluated. Initial pollinations are usually carried out by hand in a glasshouse with the object of producing a small amount of seed of each cross. Emasculation of flowers is essential to ensure that no selfed seed is produced.

Commercial quantities of F_1 hybrid seed may be produced under glass or in the field but the decision is normally a compromise between labour availability and expertise, and the financial considerations. In the USA most flower F_1 hybrids are produced by natural crossing between inbreds which are grown in the open, the seed often being harvested by machine. In Europe, however, most F_1 hybrid seed of flower crops is grown under glass e.g. antirrhinum, impatiens, pansy, petunia and salpiglossis. Most vegetable F_1's such as *Brassicas*, carrots and onions are produced in the open in countries with reliable summer climates, since higher quantities of seed are needed and the cost of glasshouse production is prohibitive. However, the economics of production for some F_1 hybrids of vegetables such as tomato, cucumber and peppers, and occasionally *Brassicas*, are such that they too can be 'bulked-up' under glass. Because they set large numbers of seeds from a single pollination (although each pollination entails the transfer of hundreds of pollen grains, of course), and also need to be emasculated by hand (except for all-female cucumbers – see p.107) production in the field cannot supply the critical conditions demanded.

The Use of Male-Sterility in F₁ Hybrid Production

(a)   Genetic
Using this technique a field can be planted with the two parent lines, one of which will be male sterile and will greatly outnumber the other (male fertile) line. Seed resulting from cross-fertilisation (the F_1 hybrid seed) will be obtained only from the male sterile parent since it must have been produced as a result of fertilisation by the other inbred line. Seed from all pollen-producing plants will be either discarded, or retained as a further inbred generation of the male fertile line.

The question which now springs to mind is – if the male sterile parent is unable to form seed by producing its own pollen, how does one obtain seed to sow it in the first place?

The most common genetic male sterility is that controlled by a recessive allele. Thus a male sterile (⚲) plant has the constitution *msms* – (homozygous recessive) while male fertile plants may be either *MsMs* or *Msms*. The heterozygote (Msms) will segregate to give 1 *MsMs*: 2 *Msms*: 1 *msms* – the usual segregation ratio for a single gene – but both homozygotes will, of course, breed true, (– except that the latter will produce no pollen to allow it to breed further!).

So, for use as a parent in F₁ hybrid production, the male sterile line is perpetuated by *backcrosses* of the heterozygous male fertile (as male parent Msms) to the double recessive *msms*. Through generations of backcrossing, each will be of the same phenotype, and the genotypes will differ only by the male sterility allele. In the subsequent generation, 50% of the progeny will be male fertile *Msms* while the other 50% will be male sterile *msms*.

For the actual production of F₁ hybrid seed in the field, the backcross generation would be interplanted with the other parental line (which is a normal male fertile inbred). Heterozygous male fertiles occurring in the backcross generation would be removed as soon as identification was possible, thus leaving completely male-sterile rows. The heterozygous (male fertile) plants would occur at random and their unwanted presence would mean that the rows should be planted at twice the normal density.

While removal of male fertiles should result in a fairly uniform stand of male steriles, it is imperative that they should be identified and destroyed without delay. Failure to remove the male fertiles will result in contamination of the F₁ hybrid seed – which must be produced after pollination by the normal male line only.

The ideal situation is one where either the male sterile plants or the heterozygous male fertiles can be recognised by the presence of a linked genetic marker, particularly one which shows up in the juvenile stage so that one class of plants could be removed before planting out. Unfortunately, such markers are extremely rare.

To summarise, the mechanics of using genetic male sterility for F₁ hybrid production require (a) a normal, fully-fertile inbred line and (b) an inbred line which is maintained (usually under glass) by crossing together known heterozygous (*Msms*) and male sterile (*msms*) plants. Seed must always be harvested from the *msms* plants and should give equal proportions of plants of the same genetic constitution as the parents. The crosses of *msms* x *Msms* should be repeated in every generation. *No Msms plants should be allowed to intercross with one another* since some homozygous male fertiles (*MsMs*) will be produced and will upset the system. In practice it would be advisable to raise isolated groups of up to ten *msms* plants with a single *Msms* plant. To ensure that the other gene differences do not build up, the heterozygous (*Msms*) parent plants can be used with different groups of main steriles in each generation. (c) For planting out in the field to raise commercial F₁ seed, seed from all groups of *msms* plants can be combined in order to provide sufficient plants.

(b) Cytoplasmic Male-Sterility

Another, less common, form of male sterility is particularly adapted to commercial utilisation and was first demonstrated practically by the production of *F₁* hybrid onions in the USA. Following some years of *F₁* hybrid onion production by this method however, various complications have been encountered due mainly to environmental influences, and reappraisals of the real value of male sterility in onions, are at present being made. Nevertheless, any search for the perfect method of *F₁* hybrid production would be unlikely to find a more workable system. Once again male sterility is controlled by a pair of recessive alleles, this time in association with an activating cytoplasm.

Thus a male sterile plant will have sterile-type cytoplasm (S), and double recessive nuclear *msms* alleles. Plants of male-fertile constitution either nullify the effect of the S cytoplasm by dominant genes for fertility, or by the presence of fertile (F) cytoplasm *Fmsms, FMsms* or *FMsMs*. Thus from six possible combinations of nucleus and cytoplasm only one gives the desired plant type.

To perpetuate male sterile lines, *Smsms* must be crossed (as female, since it has no pollen) with its genetically identical *msms* but cytoplasmically fertile *F–* to give again *Smsms*.

e.g. *Smsms* x *Fmsms*   (F is not transmitted through the pollen since only maternal cells contain cytoplasm.)

         Smsms

The male sterile line is normally referred to as the *A* line; the identical line (but with F cytoplasm) as the *B* line. To produce F_1 hybrid seed the *A* line is interplanted with a male fertile *C* line (of any genetic constitution). As will be appreciated, continual crossing of *A* and *B* together to produce the *A* line (*B* being perpetuated by saving seed separately) will, over a very short period, cause both *A* and *B* to resemble one another genetically, except for the cytoplasm, since such close mating is tantamount to inbreeding.

Cytoplasmic Male Sterility in Other Crops

In carrots, field beans (cross compatible with broad beans) and marigolds, a modified cytoplasmic-sterility system exists through which male sterile plants are able to produce seed (which again produces male-sterile plants) when crossed with related plants having 'restorer' constitutions. These 'restorers' are fertile and the proportion of male-sterile plants which they are capable of producing in the next generation depends upon their own polygenic make-up. A good restorer may produce 100 per cent male-sterile plants in every generation and therefore resembles the onion, while others may produce less, or be more subject to environment, so that the proportion of male-sterile plants does not remain constant.

The most reliable system is that where restorer males can regularly produce 100 per cent male-sterile plants. These are then used in F_1 hybrid production with a different male-fertile line – which produces only fully-fertile F_1 hybrid progenies.

Because cytoplasmic male-sterility is most desirable in those crops where there is a possibility of F_1 hybrids, it is appropriate at this point to illustrate how it may be found or identified. It is impossible to differentiate, morphologically, between nuclear and cytoplasmic male-sterility since both have the same effect, expressed either as a lack of pollen, non-release of pollen, or absence or abortion of the stamens.

Male sterile plants can be recognised comparatively easily in the field since the flower form is often distinct and they release no pollen when the anthers are brushed against the hand. When a male-sterile plant has been found, seed can only be obtained from it by using it as a female in crosses with normal plants. As long as each flower or flowering branch on the plant is labelled with the identity of the male parent, more than one male parent can be used.

Self Incompatibility in the Production of F_1 Hybrids

Many F_1 hybrids of outcrossing species have been produced by plant breeders who have taken advantage of the natural breeding system. The need for outcrossing in nature is often due to the action of an inhibitory system which prevents self-fertilisation. This results in the maintenance of hybridity and variability of genotype – avoiding the harmful effects of inbreeding and ensuring that the population retains its competitive ability.

Within such a population, however, good and bad genotypes coexist, and recognition and removal of the poor genotypes is a necessary precursor to the inbreeding, which itself precedes controlled hybridisation.

Although horticultural species comprise both gametophytic and sporophytic incompatibility systems, which give different results on self-fertilisation as indicated previously (page 19), the two types are treated in the same way during the initial stage of an F_1 hybrid programme. Desirable plants are selected from more than one mass-pollinated cultivar growing under normal cultural conditions, and are subsequently self-pollinated (in the bud stage to overcome the self-incompatible reaction). In the S_1 progeny lines it is advisable to select a fairly large number of plants ('fairly large' is an ambiguous term but must be related to the available practical facilities) within a limited number of the 'best' lines. In later selfed progenies, increasingly smaller numbers of within-line selections and larger numbers of between-line selections should be made. After the second generation of inbreeding, most lines will be homozygous for S (self-incompatibility) alleles as well as having considerable phenotypic uniformity.

In those species or cultivars with the sporophytic system, the degree of self-incompatibility can be assessed by examining flower styles with the ultra-violet fluorescent microscope a few hours after pollination. Pollen-tubes which have penetrated the stigma, and are thus able to grow down the style unimpeded, are able to be counted since they identify themselves by fluorescence. The lack of, or only a small number of pollen-tubes throughout their length, indicate a strong incompatibility reaction. If the incompatibility reaction is weak, counting will prove impossible since numerous pollen-tubes show up as a tangled mass within the stylar tissue.

A simpler, though slower, method which does not require expensive equipment makes use of the individual plant's seed-setting capacity. Open flowers of plants from a sporophytically self-incompatible population which are cross-pollinated should set the maximum number of seeds since there will be no inhibitory reactions. By comparing seed set from these against the seed set from self-pollinated open flowers (protected from all foreign pollen) a direct quantitative assessment of self-incompatibility can be made. The two advantages of this method are that pollination results should be repeatable and that the selfed seed is immediately available if it is decided to use any of the experimental plants for the inbreeding programme.

Highly self-incompatible plants (or lines composed of their selfed progeny) should set little or no seed on their own – but will set seed profusely when cross-pollinated with another highly self-incompatible line. All seed from these crosses should be of F_1 hybrid constitution. If, as occasionally happens, two highly self-incompatible inbred lines fail to produce seed when pair-crossed, it is more than likely that each line carries identical S alleles. Although lines may appear, morphologically, quite different from one another, they may be identical in their genetic self-incompatibility and will therefore act as if they were the same inbred line. The practical advantages in crossing widely diverse genotypes to bring together 'distant' groups of genes, also increase the chances of obtaining distinct S alleles.

Once self-incompatible lines have been established it is still necessary to carry out a test-crossing programme to choose the best hybrid. Even after this, constant checks must be made to ensure that the self-incompatibility of each inbred parent is not breaking down since large numbers of 'selfs' instead of hybrids may be produced under certain environmental conditions.

45

F₂ Hybrids

Now and again, references to F_2 hybrids appear in the literature or in seedmen's catalogues. In the strict genetical sense, the terminology is correct since all plants in an F_2 generation will be heterozygous and therefore 'hybrid'. Because of the implied relationship with F_1 hybrids, however, further clarification is necessary.

The commonly accepted features of F_1 hybrids have already been discussed in detail, the two major characteristics being uniformity and vigour (expressed in various ways). When F_1 hybrids are allowed to interpollinate and set seed, plants of the subsequent generation (the F_2) will consist of a wide range of types due to genetic segregation. While this may not be disconcerting (in a colour mixture of antirrhinum, for example) the yield or vigour factors will also be segregating and the general level will always be lower than that of the F_1. This may be relatively unimportant in flowers but a reduction in yield (and a possible loss of quality) in an F_2 vegetable crop cannot usually be considered. The sale of F_2 hybrid seed is confined to flower crops in the main and loss of vigour is unlikely to be greater than ten per cent.

F_2 seed is cheaper than F_1, the variable plant types can be harvested over a longer season, and because unusual types may occasionally be found, the amateur, though not the professional, may welcome F_2 vegetables.

Synthetic Hybrids

The production of an F_1 hybrid, as we have seen, is preceded by the production of genetically uniform inbred lines. If a number of these inbred lines were allowed to flower together, random cross-pollination would occur and mixed hybrid seed would be produced.

Synthetic hybrids are grown from such seed, but in this case the seed is obtained from known numbers of parent lines and plants within them. The choice of inbred lines as parents is based upon their ability to combine with others to produce good hybrid plants and to resemble all other hybrids fairly closely regardless of the crossing combinations which have taken place. Many combinations of inbred lines and varying numbers of plants within them may be used, and the overall combinations are usually finalised by trial and error – unless planned genetic experiments have provided evidence of parental combining ability.

Inbred seed for raising plants which will produce seed of the 'synthetic', is mixed in the appropriate proportions so that plants will flower and be cross-pollinated as a random mixture of inbred lines and plants. Because of the (hopefully) high levels of self-incompatibility within each inbred line, successful pollinations will take place only between plants belonging to different inbreds. Although seed of the synthetic cultivar can be reproduced regularly year after year there are bound to be slight variations in its composition. These will be caused by such factors as alterations in the placement of plants relative to one another, variations in the activity or preferences of insect pollinators, death of some parent plants etc. but the end result will probably be just as acceptable to the consumer.

Seed of synthetic hybrids is more expensive to produce than that from conventional mass-pollinated cultivars although the techniques of production are similar. The cost of research and handling of inbreds must be taken into account while, practically, seed quantities from inbred lines are usually less than from mass-pollinated heterozygous plants.

An illustration of synthetic hybrid production is given in Figure 5.

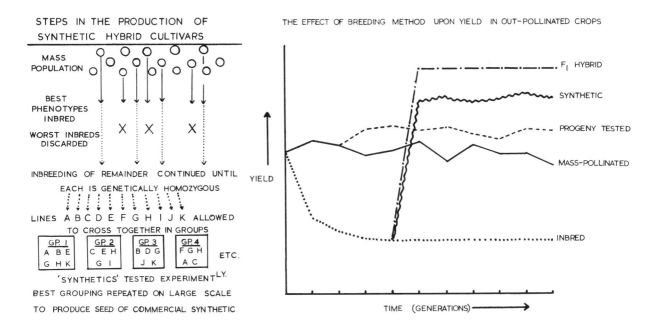

The production of hybrids – a brief summary of requirements

(a) *Inbreeding*: is essential in order to produce homozygosity and uniformity.

The 'best' plants (i.e. those with the most desirable characteristics) should be selected for initial selfing in both parental and S_1 generations.

Further selections from the S_2 generation and beyond should be of the best individual plants from the best lines only.

Inbred lines tend to be weak and those which cannot withstand 'normal' conditions should be rejected from the programme.

When male sterility is to be used, inbreeding will be accomplished by pair crossing.

(b) *Test crosses*: should be made between *complementary* plant types of different varietal origins, *which are known to flower over the same period.*

The line with the greatest seed-setting potential should always be used as female parent, but neither line should set selfed seed. Some crosses may fail to produce seed because both lines carry identical S alleles.

(c) *F_2 hybrids*: are less vigorous and less uniform than the F_1 hybrids from which they are derived.

(d) *Synthetic hybrids*: are produced by allowing a number of inbred lines to inter-pollinate.

The type of synthetic is controlled by the proportions of inbred lines in its composition.

Finally, the effects of different breeding systems upon out-pollinated crops are summarised diagrammatically in Figure 6.

Inbreeding causes marked yield reductions but synthesis of F_1 hybrids from inbreds tends to produce high yields with great consistency. Yields of synthetic hybrids are generally below F_1 hybrids and fluctuate slightly due to differential pollination. Mass-pollinated cultivars vary annually either side of an 'average' yield while progeny-tested material shows improvements in both yield and annual reliability.

Fig 5. (left) Steps in the production of synthetic hybrid cultivars.

Fig 6. (right) The effect of breeding method upon yield in out-pollinated crops.

47

Breeding for Disease Resistance

The techniques used in breeding for disease resistance differ very little from those used when breeding for any other characteristic. In this case, however, we can only be certain that the breeding programme has succeeded if the new line or cultivar withstands infection *when all associated cultivars have succumbed*. Under natural conditions it is usual to find that some plants in a heterozygous population are resistant to prevalent diseases. If these are allowed to seed, their progeny would probably also prove to be resistant and a valuable new cultivar could be in the pipeline. Because the disease organism (the pathogen) regularly produces new genetic combinations which alter its aggressiveness, however, the resistance of the new lines could be overcome in time and any resistance-breeding programme must therefore be continuous. With the repetitive 'swings and roundabouts', both plant and pathogen exist over the years in a state of balance with one another; 'resistance' is rarely absolute (when it is referred to as immunity) but is considered to be satisfactory when, despite the presence of some disease, the crop is seen to be largely unaffected.

Plants which show immunity are said to possess specific (or vertical) resistance while those which are affected by, but can overcome, the disease organism are classified as having generalised (or horizontal) resistance.

When scientific plant breeding was first stimulated by genetic theory, the most common approach to disease resistance was by field selection, resulting in a resistance of the generalised type.

Later, when it was shown that some plants owed their resistance to the presence of a major gene, plant breeders concentrated upon breeding for complete immunity, particularly with cereals and potatoes. While, on the face of it, immunity seems to possess obvious advantages, these are nevertheless only transitory. Fungal, bacterial or viral pathogens are able to show genetic variation in a manner similar to the higher plants which they parasitise and, confronted with a complete obstacle in the form of an immune crop, must overcome it in order to survive.

When disease has been a problem and an immune cultivar becomes available the tendency is for all farmers or growers to grow it. While this cannot be colonised *en-masse* by the usual parasite the cultivar has the effect of favouring those individuals in the parasite population which are able to attack it successfully. These individuals proliferate unnoticed for a time until favourable environmental conditions (perhaps two or three years hence) encourage the new form of parasite to such an extent that its numbers explode and the crop is decimated.

48   With the generalised form of resistance on the other hand, there is always

some evidence of pathogenic attack, which may be worse in some seasons than others. Because of the fact that the pathogen is not completely deprived of its food source, however, a host-pathogen balance is achieved and large crop losses are less common.

Current trends in breeding are directed towards this form of generalised field, or natural resistance which is most frequently under the control of polygenes rather than major genes which give (temporary) immunity.

Techniques of Assessing Disease Resistance

The simplest method of detecting disease resistance is by the careful observation of a growing crop attacked by a pathogen. The heavier the general level of infection the greater the possibility that uninfected plants will be truly resistant rather than 'escapes' which have somehow avoided colonisation by the disease organism.

When breeding material is being grown in a search for disease resistance, natural infection can be assisted by releasing cultures of the pathogen into the crop. Sophisticated techniques for raising quantities of pathogen may be employed but the disease organism can frequently be 'helped on its way' by the simple expedient of washing off infected tissues from susceptible plants and watering or spraying the effluent on to the test material. In the presence of heavy infection any resistant plants will be clearly seen and they should be selected to produce seed of the next generation. The degree of resistance will become apparent when progenies can be compared against one another if infection recurs the following year.

Although the most useful type of resistance is that which exploits natural infection, there are limitations to the selection of parent plants under these circumstances. It is impossible to predict that levels of infection will be similar in successive years and, consequently, false assumptions may be made about the disease resistance of some lines. A low level of infection for example, would lead to increases in the number of selected lines and the practical handling difficulties could prevent good material from being selected. A second limitation to selection under natural infection is the existence of local strains or races of the pathogen so that plants selected for resistance in one locality may prove to be susceptible in another. Supplementary cultures which are added to the local races should, therefore, be collected from as wide a range as possible. To overcome the environmental effect, next year's progeny tests would be carried out at a number of different centres, although this too may present practical difficulties.

Because of the difficulty of standardising infection under natural conditions, most programmes for the introduction of disease resistance are now carried out (at least, in their initial stages) in the controlled environments of laboratory, growth room or glasshouse. While the 'natural method' is subject to limitations, these techniques also cannot be regarded as perfect. It must never be forgotten that a breeding line will eventually be tested under cropping conditions and must produce a marketable yield or satisfactory display. Thus, laboratory tests on juvenile material may indicate disease resistance but this has to be confirmed in the crop – which will eventually be growing for months in variable weather – before the tests can be accepted as reliable.

Controlled disease-testing is practised widely in vegetables such as lettuce, tomatoes, cucumbers, peas and beans but only a limited number of flower crops (antirrhinum and sweet peas) since few diseases are severe enough to spoil the 49 floral display. The basic techniques used are those which favour the parasite rather than the host plants and the optimum conditions of temperatures, humidity and nutrients are now known for a wide range of organisms.

Thus, when testing the resistance of tomatoes to *Fusarium* wilt or *Cladosporium* (Leaf mould) seedlings are grown in temperatures of 23°C., – which gives most rapid growth of the fungi, but when testing lettuce for resistance to *Bremia* (downy mildew) the seedlings or cotyledons are held at 15°C., the different temperatures favouring different parasites.

The source of infection (inoculum) is usually maintained on specially grown plant material, or in nutrient solution extracted from plants or compounded artificially.

Tests are almost always made on juvenile material since it is easier to handle and can be used in large quantities. Apart from some tests made on seeds, the most juvenile phase is when cotyledons are used. These may be detached from the seedling or infected while attached. Methods of infection vary but usually involve spraying with a spore suspension, or absorption through contact with infected filter-paper.

Seedling plants may be tested entire or as discs of leaf tissue. The discs are usually cut with a cork borer and then treated in a similar manner to the detached cotyledons. Because of their limited life both the leaf discs and detached cotyledons must be assessed over a short period.

Practical Techniques of Artificially Inoculating Disease Organisms

Within the framework of a plant breeding publication it is possible to describe only briefly the methods used for raising and transferring disease organisms. Each pathogen requires specialised conditions but is usually multiplied by one of the following methods.

1. *Viruses*

In nature, these are transmitted from plant to plant by leaf rubbing due to wind or mechanical action, by contamination of cut surfaces when shoots are removed or grafted, by sucking insects such as aphids, by soil fungi or fauna or by transmission through seed. Some species, totally unrelated to the crop under study, may show severe symptoms of virus disease when inoculated and these are often used as 'tester' plants in an inoculation programme.

Before testing breeding material, seedlings of a cultivar susceptible to the particular virus are grown and inoculated with the pathogen – this being readily available in commercial crops otherwise there would be little need for a breeding programme against it. It may be possible to use leaf material direct from the field instead of inoculating seedlings as an intermediate stage but laboratory cultures of infected plant material are easily maintained and, therefore, regularly available.

When a programme of inoculation is to be started, breeding lines must be sown and seedlings to be tested spaced wide enough for satisfactory growth to the fifth leaf stage. When the second leaf of the test material is fully extended, leaf tissue (without large veins or midrib) from the infected plants or seedlings is ground in a mortar. Sap is strained through butter muslin or its equivalent and diluted with distilled water. Dilutions vary according to the nature of the virus but are normally greater than ten times. Breeding material is next dusted with 'Celite' – a fine abrasive powder – and each seedling is inoculated with infected sap, which is applied to the leaf surfaces by gentle smoothing with finger and thumb, or with gauze bandage. To avoid surface oxidation of the damaged tissue, seedlings should be lightly watered overhead within minutes of inoculation. To be certain that active virus was present in the inoculum one or two tester plants of the sensitive species should be treated in the same manner as all other seedlings. Inoculum deteriorates rapidly and should be renewed within five minutes unless stored in a refrigerator.

Symptoms of virus infection should first appear on the tester plants, and should then become noticeable a few days later as a typical mottling or spotting on some of the susceptible segregants within the breeding lines. Symptoms on tester and crop plants are unlikely to appear the same. To be sure that breeding lines which show no symptoms are resistant, however, the tester plants must be included in the inoculation programme to indicate that the virus was infective.

Transmission of some viruses for assessing resistance of segregating material is often more effectively carried out by using infected insects (usually aphids). These are first fed on infected plants and are then transferred to the test plants. Different viruses have different transmission times, however, and detailed techniques must be learnt from the appropriate text books.

2. Bacteria

Bacterial diseases tend to be less common than either virus or fungal diseases but are nevertheless serious – as anyone with runner or dwarf beans attacked by halo blight (*Pseudomonas phaseolicola*) will testify.

Bacteria to be used for disease screening tests are normally cultured in a 'broth' of nutrient medium after their removal as infected areas from living material. In liquid media, cultures of bacteria are difficult to separate and tend to remain mixed. The eventual application to test-plants of more than one pathogen provides a very thorough screening for resistance, however.

Before adding infected material, the basic culture medium should be made up in the required quantity, excluding those items which undergo a chemical change when heated, and sterilised in an autoclave or pressure cooker.

Tap water may be used in the basic culture medium if it has a low mineral content (small amounts of copper inhibit bacterial growth) together with enough agar to form a slight gel (approx. 0.8 per cent), dissolved at $100°C$ for one hour. Proprietary culture formulations with or without agar are widely available from biological suppliers. For a flask containing 100ml of culture media, sterilisation should be 20 minutes at $121°C$ and for 500ml, 25 minutes. Before placing the flask within the autoclave it should be uncorked to allow for expansion of the contents, and those culture media which are affected by heat should be added when the flask has cooled after sterilisation.

A liquid extract from infected tissue (a filtration of plant material which was mixed with water in a liquidiser) should now be added to the prepared culture media.

The completed culture should then be agitated continually in a mechanical shaker at room temperature for a few days until the liquid medium thickens slightly. Bacterial suspension is best applied to whole test-plants by spraying it on tissues which have been slightly damaged by abrasion with 'celite'. These are subsequently kept moist in a humid atmosphere at least until the first symptoms are seen.

Among other techniques for infecting plants or seedlings with bacterial suspensions are inoculation with multiple needles or by sand blasting; seed-leaf or root dips, or water-soaking. Most techniques are intended to duplicate the natural system through which bacteria enter plant tissues. Watersoaking   51 particularly, acts as a robust form of spraying by which bacteria are forced into the internal tissues of the more delicate plant parts.

3. Fungi

The most ubiquitous diseases are those caused by fungi. These normally invade their new host plants after being blown as spores by the wind to leaf and flower surfaces, or carried in water droplets. Spores are produced in multi-millions when the correct conditions prevail but epidemics are likely to occur only when the local environment continually favours the parasite. It is because of the enormity of spore populations and so, of recombined genetic types, that fungi are capable of overcoming in such a short period of time the resistance hitherto shown by their hosts. In order to devise experiments to test the resistance of breeding material it is first essential to know whether the appropriate disease organism is an obligate parasite which lives only on living material, or a facultative parasite which allows fungal cultures to be maintained on artificial media.

When obligate parasites are to be used for eventual inoculation to breeding material, they must be kept alive on juvenile plants in an environment which allows satisfactory growth of the fungus without causing the death of the host plants. If death occurred, the fungus being obligate, would itself succumb unless further plant material was introduced in time. Most of the downy mildew, wilt and rust diseases of flowers and vegetables are caused by obligate parasites.

Raising Inoculum on Artificial Media

Facultative parasites may be cultured on living plants if this is found expedient but where laboratory facilities are available it is easier to exercise control of the fungal material by growing it in nutrient culture. The composition of the nutrient culture is usually varied to suit the needs of the particular fungus but one substance, agar a gelatinous base, is common to all. A typical general formulation which has wide application for raising numerous fungal species is as follows:

Malt agar   2.5 gms malt
                200 gms agar
                1000 ccs water

Agar is incorporated by dissolving in hot water in proportions 1:5. Nutrient culture is sterilised by boiling for 15 minutes at 15lbs pressure and, before pouring to cool, any containers and their covers must be sterilised in an autoclave or pressure cooker. Because of the possible presence of spores which are resistant to dehydration in heat, glass containers should be sterilised dry at 140°C, for five hours. All conditions should be as sterile as possible but even without an isolated preparation room most contamination can be avoided by immediately covering the poured media. Containers may range from test tubes to conical flasks or petri dishes. In the former, the tubes are stoppered with a sterile cotton wool plug and inclined at about 45° to allow the nutrient agar to set as a 'slope'. The latter two containers are stood right way up, thus allowing all to present a large surface area for inoculation with fungus. The nutrient media should keep for months at 4°C if the flasks containing it are covered with aluminium foil to prevent dehydration.

In many laboratories, screw-top culture tubes are used, and in this case it is

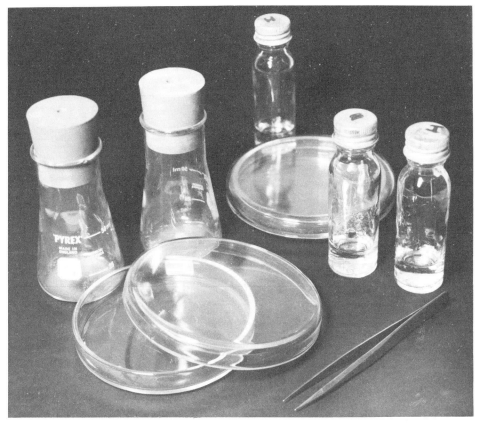

Plate 6. Range of containers for liquid or agar nutrient medium, into which inoculations of disease organisms will be made.

important that the cap should be only lightly screwed in place while the nutrient medium is cooling. After reaching room temperature, the medium is protected from chance spores by tightening the cap.

Inoculations of the nutrient agar are made by using sterile needles to transfer spots of hyphae or spores from an infected plant or from another artificial culture. Lids (sterilised in a flame, as is the neck of the tube) or cotton wool plugs are replaced as quickly as possible to avoid contamination from other airborne spores. Contamination of the agar by fungi other than the desired type may occur when transfers are made from the host plant since it has been openly exposed to other organisms, and this will be recognised in the culture by the production of different forms (and probably colours) of hyphae.

The correct species can be isolated satisfactorily however by making further transfers after cutting out the contaminant 'patch'.

Although cultures grow adequately under normal room conditions they should properly be maintained at the same temperature as that to be used for the breeding material under test. Breeding material should be ready for inoculation when sporulation of the fungus takes place. Spore inoculum is made by washing-off the spores of the agar culture into a small quantity of distilled water after which the spore concentration is determined by microscopic examination of a droplet within a haemocytometer. This is simply a means of counting a representative sample of spores so that the necessary dilution of the original solution may be made. Spore suspensions for inoculation are usually within the range 10^5 to 10^7 spores per ml (i.e. 100,000 to 10,000,000). After dilution to the correct strength, spore solutions are sprayed on to the breeding material as a fine mist until 'run-off' – when no more solution will remain on the leaves. For glossy leaves a 'sticker' may be added to the solution to ensure that some remains on the leaf surface while a 'wetter' (detergent) may be needed on other leaves in order to spread the water droplets more evenly. Because many spores enter the leaf through the stomates, or breathing pores, the under surface of all leaves must also be well covered with spore solution.

After inoculation, host plants are normally kept moist or within an atmosphere of high humidity until disease symptoms appear. Initially, these symptoms are usually quite unlike those found on a mature plant in the field but will eventually become characteristic. However, discarding of unwanted susceptible breeding material can start when the early disease symptoms are recognised.

Subsequent Handling of Resistant Material

Although laboratory and glasshouse inoculations reduce 'escape' from infection to a low degree, a chance nevertheless remains that some resistant plants will not prove so in later tests or in the field under natural conditions. In addition, the resistant part of the segregating population will comprise plants which are both homozygous and those which are heterozygous for resistance factors.

At this juncture it is important to emphasise one vital point of procedure which should never be overlooked when testing plants for disease resistance. Unless material under test is known to possess resistance through *dominant* genes the F_1 hybrid generation should *never* be inoculated. If the genetic control of resistance is unknown or is due to recessive genes, inoculation of the F_1 population could destroy all breeding material or, at best, lead to results which could be both erroneous and depressing. Instead, the F_1 plants should be allowed to seed to produce the F_2 generation *which will be inoculated*.

From the results obtained in the F_2 it should be possible to postulate the inheritance of resistance to the particular disease. If, for example, three-quarters of the plants proved resistant it would be most likely that resistance was controlled by a single dominant gene, although further tests must be conducted before accepting this first result at its face value. Resistant plants should be allowed to seed – and seed of each saved separately. With a monogenic segregation, further inoculation should produce both resistant and susceptible plants within two single-plant-progenies out of every three. The third progeny should comprise resistant plants only (see below). Diagrammatically, the system of inoculation should be as follows – where R = Resistance, r = susceptibility.

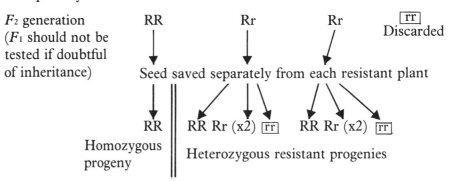

Any progenies from 'escape' plants will, of course, produce only susceptible plants.

While many systems of disease resistance are controlled by major genes, polygenic inheritance may sometimes be overlooked because of resemblances to a major gene segregation. Thus, following the previous example, one quarter of a segregating F_2 progeny may be discarded on the evidence of heavy infection although some of the remaining material may, in time, have become infected to a lesser degree. After obtaining seed of the 'resistant' plants, however, the form of resistance should be resolved when making further field or laboratory tests of the single-plant progenies. Polygenic control of disease resistance will be characterised by a continuous variation of disease symptoms within each single plant progeny and, for all progenies together, a continuous range in their mean values for resistance.

Having ascertained the form of inheritance, the further development of a resistance-breeding programme should proceed according to the general technique for major or polygene inheritance with continual recourse to the correct screening methods.

In general, resistance to a particular disease is bound to be increased if seed is taken only from plants with the least infection – which themselves should have been derived from the least infected parents.

Although many glasshouse and laboratory tests for resistance have been successful and are effective in current use, they are generally outweighed by the advantages of selecting resistant material under field conditions. This is particularly so if natural infections can be expected to occur with regularity – or by easy artificial stimulation – as happens with black leaf-spot attacks on roses in the summer when grown in non-industrial areas. By growing crops in the field, especially when segregating after crossing, there are extra chances of selecting desirable morphological types and, due to the size of population, of ensuring that only the most resistant individuals are chosen.

Where possible, particularly with soil-borne diseases such as *Fusarium* and *Verticillium* wilt, 'disease areas' can be built up by continuously growing susceptible cultivars and burying their residues. Segregating material grown on the site should then be subjected to considerable natural infection and resistant plants should be easily identified. Peas resistant to *Fusarium oxysporum* Race 1 and tomatoes resistant to both the above diseases are in common usage following such techniques of selection.

In a similar way, crops grown and selected in one environment can exhibit enhanced resistance when compared with similar crops which have been bred or selected elsewhere. This is the case with *Botrytis* (grey mould) resistance of some British-bred marigold hybrids composed with that of their American counter-parts which are more accustomed to sunny skies. Internal browning of Brussels Sprouts (a zonal deterioration inside sprout buttons of perfect external appearance) is more pronounced in the wetter, more humid, regions of Ireland than in Great Britain. Although this appears to be a physiological disorder rather than a disease, the implication is that true resistance is most likely to be found by examining genetic segregants grown in the Emerald Isle. Since this disorder can only be assessed by cutting 'buttons' in half, plants which are 100 per cent healthy can be propagated vegetatively by rooting the dissected plant material.

A compromise technique similar to that outlined for Brussels sprout, and making use of the better aspects of both field and glasshouse testing, can be evolved with a range of crops. Antirrhinum rust, for example, is a serious disease which can often cause deleafing and browning of plants at or immediately after flowering. If cuttings of axillary shoots are taken from selected plants in the field these can be quickly rooted in a sand bench under mist irrigation. The small number of rust spores present in the vegetative population will very rapidly multiply with no extra encouragement, and within three or four weeks of removal from the parent plant some cuttings will have proved to be very obviously susceptible.

Now is the time to discard the original field selections which are known to lack resistance. To be able to do this, of course, both vegetative cutting and field plant should have been identically labelled!

The mist propagator, used in this way, can greatly simplify resistance breeding, particularly for those disease organisms which thrive in high humidity such as the downy mildews, leaf and flower moulds, and bacterial spotting diseases.

The Introduction of Disease Resistance from Wild Species

All cultivars are adapted forms, derived many generations ago from uncultivated, wild, plant species. Selection through the years has been directed towards economic and competitive advantages, with the consequence that hidden characters, such as disease resistance were preserved only when their value was evident at the time of initial selection. Derived plant forms are therefore unlikely to carry all available genes concerned with disease resistance – nor, in fact, will they carry other genes affecting even less noticeable characters.

In the present state of intensive plant production, disease epidemics can cause serious losses of income, or disruption of planting schemes which disease-resistant lines would escape. While some cultivars may be proved disease-resistant, the greatest chance of finding 'new' resistance-genes lies in the use of their wild progenitors. Plant species tend to have characteristic centres of origin (such as the area including Ethiopia for peas and *Lathyrus*, or Northern India for *Primulas*) and the more primitive species remaining in (or obtained from) these areas, if cross-compatible, would probably provide the right genetic material. Because of the greater need to build up disease-free food stocks the search for disease resistance has hitherto been concentrated mostly upon vegetable and cereal species, although flowers are currently receiving greater attention.

In general, wild species are far removed in appearance from the cultivated types and most crossing programmes for disease-resistance inevitably follow the backcross pattern. By this means, only those genes concerned with resistance are ultimately incorporated into the new cultivar. 'Backcrossing' in this case, however, can be accomplished by using different cultivars in each generation ending with a new disease-resistant form.

Because of the long time and development interval between present-day cultivars and their wild ancestors, mutational or chromosomal changes will have proceeded independently, resulting in varying degrees of incompatibility between species or types. In some instances the cross-incompatibility may be so complete that the only chance of transferring a resistance character is by using other related, and more compatible, species in the form of a genetic 'bridge' between the two cross-incompatible parents. Another form of cross-incompatibility is found when the cross can be made in one direction only. The reciprocal cross may prove fully ineffective in fertilisation. Thus *Lycopersicon* (tomato) will set seed when pollinated with one of its wild ancestors *Lycopersicon hirsutum* which is resistant to *Didymella* disease, but no seed set is obtained when the cross is made reciprocally.

Such unilateral cross-incompatibility between wild parent and derived cultivar, is most frequent when the wild ancestor is used as female, and appears to be due to relics of the *self*-incompatibility system.

Unless there are basic reasons for one-way-crossing it is imperative that crosses involving wild species should be made in both directions to be certain that hybridisation is possible.

56

PART II: THE BREEDING OF SPECIFIC CROPS

The Breeding of Specific Crops

Technical Application of Genetic Principles

Although genetic knowledge can be applied in the improvement of both animals and plants, the techniques used for breeding different genera even within the same botanical family may be almost as diverse as between fauna and flora. The breeding of any crop species can only be successfully attempted after gaining knowledge of the characteristic breeding system and the (usually) unique floral morphology. In this section it is intended to provide as many practical details of emasculation, pollination, etc., as are essential for the smooth running of breeding programmes in most common crops or species.

A breeding programme does not start with a series of cross-pollinations and end with a seed harvest. It begins with the choice of parents and the timing of seed sowing to produce coincident flowering; it continues with close-observance of any handicaps at flowering time such as stigma receptivity or self-sterility, while after pollination, the length of seed maturation is noted so that valuable crosses are not wasted by seed shedding. During the whole period the cultural requirements of the plants must be met, since many good pollination schemes have been ruined by allowing the seed bearers to die from lack of attention.

The Importance of Emasculation

Certain characteristic features of the flowering and reproductive physiology of plant families must be recognised before embarking upon a programme of emasculation and hybridisation. The number of anthers (male organs) within each flower is constant for a family although anthers of species belonging to the same family may differ morphologically, or by their position or arrangement within the flower. Thus, plants and species of the family *Cruciferae* all have six anthers within each flower – whether they are from Brompton Stock or Watercress. The Iris family has three anthers per flower but Sisyrinchium, a member of the family, which is obviously a dwarf iris, joins its anthers into a tube and could thus be confused with other groups of plants. Occasional disfigured flowers in all species may bear more or fewer anthers but these can usually be traced to developmental upsets earlier in the life of the plant.

Whenever cross-pollinations are to be made they must be preceded by emasculation – removal of the anthers – in order to prevent self-fertilisation. Even though the plant or species is thought to be sterile, while the anthers remain there is always the chance that a seed may be formed from self –, rather than cross-fertilisation. Anthers should be removed in the bud stage so that no 57 pollen is shed, and counted to ensure that the expected number have all been detached. In some species, anthers can be removed individually but others are fused together (e.g. *Impatiens*, Tomato) and must be removed as a whole. In such instances it is essential that the whole anther mass is detached since any remaining pieces will mature to produce ripe pollen and could contaminate a controlled pollination. In general, single – as distinct from fused – anthers are borne on long filaments and can be easily detached by a gentle tug with the forceps. If possible, it is best to grip the tip of the filament, rather than the anthers, with the forceps so that no rupturing of the anther wall takes place.

Pollination of some species cannot be carried out at the time of emasculation. Many umbelliferae – carrots, parsnips, and *eryngium* tend to exhibit *protandry* as do godetia and impatiens, by shedding their pollen before the stigmas are receptive. If emasculation (which is difficult in *Umbelliferae*) is practised, the treated flowers cannot be pollinated for approximately two more days. The converse – protogyny – when stigmas are receptive before pollen of the same flower has been shed, – occurs in a limited number of species. With these species cross-pollination is likely to be successful more often.

Although many flowers and vegetables belong to the same family (e.g. Aster, marigold, sunflower, globe artichoke, lettuce and chicory are all members of the *Compositae*) they are dealt with separately in this section under the two headings 'Flower crops' and 'Vegetable crops' unless pollination and related techniques are so similar that their descriptions would involve duplication. Only the more common species are described in detail since the general pollination technique will be applicable, with slight modifications, to the whole family. *For all pollinations it must be remembered that one pollen grain can fertilise only one ovule,* no matter how large a quantity of pollen is applied.

A. Flower Crops

Family Amaryllidaceae

Comprises Daffodil, narcissus and snowdrop. Anthers six; emasculation in the loose-bud stage, after emergence of the flower through the spathe, by inserting forceps through the bud petals and removal of anthers singly. Cross-pollination at mature flower stage using a small paint-brush covered with pollen, or by using whole anthers from a recently opened flower of the appropriate male parent. Pollination procedure should be carried out in a warm (55 – 65°F) glasshouse and successful pollinations should be recognised by ovary swelling within three weeks. Successful pollinations should give up to twenty seeds per flower. These should be sown immediately upon maturity otherwise natural dormancy will occur. Because this family belongs to the monocotyledon class, germinating seeds will be recognised by their single green shoot, rather similar to a seedling grass though with a more 'rounded' leaf. Seed sown when first ripe should germinate in the Autumn although some may not appear until the following Spring.

From date of initial pollination to production of first flower usually takes five years. If any of the new hybrids show promise the initial bulb will be propagated by offsets to multiply the line. Due to the fact that most varieties are genetically hybrid, results from self-pollination should be as good as those from crossing.

Balsaminaceae

Comprises *Impatiens* species. Anthers five, fused, tightly surrounding a shiny ovary which is tipped by short, feathery stigmas. Mature anthers may release pollen which tends to fall upon the stigmatic surfaces. Alternatively, the fused anthers become forcibly detached from the petals by upward growth of the ovary, fall upon the lower petal and make contact with the stigmas. Self-pollination with profuse, mauve-coloured pollen then takes place. Since self-fertilisation is very common in this species, emasculation should be carried out when flowers have just started to open. Forceps should be inserted above and behind the anthers, giving a gentle forward pull but avoiding damage to the ovary. This forces the anthers to fall forward and downwards. Alternatively, the anther filaments, which may be recognised as thin pieces of tissue resting upon the ovary, can be broken one by one using the forceps.

Pollination is most successfully carried out (using the anther tube from the appropriate male) one or two days after emasculation when the stigmatic tufts can be easily distinguished. Seeds should mature within two weeks under glass, 59

Plate 7. Impatiens flowers showing unemasculated (left) and emasculated (right) floral parts. Anthers of right hand flower are still present on the petals.

at approximately 65 – 70°F. Pods should be harvested carefully when swollen to the size of an apple pip since the walls rupture sharply to eject and disperse their seeds. Each pollination should result in the production of approximately ten seeds. These germinate readily and are not subject to dormancy.

Begoniaceae

Comprises numerous species of *Begonia*. Most species appear to be polyploid and the cross-compatibility between them cannot be predicted with accuracy, thus indicating the desirability of test crosses for introducing new characteristics. The commonly cultivated species (*Begonia rex* and *semperflorens*) are monoecious, bearing male and female flowers separately upon the same plant, (see Figure 7). Plants with flowers of different sexes have a prepotency for cross-fertilisation although self-fertilisation can be carried out just as easily. Emasculation is unnecessary but female flowers must, of course, be protected from contamination by pollen from male flowers of the same plant if controlled pollinations are to be made.

Stigmas are receptive when flowers are fully open but anthers may not willingly release pollen and should, under these circumstances, be rubbed or squeezed on a hard surface. Pollen will then be picked up and applied by brush. When using a male parent with dehiscent (easily splitting) anthers, numerous pollinations can be made direct by detaching and pollinating with male flowers. Since female flowers occur on both parents, reciprocal pollinations should be made to increase seed amounts. Begonia seed is smaller than that of most other flower species and one pollination should produce approximately 500 seeds, within three or four weeks. Seed germination is high with freshly harvested material. *Begonia semperflorens* is particularly suited to a programme of F_1 hybrid production–which must be preceded by inbreeding to obtain uniformity.

Boraginaceae

Few common horticultural flowers but including *Heliotrope, Echium, myosotis*

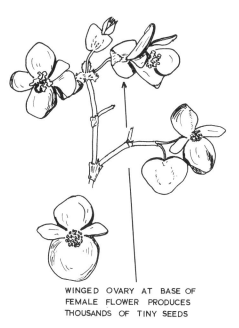

BEGONIA SEMPERFLORENS
(SEPARATE MALE & FEMALE FLOWERS)

WINGED OVARY AT BASE OF
FEMALE FLOWER PRODUCES
THOUSANDS OF TINY SEEDS

Fig 7. Begonia flowers, having
separate males and females
upon the same plant
(Monoecy).

and *anchusa*. Myosotis (forget-me-not) tends to be self-incompatible but since
this characteristic is rarely absolute, for certainty of cross-fertilisation it is first
necessary to emasculate. This should be done in the bud stage, removal of the
five anthers being followed by immediate cross-pollination.

When breeding *Echium*, advantage may be taken of the fact that some plants
possess only female flowers (they are, in fact, male sterile) or flowers may be
mixed female and hermaphrodite. For crossing purposes, the female flowers are
obviously invaluable.

Campanulaceae

Comprises Canterbury Bell, rockery campanulas and Lobelia. Five anthers,
which are attached to the base of the petals and which cluster together around
the top of the style in the immature flower or bud. Flowers are sometimes found
with more than five anthers, in which case it will be seen that the petal number
matches them exactly.

Although the Lobelia flower is irregular in form, its reproductive organs are
nevertheless arranged similarly to those of the uniform campanula flowers, and
emasculation and cross-pollination are identical for each species.

Anthers and stigmas appear very similar to one another at the time when
emasculation should be practised i.e. in the young bud stage when flower colour
is becoming recognisable, and great care must be exercised. The three stigmas
on the top of the style tend to intermingle with the similarly coloured anthers
and are vertical in the bud stage, later opening out and becoming receptive.
Anthers tend to resist being detached, but if one of the stigmas is pulled by
mistake the extra resistance makes the error quite obvious. Cross-pollinations
should be made as the flower reaches the opening stage.

61

Caryophyllaceae

The pink, Carnation and Sweet William family which also includes Lychnis (the field Campion in its garden forms) and Gypsophila. Usually ten stamens but these can vary from flower to flower even on the same plant, and are especially variable in number in the very double carnations and pinks. In Lychnis and some of the single pinks, anthers are arranged in two groups of different heights. The stigma (which is deeply split) tends to be higher than the anthers within the pinks and carnations, but lower than them in Lychnis.

Cross-pollinations can be made immediately following emasculation, which is best carried out in the late bud stage when the petals are showing colour.

In Sweet Williams the head of flowers comprises individuals which mature at different times, usually starting with the centre flower of a cluster. For pollination purposes it is best to be drastic with the flower head, either by removing all but a single flower cluster, or by pollinating members of the head which have reached the right stage, followed by removal of all other buds. Emasculation and pollination are the same as for Pinks, and each flower pedicel is long enough for the appropriate label to be attached.

Because of the density of carnation flower buds cross-pollinations are most successful when made at the mature-flower stage, as long as the female flower has been protected against insect pollination. The stigma is easily seen amidst or above the petals, and no emasculation should be necessary.

Numerous new cultivars within the carnations have resulted from bud sports, the high incidence of these mutants being related to the widespread dissemination of plant material as cuttings which are therefore subjected to a wide range of environments.

Compositae

Comprises many species, of which the most commonly cultivated are *ageratum, arctosis, aster, chrysanthemum, cornflower, dahlia, daisy, echinops, gaillardia, marigold, pyrethrum, rudbeckia, sunflower*. Most flowers assume a 'double' form because of the numerous petals but a central disc may be seen when petals are pulled aside. Each flower is, in fact, composed of a mass of smaller flowers which together make up the 'composite' head. Each flower within the head is perfectly formed with five anthers (there are exceptions, mentioned later, however) and five petals surrounding a central style. Because of the tightly packed individual flowers emasculation is almost impossible, and methods of cross-pollination therefore range from the very involved to the haphazard.

The sunflower illustrates most clearly the result of satisfactory pollination, *with each seed representing the outcome of a single fertilisation upon a single floret.* Each floret bears only a single ovary.

Two forms of floret exist in every compound flower of the cultivated *compositae*: those on the outside of the disc possess five long petals which are fused together on four edges thus forming a flat or ligulate petal. Towards the centre of the disc petals become diminutive and are fused on all edges to form a tube. Anthers are regularly fused in the form of a tube within both types of floret. Because of the sequential opening of florets, a compound *compositae* flower is fit to be pollinated over a period of days. Mature seed may be forming in the outer (or ray) florets while the central ones are either still receptive to pollen or may not yet have opened. In a glasshouse or on a hot day, the sequential opening of the tubular florets may be studied with the use of a hand lens.

Both self-sterility and self-fertility occur widely in *compositae* species. In order that the breeding system can be assessed and the correct pollination procedure adopted, the seeding potential of a chosen flower or plant should be studied by protecting it from insects and thus from foreign pollen. If no seed is set, the plant or species is probably self-sterile and cross-pollinations can be made merely by brushing the compound head daily with a pollen-covered brush or by dusting it with a detached flower from the male parent.

If the species is self-fertile (cornflower and ageratum plants vary in their reaction, arctosis and marigolds are self-fertile, and daisy and sunflower are self-sterile) cross-pollination is complicated by the crowding of florets and the difficulty of emasculation. Although a number of florets may be satisfactorily emasculated, the presence of pollen upon so many adjacent untreated florets means that self-pollination may still take place. Because of this, to be certain that cross-fertilisation has been successful, plants used as male parents should carry 'marker genes' which can be identified in the mixed progeny of the pollination.

Florets at the outside of the compound flower – the 'ray' florets whose petals are flattened – are frequently found to be unisexual, female only, and successful cross-pollinations may therefore be carried out on these without resorting to emasculation. At seed maturity, only the outside ring of seeds should be harvested as hybrid seed – any seed forming upon the central disc can be regarded as selfed and should be kept separate or discarded.

Two further techniques for ensuring cross-fertilisation may be used independently or in conjunction with one another. The first is emasculation of a number of newly opened florets with a finely pointed pair of forceps – the florets may remain part of the whole flower or may be isolated by removing all associated, untreated, florets. The main advantage of isolating florets is that it allows easy identification of hybrid seed, but this may be offset by the excessive damage suffered by the compound flower when a large proportion of its florets are removed. Furthermore, ovules in a compound head which are adjusted to the micro-climate often abort when suddenly exposed on every side to rapid drying conditions.

Successful emasculation requires considerable practice because of the delicacy of the operation. The five anthers surrounding the style must be removed when the style first becomes exposed in the apex of the anther tube. Forceps should be placed around the base of the anther tube just above the filaments, (although these will not be visible), which is then gripped firmly and pulled sharply upwards. The anther tube is thus lifted up over the style which should remain undamaged, like removing a child's vest! Until the technique is fully understood, initial attempts at emasculation will probably result in the decimation of complete florets but the loss of small numbers will not harm the head. When a sufficient number of florets has been emasculated, the remainder should be cut just below the anthers with fine pointed scissors. In this way, the release of self pollen is prevented while the micro-climate is partially retained and dehydration avoided because all the lower halves of the florets are left intact. Pollination should be carried out upon the emasculated flowers when all stigmas are seen to have split and have become receptive. The only seed produced on such a compound head should be hybrid.

The second technique is used either as a sequel to the previous treatment in order to remove adhering pollen, or as a separate method of emasculation. Briefly, (described in more detail under lettuce) a fine jet of water is sprayed on the compound flower just as pollen is released, causing it to be washed away. After a time-lapse of approximately half an hour the treated head can be pollinated.

Neither of these techniques is entirely satisfactory for crops such as cornflower since the production of pollen from any one floret continues over a long period and when removed by water-jet is later replaced. In addition, the cornflower anthers are exceedingly tough and not easily removed from the florets although some success is possible after practice.

Of all pollination techniques for self-fertile *compositae* that using only ray florets is probably the most reliable. Where ray florets are absent, however, emasculation by forceps is probably most effective although requiring much practice.

For *compositae* with a self-sterility system, cross-pollination is quite straightforward. A small pollinating brush should be covered with pollen of the male parent by rubbing it around the pollen-covered disc and it should then be rubbed over the female disc in exactly the same manner. The brush will, of course, become contaminated with 'self' pollen but this is immaterial as long as crosses are being made only between the two parents. When recharging the brush on the male parent reciprocal pollinations will inevitably be made and flowers should be labelled accordingly. On no account should one brush be used to pollinate more than one female plant unless sterilised in methyl alcohol (or absolute alcohol) between pollinations.

Apetaly and Male-Sterility
Because of a floral mutation, the cross-pollination of marigolds has been made very much easier in recent years. The mutation (apetaly) has probably occurred many times in previous decades or centuries but plants with this flower type are most likely to have been discarded from a normal crop as an embarrassment. Apetalous marigold flowers resemble a sawn-off shaving brush in bright yellow or orange since they are completely devoid of petals. The great advantage of this flower form lies in the fact that the gene causing loss of petals is genetically linked to a gene for male-sterility and, in consequence, apetalous flowers have neither petals nor pollen and can be cross-pollinated without difficulty.

Male flowers can be differentiated from male-steriles in the bud stage, thus allowing early roguing of the crop before male flowers can mature and cause contamination.

Plate 8. 'Apetalous' (male-sterile) and normal marigold flower heads.

The inheritance of apetaly/male-sterility has not been fully determined but is basically polygenic in association with restorer plants of varying efficiency. New evidence now indicates that some restorers are also inherited as major genes.

Pollination of male-sterile flowers is achieved by using whole heads of the male parent or by transferring pollen by brush. In cases of extreme pollen-shortage in the male flower (applicable only when making experimental crosses) florets can be removed from the male, slit to release pollen and their inner surface applied direct to the female.

Cruciferae

This family is extremely diverse but, regardless of the form of the inflorescence whether large-flowered (as wallflower) or small-flowered and compound (as candytuft), identification is based upon the cruciform shape of individual flowers – each of which possesses six anthers and produces its seeds in a pod or silique. The best known flower species are *Alyssum*, sweet-scented stock, honesty, wallflower, and siberian wallflower. *Cruciferae* possess a self-incompatibility system of the sporophytic type but degrees of intensity vary both within and between species. In general, wallflowers are fully self-compatible and exhibit little or no loss of vigour subsequent to inbreeding. *Alyssum* is more self-sterile but inter-pollination of closely related plants is possible and provides the morphological uniformity which is associated with this perennial border plant. With all *cruciferae*, whether flower or vegetable, the self-compatibility of individual plants must be tested, since it is dangerous to plan a breeding programme based upon generalisations for the whole species.

The test for self-incompatibility in wallflowers is most easily made by self-pollinating a known number of flowers upon a branch and comparing their seed-set with that from flowers of an associated branch which has been cross-pollinated. From the result of several experiments it appears most likely that full self-compatibility will be found, thus indicating the necessity of emasculation whenever cross-pollinations are to be carried out. Flower buds are emasculated about one or two days before they would be expected to open, the sepals of each bud being split from just above the base to the tip. With practice the flower buds can be slit and anthers removed in under ten seconds with very little deformation of the bud. Pollination, usually by brushing, can be done immediately. With 'racemose' inflorescences like *cruciferae* it is possible to carry out many pollinations on a single branch; each flower may be labelled separately after different pollinations, or several groups of successive flowers may each be pollinated by different males. If a flowering branch is completely utilised in this way the pollination period could extend for three weeks and while the apical flowers are being pollinated, pods would be forming in the lower part.

Pods of wallflowers contain up to 40 seeds, produced either side of a dividing *septum*. These will germinate immediately after ripening but are also liable to germinate inside the pod if pods are collected and stored tightly when green. Although the various types and colours of wallflowers are well-known their seeding capacity is not. In general the violet types are shy seeders with only just over half the number of seeds per pod which are set by the yellow and scarlet-flowered types. Pink-flowered forms tend to produce slightly less than the scarlet types. Studies on over four hundred plants gave average seed numbers (per pod) of 11.3 for Dwarf yellow, 10.9 for scarlet and giant ruby, 10.4 for giant pink and 7.4 for dwarf violet types. The seed potential of wallflower ovaries (i.e.

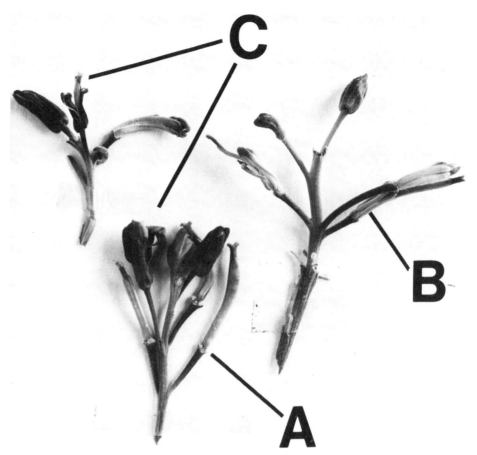

Plate 9. (i) normal (A) wallflower pods, buds and flowers — male-sterile (B) wallflower flower-head. No petals, but fertilised pod grows through 'sterile' ovary. C. indicates normal (lower) and male-sterile (upper) flowers.

the number of ovules available for fertilisation) may be as high as 60, but complete fertilisation is rarely achieved.

Male sterility has been found in wallflowers of the dwarf violet and cream types. Petals of the flowers are absent and appear to be replaced by a distorted ovary/sepal strucure. From the centre of this structure arises a normal stigmatic surface which, after pollination, is seen to be the apex of a perfect silique containing normal seeds. Insect pollination of these male-sterile flowers does not seem (and is unlikely) to occur but much hybrid seed can be obtained by hand-pollination techniques. The inheritance of this form of male-sterility is unknown at present.

The pollination of *Alyssum* and candytuft is rather more complicated than that of wallflower or stock, because the very small flowers are borne in compact heads. As there is a tendency towards self-sterility in *Alyssum*, emasculation can sometimes be disregarded, and cross-pollinations of limited effect can be made upon a small cluster of flowers by dusting them profusely with pollen from the male parent. If the male parent carries a marker gene of flower or foliage the hybrids should be quickly identifiable. In the absence of a marker gene the 'crossed' population should be grown adjacent to the variety from which the female was derived and hybrids should be easily identifiable at or before maturity. Although this pollination system may seem rather casual, the chances of producing hybrids in the progeny are good due to the large number of flowers available for pollination.

Candytuft may be treated as wallflower or *alyssum*, but if wishing to limit the number of female flowers, it is best to remove all unwanted ones at time of pollination and ensure that the remainder are correctly labelled. Pollinations

Plate 10. (ii) Seed setting on a
cross-pollinated male-sterile
wallflower plant.

are best made upon the outer flowers since they are larger, easier to manipulate, and are less affected by the altered environment when the inner ones are removed.

Dipsaceae

With scabious as its best known representative – is colourful and genetically variable but appears to have been largely neglected for breeding work. Both annual and biennial forms produce their flowers in umbels and cross-pollination is consequently subject to the same conditions as in the *compositae*. However, florets within umbels are larger and more distinct, so that emasculation, though tedious, is by no means impossible.

Florets of scabious possess four anthers which must be removed in the late bud-stage before they have shed their pollen (anthesis). In some plants, particularly those of annual scabious, the style of each floret is extended well beyond the anthers from early maturity and cross-pollination is possible without resorting to emasculation. Because the possibility of self-pollination still remains, however, it is essential to avoid shaking the flower head – which means that outdoor pollinations under insect-proof bags are impracticable. If there is any choice of the method for cross-pollination it is advisable to use plants with elongated styles since numerous florets may be fertilised and the removal of untreated ones will be avoided – thus improving the likelihood of successful seed production. For only limited numbers of cross-pollinations it is best to use a newly opening flower. The outer, ray florets, open first and can be emasculated without difficulty – pollinations being made immediately.

67

Gentianaceae

The best known species in this family are the numerous *gentians* and *Exacum affine*. While the former comprise many different garden forms – some of which can be cultivated only with difficulty – the latter is rapidly gaining popularity as a reliable house plant. Its many scented blue blooms (each of approximately 20mms diameter) replace one another over a period of three months or more and, since they are easily manipulated and give prolific seed, it seems likely that this species will in future receive much greater attention from breeders. The species has attributes which are capable of stimulating biological or botanical interests among school-children. The long styles of young flowers are diagonally aligned like a hand on a clock face and, with ageing of the flower, the position of the 'hand' changes from 'four o'clock' to 'eight o'clock'! This sign of maturity is coupled with fading of the flower and swelling of the basal ovary.

Cross-pollination is easily carried out after removal of the five anthers when the flowers have first opened. Flower seeds are capable of germination immediately after harvest.

Geraniaceae

The best known members of this family are the various *pelargonium* species, in particular X hortorum which is noted for its concentrically patterned leaves. Many improvements have recently been made to the common bedding forms by American and British plant breeders who have overcome the need for vegetative propagation to a large extent by producing F_1 hybrid cultivars which can be raised as annuals from seed. Further improvements must be made in the time from sowing to flowering before these forms are entirely acceptable, however, but the virtues of F_1 hybrids are very apparent in the marked uniformity of flower and leaf colour, plant height and simultaneous flowering time.

The *geraniaceae* are self-compatible and emasculation is necessary in the bud stage prior to cross-pollination. The family is quite uncomplicated as far as breeding techniques are concerned but anomalous behaviour can be experienced due to the existence of two 'classical genetic' types.

One small flowered form has been shown to be a *haploid* with a normal chromosome complement of nine. No seed is produced because chromosomes cannot pair at *meiosis* to start the formation of ovules and pollen mother cells and the cultivar can therefore only be propagated by vegetative means. A diploid cultivar which, apart from the increased size of its floral and vegetative organs, exactly resembles the haploid 'Kleine Liebling' has been derived directly from it by chromosome duplication.

Variegated plants of Pelargonium X hortorum are periclinal chimaeras, some of which have green inner, and white outer, cells – a condition shown most clearly in the leaves. Because the chlorotic areas (those without chlorophyll) may be perpetuated through the reproductive organs, selfing or crossing together of green and white variegated plants is likely to result in completely white seedling progeny. When reproductive structures on a variegated plant arise from the green tissues only, selfed seedlings should be completely green.

P. X *hortorum* has been crossed with P. *peltatum*, the ivy-leaved Geranium used widely for hanging baskets, although hybrid seedlings are very unthrifty. Other interspecific crosses have failed even though pollen has penetrated the stigma.

'Mutations' can be produced in the chimaerical perargoniums by taking root cuttings since new vegetative tissue arises from the cell layers which, in other species, give rise to bud sports. Such mutations are spasmodic, however, and greater genetic variability is to be produced by cross- or self-pollination. Because of the fact that pelargoniums have been constantly propagated by vegetative means, cultivars are probably highly heterozygous in genetical terms. For this reason self-pollination should give progenies which vary as much as those resulting from cross-pollination and from which it should be possible to select new and desirable types. Each flower of geranium (in its single form) is five petalled and can produce only five seeds. The more double a flower becomes the less seed will be set per pollination and on average only ten to twelve seeds will be set for every 25 flowers pollinated.

Tetraploid geraniums, notably Pink Cloud, have been produced but tend to be disregarded because of their excessive vigour and late flowering season.

Gesneriaceae

The 'house plant' family with the fleshy leaves and somewhat flamboyant flowers of *gloxinia*, *Saintpaulia* and *streptocarpus*. All are normally propagated easily by tubers or by leaf cuttings (streptocarpus and saintpaulia) and breeding techniques have been used only in recent years to extend the range of flower colours and leaf form. Flowers of gloxinia are tubular but split into seven or eight petals on the edge of the reflexed corolla. The number of petals is normally matched exactly by the number of anthers, except in the double flower forms. Pollinations should be made when flowers are fully open, having been preceded by emasculation in the bud stage.

Progeny will flower as annuals from seed and any highly desirable form can be perpetuated immediately by growing the tuber which will also have been produced.

Streptocarpus flowers are also tubular but are *symmetrical* only in one plane (zygomorphic) while Saintpaulia flowers have a more flattened face. Saintpaulia roots well when leaves, with their petioles, are detached and the petiole embedded about an inch deep in peat or fibrous compost. Both forms may be propagated from leaves cut in half longitudinally which are placed into a peat, sand and soil mixture after the midrib has been removed so that the outer edge lies above the soil surface. Rooting should take place within three to six weeks and plantlets will form along the edge in contact with the soil. By utilising this easy-propagating character after treatment by irradiation, new commercial forms of *streptocarpus* have been produced. Irradiation has been used to cause mutations in single cells which have then developed into plantlets of uniform genetic type to such good effect that it has proved possible to commercialise new cultivars within three years from treatment.

Improved forms can also be produced sexually by removal of the pair of fused anthers (the filaments are already separate) in the bud stage. If left until the open flower stage, the anthers deposit self-pollen upon the stigma which becomes enclosed by them as if in a catapult. The twisted seed pods should be harvested when still slightly green in order to prevent loss of hybrid seed which would be caused by sudden movements of ripening pods. It is thought that the popularity of Streptocarpus as a pot plant would be increased if its leaves could be reduced from their present ungainly size. Breeding programmes now being conducted appear to be making headway – the inheritance of leaf size being a classical example of polygenic control.

69

Iridaceae

This is a very large family comprising *crocus, iris* and *gladiolus* as well as lesser known genera such as *sparaxis, tigridia, ixia* and *freesia*. Their common characteristics, apart from attractive colourful blooms, are the normal method of propagation – by corm or rhizome and the arrangement in threes of their floral and reproductive organs. As with the *Gesneriaceae* and *Amaryllidaceae*, successful genetic combinations brought about by selfing or crossing can be immediately capitalised because of the species' capacity for vegetative propagation. In the case of gladioli in particular, a full-sized corm will produce up to 50 cormlets in any one season – these will reach full size in two years – and multiplication of a new cultivar can proceed without delay. For this reason, and because cross-pollinations are easily carried out on the large flowers, new cultivars of gladioli are continually introduced – largely by amateur plant breeders.

As with pelargoniums, just as much variation should be obtained in the progeny of a self-pollinated flower as from one which has been cross-pollinated.

A common query of horticulturists and private gardeners concerning gladioli, which can be explained by one or both of two conditions, is the so-called 'reversion' of coloured gladioli to the white flowered form over a period of years. Its cause is either the more rapid multiplication of cormlets on white flowered cultivars – thus swamping or outnumbering cormlets of coloured cultivars – or the occurrence of somatic mutations i.e. those which occur in vegetatively multiplying tissue. Following somatic mutation to 'white' the affected cells may produce white-type cormlets which, when they develop, lead to increased proportions of white flowering forms in the general population.

Pollinations are easily made within species of the *Iridaceae* but flower forms vary so widely that each species should be studied in detail in order to establish successful pollination techniques. Crocus for example, has well defined and easily manipulated reproductive structures (and the various species seem to have been remarkably neglected by plant breeders). Iris flowers are markedly tripartite with single anthers below each stigma which forms a petaloid tube above the decorative larger petals. Bulbous forms of iris are not cross-compatible with the rhizomatous forms. Because of the fairly complex arrangements of floral parts, when crosses are to be made it is advisable to postpone emasculation until the flowers have opened, *as long as the anthers are not shedding pollen*. Insects are scarce at this time of year and precautions to avoid contamination may be somewhat relaxed although Iris, for example, is frequently self-fertilised and emasculation is desirable.

Gladioli, by contrast, flower at a time of intense insect activity and all treated (and to be treated) flowers should therefore be protected either in an insect-proofed glasshouse or by a sleeve of insect-proof material. If the latter, the enclosed flowers should be allowed free movement; if possible, their styles and stigmas should never come into contact with the material otherwise they become accessible to insects which rest on the outside of the material and possibly cause accidental pollination. Pollinations of gladioli should be made in the bud stage with each flower labelled separately. Because seed-setting after pollination absorbs much of the plant's energy reserves it is advisable to pollinate no more than five flowers on any main spike.

The papery seeds should be sown in seed boxes when mature in the late autumn (as for Iris species) and replanting should be related to the rapidity of growth. Flower form and colours should be seen within two years after the initial pollinations (except for the bulbous irises which will take three to four years). Each seedling from a particular cross-fertilisation will be an F₁ hybrid but because of the heterozygous nature of each parent it is unlikely that many of the seedlings will be identical. Instead, a flower colour range exceeding that of both parents should be expected, thus increasing the chances of obtaining a good form. By the time a desirable new type has been evolved, the large corm should be producing cormlets. *Since these will produce replicas of the new flower form,* the safety of the new line will be assured.

Freesias have gained increased popularity since the introduction of more diverse tetraploid material although diploids are still used extensively in spite of their smaller flowers, especially for raising bulk populations from seed. In the tetraploids the cross-pollination of clones or plants is encouraged by the fact that good pollen-producers are poor seed-setters, and vice versa. Temperature during flowering and pollination affects flower fertility and seed yield; pollination at 20°C gives good seed yield following growth at 14°C.

Labiateae

While this family is best-known for its wide range of herb species; mint, sage, rosemary, thyme, hyssop, savory, marjoram, balm and basil (none of which can be crossed together) it also contains the decorative flower species such as lavender, catmint and salvia, as well as the coleus, noted for its brightly coloured foliage. The three main diagnostic features for the whole family are the 'hooded' flower form, the four seeds or 'nutlets' per flower and the square (in cross-section) stem. Because each pollination can produce a maximum of only four seeds per flower (at least four pollen grains must therefore be available on the stigma) there is very little likelihood that seed of Labiateae could ever be produced as F₁ hybrid on a commercial scale. Nevertheless, male-sterility in salvia is known to exist, thus making F₁ hybrid production of this crop more possible on a field scale.

In spite of the shape of the flower, which appears very well adapted for insect pollination, self fertility is common to the family and self-pollination can often take place unaided because of the juxtaposition of stigma and anthers. The stigma is not receptive to pollen until the flower has opened fully and the tip of the style is seen to have split into two reflexing parts. Pollination in the bud stage is very unlikely to succeed and, because emasculation of the bud is difficult, transfer of pollen is best attempted at the time of stigma splitting (bifurcation). After a large amount of trial and error, most successful pollinations (mainly on salvia) have been made in a calm atmosphere under glass, without prior emasculation, by lightly touching the open stigma with foreign anther or pollen-covered brush, and by taking care not to touch the maternal anthers.

If one observes closely the behaviour of pollinating insects the reasons for self-fertilisation in *salvia* become apparent. Within the glasshouse insects rarely visit the flowers, and seed production seems to be achieved largely by self-fertilisation – the pollen dispersal and placement being caused by local disturbances which agitate the flowers. In the field, the flowers are visited frequently by insects, but instead of a direct approach to the side of the corolla (which would result in automatic cross pollination) the bees often extract nectar from the base of the flower by approaching it between the corolla and coloured bracts. Thus, in the field also, self-fertilisation appears to be the general rule.

The most common horticultural salvias belong to the *splendens* species, represented by the red, pink, purple and white flowered forms. Other species, e.g. *farinaceae* and *horminum* possess blue flowers and coloured foliage   71 respectively but no hybrids between the various cultivated species are known. The wide range of species owe their distinctness to differences in chromosome number which prohibit inter-specific crossing or, if crossing is successful, produce sterility in the hybrid. Nevertheless by using modern techniques of chromosomes doubling, embryo culture etc., the salvia genes should provide a wealth of new, profitable forms for the specialist plant breeder.

In the more common garden forms the various flower colours appear to be inherited in an 'epistatic' relationship – Purple is dominant to deep red, deep red is dominant to Scarlet. Scarlet is dominant to pink which is dominant to white.

Linaceae

A very limited garden family, being confined to the delicate-foliaged blue, yellow and red flax. Because of the limited species range, there is little evidence that the present garden forms can be expected to show much improvement by inter-crossing. In spite of this, there is still the possibility of finding an unexpected segregant which would help to upgrade the family image if crosses were attempted. Emasculation of the five large stamens which surround the style and stigma should be made in the late bud stage by first unwinding the overlapping petals to allow entry of the forceps. As is well known, *linum* sheds its petals very rapidly and this may occur during the emasculation process unless great care is taken. Pollination follows emasculation immediately.

Liliaceae

This is a very large family covering a multitude of different phenotypes whose common factor is the arrangement of floral parts in threes, (the most common number of anthers and petals is six). Since the range extends from hyacinth and bluebell to tulip, a large number of lily species and lily of the valley, no breeding technique can be described which will be satisfactory for all genera or species. Apart from the more appropriate details such as ensuring that three or multiples of three anthers are removed during emasculation, the most important consideration for the breeder is that the family is vegetatively propagated. Thus, any single plant resulting from a successful pollination can be perpetuated *ad infinitum* without any alterations of characteristics. Within the family, many interspecific crosses have been attempted, particularly of lilies, with varying degrees of success.

Seeds derived from crosses, notably those between *Lilium speciosum* x *L. auratum* in work by Emsweller, have been found to deteriorate after sowing although plump and healthy when harvested. The wastage of material was overcome by resorting to embryo culture in test tubes. In further lily crosses (*L. album* x *L. auratum, rubrum* x *auratum* and *album* x *rubrum*) the hybrid seed was washed in running water for 14 hours, sterilised with calcium hypochlorite and then cultured successfully as for embryos. Because the running water removed ferulic acid – a germination inhibitor – the embryos were able to grow normally through the seed coat.

Lily seed may germinate quickly when freshly harvested, but if older, may not germinate for a year or more. The newly formed cormlet deteriorates if roots are damaged when transplanting and seed of hybrids should therefore be sown thinly. In general, pollination etc. techniques closely follow those described for the *Amaryllidaceae* or *Iridaceae*.

Plate 11. Flowers of Oenothera
showing the receptive
cruciform stigma.

Malvaceae

The Mallow, Lavatera and Hollyhock family. One of the greatest breeding
achievements within this family has been the introduction of dwarf hollyhocks.
Dwarfism is a common expression of genetic variation in all families but in no
other family could its impact have been more pronounced. The first dwarf
hollyhock 'Powder Puffs' is believed to have resulted from selection rather than
genetic manipulation thus emphasising the benefits of keeping ones' eyes open.

Floral arrangements are very similar to those of *Linaceae* with the anthers
surrounding the styles. Anthers are more numerous, however, and styles are
separate from one another, resembling a small tuft in the centre of the flower.
Emasculation is as for Linaceae but the petals of the bud are much more strongly
attached. Anthers should be detached until none are visible although in practice
this is extremely difficult because they 'clothe' the central portion of the flower.
The easiest method of crossing is to ignore emasculation and to apply pollen to
the stigmas in the bud stage, about two days before the flower opening. In this
way the foreign pollen is able to effect fertilisation before self pollen is shed.

Oenotheraceae

In spite of wide discrepancies of chromosome number, this is another family
where it appears possible to make considerable horticultural advances by
breeding new plant forms. As well as others, the family is represented by *clarkia,
godetia, oenothera* (the evening primrose) *gaura, fuchsia* and the showy, wild,
rose bay willow herb (*epilobium* or *chamaenerion*). Within the white, red or pink
garden forms of *godetia* and *clarkia* there is complete cross-compatibility, but so
far the introduction of yellow colour from the *oenothera* genus has been
unsuccessful.   73

Emasculation and pollination are straight-forward, particularly since the
buds and flowers are fairly large and easy to manipulate. Flowers contain two,
four or eight anthers; emasculation should be carried out in the late bud stage a
few hours before the flower is expected to open, but pollinations cannot be
carried out until the style has split at its apex into a cruciform stigma. In the
unemasculated flowers the pollen is frequently seen covering the stigma in a
cobwebby fashion. Successful pollinations can be identified within a week
because of the rapid swelling of the basal ovary. Seed should be ready for
harvesting within three weeks of pollination and will be capable of germinating
immediately.

Orchidaceae

Breeding work within the *orchidaceae* is so advanced and sophisticated that it
forms the subject of a number of books, and for this reason any degree of detail in
this present section would be superfluous. Orchids of the more flamboyant types
are mainly tropical in origin although the distribution of the Orchid family is
world wide and ranges from the exotic to the less significant temperate types
which can be found as ground plants in this country.

The culture of orchids requires high temperatures and humidity under glass,
while the breeding of new cultivars involves techniques which differ basically
from those discussed previously. Instead of applying pollen from anthers or
brush, the pollen of orchids is applied directly to the stigma of mature flowers
from pollinia – a pair of detachable lozenge-shaped pollen sacs. The thousands
of seeds resulting from fertilisation must be germinated and cultured initially in
a nutrient medium which varies with the species. When the new form is judged
on its floral characteristics (six to seven years after the pollination), any
successful type is propagated and multiplied vegetatively. Because of the long
'shelf life' or period over which they remain attractive, the individual orchid
flower amply rewards the continued effort of making improvements by
breeding.

Papaveraceae

This family of poppies, including the blue *meconopsis*, the opium and iceland
types, differs in two important respects from any family discussed hitherto. Both
differences affect breeding techniques since the poppies possess numerous
anthers, of no constant number, thus making assurance of emasculation
difficult, while the other characteristic is concerned with the harvesting of seeds
after fertilisation. The ovaries of the *Papaveraceae* vary in shape according to
species and even cultivars, but all contain myriads of minute seeds which are
released from the ovary through apical pores. Great care is therefore needed at
harvest time if the valuable results of pollinations are not to be lost.

Because of the phenomenal seed production from a single pollination, poppies
are ideally suited for the production of F_1 hybrids. However, until male-sterility
is found and can be utilised it is impossible to produce F_1 hybrids in the field,
while the financial return from poppies is at present inadequate to contemplate
hand-pollination for F_1 hybrid production under glass.

Cross-pollination and the production of F_1 hybrid poppy cultivars is practically very feasible, however, as long as competent emasculations are carried out by hand in the bud stage. Pollination by the male parent can be done in the conventional manner when emasculated flowers commence to open, and in order to economise on glasshouse space only a small number of plants of the male parent need be grown. Pollen production is prolific and, by using a brush instead of detached poppy heads, wide distribution is possible. Most poppy species are annuals or even ephemeral (more than one generation per year) so that rapid assessments may be made of the value of any breeding material.

Papilionaceae

As with the *Orchidaceae*, many specialist books have been written upon at least one of the genera within this family, namely sweet pea *Lathyrus odoratus*. To a large extent this is a reflection of the interest shown in the flower but it is also evidence of the ease with which new cultivars may be bred. All the leguminous flowers are found in this family, the range thus covering annual and perennial herbaceous plants, shrubs and trees; from sweet peas, lupins and wisteria, to broom, laburnum and acacia.

In general the flower form is fairly complex, consisting of five petals – a single 'standard' at the back of the flower, two 'keel' petals (often joined) surrounding the style or ovary and these in turn being bordered by a pair of 'wing' petals. Around this basic conformation lie specific differences in detail which may cause reduction in size of the standard petal, twisting of keel petals (and ovary), enlargement of wing petals or similar modifications. Each species must be studied on its own account and pollination procedure deduced from the form and function of a typical flower.

For an initial guide to pollination techniques the sweet pea flower will be discussed. This, similar to that of the lupin, is basically simple but the subsequent section on vegetables will deal with the greater complexity in *papilionaceae* flowers as exemplified in the dwarf and runner bean.

Pollen in the sweet pea is shed very early, before the flower opens. In spite of their attractive appearance and scent, sweet peas are rarely visited by insects but they set seed very freely as a result of self-pollination.

Pollen is released in the region of the stigma and, as the keel petals are joined at the tip, the pollen is retained in a 'pocket' which also accommodates the stigma. Self-fertilisation is thus inevitable unless emasculation can be carried out in the bud stage. The correct size is reached when the bud is the same length or slightly longer than the calyx; emasculation earlier is likely to cause death of the bud while at a later stage pollen will probably have already been released.

Ten anthers (with their filaments attached in a tube at the base of the ovary) should be counted to be certain of success and, following their removal (by splitting the top of the keel petal through the folded standard to allow access to the bud), pollen from the appropriate parent can be applied. This is done either by pollen-covered brush, or by inverting a flower from which standard and wing petals have been removed and in which the pollen-covered style is exposed by withdrawing the keel petals. Each pollination should result in a pod with approximately ten seeds maturing about three or four weeks later.

If cross-pollination has been successful the resultant F₁ progeny will all be alike; their progeny, however, will segregate into different flower colours and shapes. Selection of single plants over five generations, however, should produce a number of almost uniform, though distinct from one another, lines.

75

Polemoniaceae

The Phlox family with Sweet William-sized flowers combined into a flattish terminal head. The five anthers can be removed in a similar fashion to those of *Linaceae* but in this case the petals can be unwound without becoming detached.

Primulaceae

In addition to the many common and rare species of *primula* and *polyanthus*, the family comprises *cyclamen* and creeping jenny (*Lysimachia*). The different style lengths and anther levels within corollas are characteristic of this family and act as an adaptation towards cross-pollination, with the consequent preservation of genetic variation. Numerous genetic investigations have been made into the natural breeding system of primula species and, while many are self-fertile, probably due to selection under cultivation, the species favouring cross-pollination tend to possess two forms of flowers. These are the 'pin' and 'thrum' types shown in Figure 8.

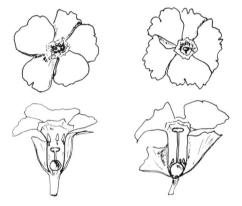

Fig 8. Thrum (left) and Pin (right) flowers of Primula as seen from above and, with part of the corolla removed, from the side.
On a single plant, all flowers will be of PIN or THRUM-type only.

Pollen from thrum anthers normally fertilises pin flowers (i.e. those whose stigmas are situated at the mouth of the corolla tube) while anthers of pin plants provide pollen to fertilise the short styles of the 'thrum' types. Some plants, particularly of the common primrose (*primula vulgaris*) may show homostyly – where anthers and stigma within the same flower are of the same height. These are normally quite self-fertile. Plants of *Primula sinensis* and *malacoides* are all 'pin' types, but *Primula obconica* comprises equal proportions of 'pin' and 'thrum' flowers. The production of F1 hybrid lines is facilitated in heterostylous species since the 'pins' may be pollinated by hand with 'thrum' pollen without resorting to tedious emasculation. 'Thrum' plants make no seed contribution to the F1 hybrid but since they are required to function only as males, a small number will be sufficient to provide pollen.

The inheritance of pin and thrum flower types is an example of single gene activity with a difference. The recessive dd gives 'pin' while the heterozygous Dd gives 'thrum'. When crossed, the typical 1:1 ratio should be produced as follows:

$$\text{Pin (dd) x Thrum (Dd)}$$
$$\text{F}_1 \text{ 1Dd : 1dd}$$

Counts of Primula obconica plants from a number of populations of breeding lines have shown a surplus of 'pin' types (1488) over (1232) thrum types however. These figures do not conform to the conventional 1:1 ratio of classical genetics but the bias towards 'pin' types is very satisfactory from the point of view of F₁ hybrid production.

Selfing or intercrossing of pins (when possible) gives pin types only, as would be expected from a 'double recessive' gene, while selfing or intercrossing of thrums (which is very much more difficult) gives 2 thrum; 1 pin instead of the expected 3 thrum: 1 pin. This is because the dominant gene is lethal when homozygous and consequently, seeds bearing the double dominant never mature. Primula seed is minute and should be sown on the soil surface in a pot since any depth of cover could restrict the germination of seed which may be bearing valuable genetic combinations.

The *cyclamen* exists in a number of garden forms which are used for naturalising to give the same effect as the wild species of the Mediterranean areas. The most commonly grown types, however, are the large and small-flowered pot-plant forms of *cyclamen persicum*. These normally take a period of 12 to 18 months from time of sowing to the large scale production of blooms, since a corm of at least two centimetres diameter must first develop. Germinating seeds form a single true leaf at the apex of a lentil-sized cormlet.

Cyclamen flowers are self-fertile but inbreeding is followed by a fairly severe loss of vigour and the normal method of cultivar production is by mass-pollination of similarly coloured plants. Because the flowers normally 'hide their faces' the five anthers (which shed prolific pollen) tend to deposit little upon the downward-facing, and slightly projecting, stigma. Mass-pollination is normally carried out under glass from January to early April either by tapping a flower with one index finger and catching the pollen upon the thumbnail of the other hand (which is then used to pollinate another plant) or by catching pollen in a plastic 'spoon' and transferring it from plant to plant in larger quantities. With either method, sterilisation of thumbnail or spoon is necessary between group pollinations – the spoon in boiling water or alcohol, the thumbnail with the latter only! It will be realised that when using either of these methods some self-fertilisation is inevitable – the subsequent inbred plants probably being discarded at potting-on because of their poor vigour, or surviving to give possibly lower quality plants.

Because the proportion of self-fertilisation seems to be limited even when self-pollen is available there is considerable opportunity with cyclamen for the production of F₁ hybrids. Emasculation, though easy to perform, is not absolutely necessary as long as the flowers being pollinated are not disturbed, causing contamination of the pollen. In practice, supplies of pollen should be divided into smaller quantities for application to single plants.

Emasculation may be performed in the late bud stage while petals remain tightly twisted. By continuing the petal twist (and pulling slightly) with one hand whilst holding the ovary with the other, all petals and anthers can be removed simultaneously – exposing the stigma for pollination. Plants differ in the ease with which they allow emasculation and, if it was of value, selection for this character could easily be carried out. The drawback to the technique, however, lies in the fact that the anthers possess a growth hormone which is essential for the continued growth and development of the ovary after pollination, and their removal paradoxically prevents the very operation (F₁ hybrid seed production) it was designed to assist.

Successful pollinations are followed by the production of spherical seed capsules – which should be supported by a metal ring or equivalent since they are forcibly returned to the soil by their rigid pedicels. Capsules form a ring of broken tissue at the apex when mature and although the ripe seeds are exposed they are retained within the capsule by a gummy mucilage for up to a week.

Fresh cyclamen seed tends to germinate erratically because of the presence of a germination inhibitor. This can be removed by washing the seeds in a muslin bag under running water for 24 hours. Seed should be dried on blotting paper and then sown normally.

Although considerable breeding of cyclamen has taken place, very few details of character inheritance have been recorded. Characters such as the presence of perfume, silver leaf, early flowering, and the deeper flower colours (magenta and dark red) appear to be controlled by dominant genes while polygenes are responsible for the expression of flower size, pedicel length and number of flowers per plant.

Ranunculaceae

While the floral structure of this family is regarded as primitive by taxonomists, the many species it contains are represented wherever flowers are grown. The most common species are *anemone, aquilegia, clematis, delphinium, nigella* and *paeony* whose greatest similarity is the possession of numerous anthers. In double paeonies a number of anthers have been replaced by petals, and although delphinium flowers appear complex, their reproductive organs comprise the characteristic separate styles surrounded by anthers.

Although considerable genetic variation exists within each genus, very little constructive breeding work has been attempted apart from that in *delphinium, paeony* and *clematis*. This is probably due to the difficulty of ensuring successful cross-pollination by the prior removal of all anthers. In general, the inner whorl of anthers tends to dehisce (split) first and is followed in sequence by the other anthers in their spiral arrangement. If the inner anthers are removed at the late bud stage the remainder can be extracted when the flower is fully open without danger of self-fertilisation by premature release of pollen. Sometimes, however, it may prove easier to wait until the young flower has opened fully and under these circumstances it is imperative that the plants for pollination should either be grown under glass or should be covered with a cellophane bag in the field or garden. Pollen from the male parent can be dusted on the stigmas with a brush or by placing a de-petalled flower directly upon the emasculated one.

The St. Brigid (double flowered) and de Caen (single) anemone cultivars have remained relatively unimproved ever since their introduction, but work is currently in progress to produce F_1 hybrids with great potential in flower size and number. Inbreeding causes marked reductions in vigour but this is more than compensated by the quality of subsequent F_1 hybrid plants. Anemone flowers are protogynous (stigmas are receptive before pollen is released by the anthers) and self-pollination is therefore possible only after the second flower of a single plant is produced. The anthers of the first are then used to pollinate the receptive stigmas of the newly opened second flower. Seed set is indicated by slight swelling of the central cone of the flower, petals fall away and the seed is released in a cobwebby mass which peels back from the receptacle six to eight weeks after pollination.

With the exception of *Nigella*, desirable hybrid plants in the Ranunculaceae can be multiplied immediately by vegetative propagation where applicable to give uniform cultivars, and we may expect to see many improvements in this family as it becomes more familiar to plant breeders.

78

Rosaceae

Compared with the previous family this one has been almost overworked. It contains our most popular garden flower or shrub – the rose – in hybrid tea, floribunda, species or miniature form, but also comprises numerous species of strawberry, rubus (raspberry, blackberry etc.), apples, pears, peaches, apricots, plums, cherries and quince. The ornamental flower forms of *potentilla, geum, spiraea, pyracantha, cotoneaster*, and hawthorn also belong to this family, all forms being noted for their well-protected seeds in fleshy fruits of varying shapes and sizes. The two basic fruit forms are the fleshy receptacles which bear naked (strawberry) or protected (raspberry) seeds and the larger, pithy, hips (rose, hawthorn), drupes (plums) or apples.

So many publications have been produced dealing with rose culture and breeding that any further detail here would be superfluous. Nevertheless, it should be stated that the basic technique for rose pollination can be generally supplied to flower forms throughout the family, with the possible exception of the fleshy receptacle species. Here, the styles are more numerous and less compactly located thus necessitating a more liberal application of pollen than for the discrete ovary types. Like *Ranunculaceae*, the *Rosaceae* family is noted for its large number of anthers. These, however, are present in concentric rings rather than a spiral – although the principles of emasculation in late bud and early flower maturity apply equally to both families.

Since many members of the family have double flowers, pollen may be limited and it should be collected by inserting a small brush into the petal bases of as many flowers of the particular male as possible. Pollen may also be collected from male parents by emasculating them and storing anthers at low humidity for 24 hours at 1°C. At emasculation time the petals of the more extreme double forms to be used as females (particularly of roses) may need to be cut away at the base with a pair of scissors so that pollinations can be carried out more easily. Because of a greater tendency to seed dormancy in the rosaceae, vernalisation of moist seeds in a refrigerator or in an overwintered seed box for the equivalent of four months at 0°C is often necessary for even germination.

Scrophularaceae

There is a close resemblance between this family and the *Labiateae*, but the major difference lies in the protection given to the seeds which are formed inside a capsule instead of being naked at the base of the petals. Flowers of *Scrophulariaceae* are frequently highly decorative, are borne on long spikes and are adapted for insect pollination as can be seen in *foxglove, antirrhinium, pentstemon, calceolaria* and *nemesia*.

While this family is well adapted for the production of F_1 hybrid cultivars because of the large seed-sets from few pollinations, only *antirrhinums* appear to have been worked on intensively.

Although they are fully self-fertile, species tend to be more receptive to pollen from other plants of the same crop than their own and, providing that care is taken to avoid disturbing the self anthers, cross-pollinations may easily be made in the glasshouse without resorting to emasculation. In the field, however, flowers are so attractive to bees that all flowers become pollinated repeatedly as soon as they are open wide enough for entry, and only protected buds can be used for deliberate crossing. For complete certainty, buds should be emasculated about two days before they can be expected to open – removal of the four anthers is very straight-forward – but because the style so closely resembles 79

Plate 12. Antirrhinum. 'Bunny-face' and pentstemon-type flower.

anther filaments in the confines of a bud some practice is required, and a few flowers will probably end up being both male and female sterile! A fairly recent mutation in the flower form of *antirrhinum* has produced an open throated pentstemon-type flower and although the bud shape still remains very similar to the normal 'bunny face' type, the young open flower is very much easier to emasculate and pollinate. Crosses between pentstemon-flower and 'bunny face' produce a bunnyface F_1 with a 3:1 segregation of bunny:pentstemon in the F_2, thus indicating that inheritance of the conventional flower form is controlled by a single dominant gene.

Tetraploid cultivars of *antirrhinum* are now widely grown, being noted particularly for their large flowers, while triploids have been made by crossing them with conventional diploid cultivars. In theory, the triploid plant forms should prove valuable additions to the range of antirrhinums, having a tidier appearance because of the absence of seed pods. Triploids normally fail to set seed because of breakdown in the formation of pollen grains and ovules, but it is apparent that all triploid antirrhinums produced to-date are highly fertile (and set the normal number of capsules). This is probably due to the fact that ovules and pollen grains are produced in such abundance that failures in fertilisation pass unnoticed.

The prospect of crossing antirrhinums with pentstemon is worth some investigation since the two species are closely related morphologically and possess the same chromosome number. Crosses between the conventional cultivated forms have been unproductive. It may be possible, however, to combine the separate genomes by persistent crossing between the less-well-known species which, being less modified, may be more likely to bear common chromosomal and genetic backgrounds.

Most successful *antirrhinum* cultivars possess a high degree of resistance to rust, the fungal disease which causes black and brown leaf spotting at and just after flowering time, and eventually causes leaf yellowing and death. Resistance is inherited as a single dominant gene and resistant parent lines may therefore be used widely for F_1 hybrid production with large numbers of other (susceptible) parents.

THE BREEDING OF
SPECIFIC CROPS

Solanaceae

This, the potato, tomato and tobacco family, is noted for the popularity of its flower species and genera – *petunia*, *nicotiana* (the floral forms of tobacco), *schizanthus* and *salpiglossis*. Petunia and nicotiana have been studied widely over many years since the theory of gametophytic self-incompatibility (see page 18) was first postulated from studies with nicotiana. Although self-incompatibility implies that cross-pollination is the only means of seed production it is not absolute, and is absent altogether from *salpiglossis*, though present to some extent in *schizanthus*.

In theory, the many F_1 hybrids of petunia should be produced by natural cross pollination of inbred lines, but in practice most F_1 hybrid seed is produced by manual pollination, often preceded by emasculation to prevent any chance selfing. Insects are reluctant visitors to petunias and natural pollination cannot therefore be relied upon to give a full seed yield. The added compensation of manual pollination is that the production of one hundred per cent F_1 hybrid seed is almost assured.

Most of the solanaceous flower genera and species possess hairs or glands which produce a sticky secretion and act as deterrents to insects. *Salpiglossis* is particularly glutinous and insect visitors are rarely seen even when a crop is in full flower. When self-pollination (by brush) of separate plants within mass-pollinated cultivars has been carried out, the subsequent S_1 progenies of any one cultivar have shown very marked uniformity both within and between lines. S_1 lines of other cultivars have shown similar intra and inter-line uniformity while cultivars themselves remained distinct.

From these results it can be assumed that cultivars reproduce themselves largely by self-pollination of individual plants. Any 'off type' plants in the progeny of a plant would be removed from the population during roguing since they would be very noticeable within a generally uniform population. In *salpiglossis*, as much seed is set by self as by cross-pollination and selfed progenies show no loss of vigour.

To prevent self-fertilisation, the anthers (two large situated below two smaller ones and a single insignificant anther below all others) can be removed at the late bud stage, only 24 hours or less before the bloom opens fully. In the young flowers the five anthers are situated slightly below the stigma and, with care, may be removed even when pollen has just been released. Towards the end of a plant's flowering season very small, insignificant hooded flowers may be produced. These automatically pollinate themselves – and are totally undesirable when F_1 hybrids are being produced. There is evidence, however, that the facility for small flower production is genetically inherited and it should therefore be possible to select lines which are free from this embarrassing characteristic.

For the production of selfed seed, petunia and nicotiana should be self-pollinated in the bud stage, thus overcoming the incompatibility reaction. Salpiglossis selfs readily through its minute, late flower. Crossing of the other species is carried out on the mature flowers – without emasculation if the degree of self-incompatibility has been adequately tested.

Schizanthus has been somewhat neglected from the point of view of overall improvement by selection, and for the production of F_1 hybrids, but it should be 81

Plate 13. Salpiglossis. Small flowers (arrowed) which are difficult to spot, almost impossible to emasculate, and set selfed seed with ease.

as responsive to pollination, and as well-appreciated, as petunia. Seed of most petunia cultivars – F₁'s in particular – is grown in the USA, and the cultivars may occasionally be only marginally suitable for cultivation within the UK. Selection of parent types at the lower latitudes of USA encourages flowering in short days. In consequence, some cultivars grown in Scotland or Northern England tend to remain vegetative or to produce only limited numbers of flowers under the long days of summer.

Valerianaceae

Only *Valerian* (or *Centranthus*) are well enough known in this family to be considered for improvement as garden flowers. Totally neglected by selectors or breeders, they nevertheless have great potential and, if large enough populations are grown and genetically manipulated for a few generations, there is a good chance that rapid advances could be made. The reason for this optimism is that, while they are still undeveloped, they nevertheless form a showy flower head, with numerous individual flowers, which lasts over a long period in mid-summer. An increase in the flower size of only ten per cent, or a departure from the red, pink or white shades, would give an immediate response, and should be the foundation for even greater improvements.

Pollination of the tiny flowers involves patience, but is generally fairly easy and, as each one has its own short pedicel, labels denoting the type of pollination can be attached. Newly opened flowers contain up to four anthers, usually one or three, and these can be removed before they have shed pollen. The stigma is receptive at this stage and should be pollinated by detaching an older flower and applying pollen directly from the plant being used as male. Each pollination should result in a single seed which is mature when it produces a feathery head or 'pappus'.

82

Verbenaceae

The only widely grown member of this family is *Verbena hybrida* with its tight heads of small, highly coloured, tubular flowers. Seed is notoriously poor in its germination percentage but there is evidence that simple selection methods can quickly overcome this defect. Apart from the variability in flower colours, cultivars show considerable uniformity for plant type and the breeding system allows both self and cross-pollination (the latter often by butterflies).

Cross-pollination should not be attempted without prior emasculation (four anthers) in the bud stage although small, confined, flowers make handling difficult. It is best to remove from a head all but the few flowers to be pollinated – which should then be labelled with their appropriate cross by tying below the calyx, *not around the tubular corolla* which will fall away as the ovary matures.

Violaceae

To this family belong our most popular border or edging flowers – the violas and pansies. The large-flowered pansies have been improved considerably by the introduction of F_1 hybrid strains and the time now seems opportune for selection and development of free-flowering, pastel-shaded violas. Open-pollinated varieties of pansies and violas are often found to be uniform for height, flower size and colour, while the ease with which they set seed is well appreciated. Self-pollination is very straightforward and occurs naturally when the five large anthers release their pollen.

After the production of numerous inbred lines the next step (F_1 hybrid production) is practised commercially in large glasshouses by emasculation, followed by pollen application with detached flowers of the male inbred. To avoid repeated pollination of the same flowers, the basal petal of each pansy or viola is detached to indicate that pollen has been applied. Casual visitors should be excluded from the glasshouse at this time since it is difficult to convince them that a good cultivar can result from such a deformed parent.

Vegetable Crops

Because the number of common vegetables is more limited than the many flower species, the main headings in this part are listed alphabetically using the generally accepted name of each crop or species, with the family name bracketed alongside. The various botanical varieties of *Brassica cleracea* are incorporated under the heading 'Brassica' however, since they are completely cross-compatible although morphologically distinct.

Asparagus (Liliaceae)

Although this vegetable crop is regarded as a delicacy it is declining in acreage due to the fact that labour costs (most harvesting is done by hand) are not being matched by increasing yield. Without doubt, asparagus continues to offer the most resistance to improvement by plant breeding, due in large part to its own breeding system which is based upon differentiation of the sexes. Plants may be male, female or hermaphrodite to varying degrees following the genetic interpretation XY or YY = male and XX = female.

The clear cut genetic distinction between sex types is less apparent morphologically, however, and male plants may comprise a range of andro-monoecious types (male and hermaphrodite flowers on the same plant) which are capable of setting variable numbers of berries. While plants may be regarded as pure males at immaturity (one year), by three years of age they give their maximum expression of andromonoecy and after this time gradually revert to almost complete maleness.

The importance of sex in the improvement of asparagus crops is through its association with yield. Male plants outyield female plants by weight by nearly fifty per cent (Wellenseik) through producing larger numbers of medium-sized spears. Female plants (which tend to produce fatter spears) use considerable energy for seed production, resulting in fewer spears in the subsequent season.

Because of the uncertainty that genetic males will remain unisexual all their cultural life, any system which identifies true males would be of great value. Cytological studies tend to be unreliable, as well as time-consuming, because the male and female chromosomes cannot be accurately identified. Selection of male plants by a Japanese technique (Hagiwara and Kusamitu) could have a particular value as a speedy process if it were proved reliable but unfortunately, the method does not appear to have been widely tested. Shoots of seedling plants were grown in tap water for two days and then placed in a 0.02 per cent solution
84   of Potassium chlorate (K Cl$_2$) – in the dark – for one or two days. For a further

two day period the shoots were returned to tap water and kept well illuminated, after which the male shoots faded while the females remained healthy. The significance of this behaviour was not fully understood by the authors and it is encouraging to find that sex may still remain slightly mysterious!

Improvements to asparagus yields have been attempted both by selection methods (whereby plants with the highest yields are mated together in pairs or greater numbers) and also by the induction of tetraploidy. The second method has increased yield somewhat, though also increasing the diameter of the spear which is not always desirable. The selection method has been used by numerous workers and shown to succeed within limits, but its main defect has been the long period needed to test both parents and progeny.

Some evidence has been given (Ellison J.H. and Schermerhorn, L.G.) that early yielding plants (those with five or more spears on the first day of harvest) give significantly higher total yields than the remainder of the population, so identification early in the growing season should allow them to be used as parents.

Asparagus crowns from seed produce only low yields until about three years old. From this time, yield of each plant should remain reasonably consistent for another seven or eight years. To produce a commercial crop of high yielding crowns the best system would appear to be:

(a) Sow seed to give more than double the number of asparagus plants ultimately required. This seed should have been derived from plants bearing only small numbers of berries.

(b) Plant all crowns when ready into permanent beds at half the eventual spacing.

(c) At three years of age select and interpollinate the plants with the greatest expression of maleness (some hermaphrodite flowers will be available for pollination on most plants). Save all seed from these pollinations and, at the same time, remove the female (excessively berried) plants from the field. The remaining plants should comprise the commercial planting and will be cropped as long as is thought desirable.

(d) Freshly produced seed from the crosses should be sown and the crowns subsequently planted in new beds. The new bed should then contain plants of a fairly consistent male type, capable of outyielding the original crop.

This method is not designed to apply genetic information directly, for the simple reason that the crop is difficult to assess in genetical terms and progenies frequently fail to reveal expected gene ratios. However, the method attempts to associate genetical theory with practical expediency on the basis of higher male yields. After two or three spears have been allowed to produce green foliage, emasculation (where necessary) and pollination of flowers should cause little difficulty. Hermaphrodite flowers (identifiable by their fatness due to the six large orange anthers) should be emasculated in the late bud stage. Since selected plants should bear largely male flowers, however, few hermaphrodite flowers will be available for pollination.

Aubergine (solanaceae)

This vegetable is polyploid and inheritance of characters is inevitably complex. It has given good results in programmes for the production of F_1 hybrids in   85

Japan, but probably warrants little practical study here because of the low demand and marginal growing conditions. Pollinations may be made as for peppers or tomatoes (pps. 113, 119).

Beans (Leguminoseae)

The broad bean (*Vicia faba* var *major*) is cross-compatible with the field bean, horse bean or tick bean used in agriculture but differs from them in size of seed and also the natural breeding system. While the field beans show approximately 70 per cent natural crossing and 30 per cent selfing, the broad beans are completely reversed with 30 per cent crossing and 70 per cent selfing. The preference for selfing is considered to be due to more stringent selection in the past for good seed-setting and uniform plant types – overcoming to some extent, the remnants of a self-incompatibility system as found in the field beans. Although tapping of the flower is normally necessary to ensure deposition of pollen upon the stigma, when plants were kept in an insect proof house and flowers were untouched the following results were obtained.

TABLE 9 – AUTOFERTILITY IN BROAD BEANS

Cultivars	No. of plants tested	No. of plants setting seed (Autofertile Plants)	Range of Seed Nos.
Triple-white	195	113	1-34
Bunyard's Exhibition (Seville type)	20	7	2-30
Beck's dwarf green gem (Winter hardy small podded)	31	18	13-32
Eclipse white longpod (Windsor type)	16	11	3-15

The result of preferential selfing is that Broad bean cultivars show good uniformity although crossing may occur between plants within the cultivar – or between cultivars if planted too closely. Seed harvested from a triple-white type with white flowers which has been contaminated by a Seville or Windsor black-and-white-flowered type will, in the next generation produce plants with similar colouration to the pollen parent.

Three basic types of broad beans are known in horticulture, the triple-white type with seeds which remain green when dry, the Seville type with brown coloured seeds slightly larger than those of triple-white – and averaging six to nine seeds per pod, and the Windsor type which has the largest seeds (brown when dry) but only about three per pod. The colour in the latter two plant types is present as a black patch on the flowers, and black spot on the stipules (where leaf is attached to stem) which resembles an ink blot, a reddish stem base and a black hilum (seed attachment point) with general browning of the seed coat. Because the pigmentation diffuses into the water when the bean seeds are blanched, these cultivar types are unsuitable for canning purposes. Although the non-pigmented triple-white types are used exclusively by canners, these too have their limitations because they are less winter-hardy than the other types and consequently mature later in spring. A single dominant gene controls the expression of colour at these four locations, producing what is known as a pleiotropic effect since it affects more than one character at the same time.

Plate 14. Broad Bean. Close-up of pigmented axil spots (circled) and flowers of Seville types compared with non-pigmented Triple white type.

Although broad bean flowers shed pollen in the stigmatic region in a similar manner to the sweet pea, thus implying self-fertilisation, the flowers are highly perfumed and attractive to insects and cross-pollination is common. Bees may visit flowers but fail to pollinate them, however, since they frequently obtain nectar by biting a hole at the base of the corolla. Early in the flowering season most bees visit and pollinate flowers in the orthodox way, but learn the new techniques as the season extends.

Where controlled crosses are to be made, flowers must be emasculated while still in the bud stage by slitting the top of the flower with forceps and forcing the petals apart to gain access to the ten anthers. Because of the abundance of pollen it should be applied from the male parent either by brush or by using the (pollen covered) stigma of the male flower. If pollinating by the second method, no more than two female flowers should be treated with one male flower. Seed production after a cross pollination will, of course, be genetically F_1 but will appear exactly the same as any other seed on the mother plant.

Dwarf Beans (Phaseolus vulgaris)

Apart from obvious morphological differences, the main characteristic separating the dwarf from the broad beans is the complete self-fertilisation which occurs in the dwarf type. Although its flowers are as modified for cross-pollination as any other legume, self-fertilisation is nevertheless the rule and natural hybrids are rarely found. When conducting a crossing programme it is advisable to use male plants which carry a marker gene to identify true hybrids since, even with emasculation, complete cross-fertilisation is difficult to achieve.

Anthers of dwarf bean flowers are completely enclosed within a tight sheath of keel petals which form a complete loop. Because of this construction, certain emasculation is difficult and damage to the buds is frequent. Possibly the most reliable method of crossing is to gently expose the stigma by applying pressure to the wing petal after the bud has just started to open. All dwarf bean flowers are 'left-handed' in that the stigma will be exserted only when the left-hand wing petal (as seen from the front of the flower) is depressed. If the movement is

87

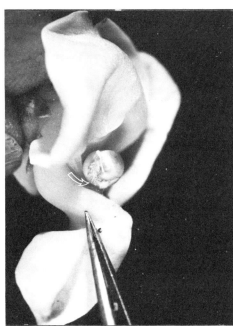

Plates 15 and 16. (i) Dwarf
bean flower with stigma
protruding (arrowed).
(ii) Dwarf bean flower style
extruded when left-hand wing
petal is depressed. Arrow shows
stylar hairs behind stigma.

carried out gently upon a newly opened flower, the pollen will remain loosely attached to the anthers and will not fall upon the inward-facing stigma; on late buds, it is unlikely that pollen will have been released. After the application of the chosen pollen to the stigma (by brush or, preferably, a detached mature flower), pressing on the wing petal should be relaxed gradually to allow the reproductive organs to return to the protection of the keel petals – taking care to avoid disturbing the loose pollen of its own anthers.

The element of uncertainty about full cross-fertilisation is quite unsatisfactory when crosses are made for genetic experiments (unless hybrids are identifiable by marker genes). For plant breeding work, however, the technique of crossing without emasculation is more suitable since it gives a higher number of successful crosses, and selfed and hybrid plants can easily be identified in the field. American workers have achieved 99 per cent successful crossing by this method.

Dwarf beans have a very marked threshold for pod production and if pods (other than those resulting from deliberate pollinations) are allowed to develop upon plants used for crossing, subsequent flowers will fail to set. When plants are grown in a glasshouse for crossing purposes it is unlikely that a plant grown in a 4½ inch pot will support more than eight pods to full seed maturity. Occasionally, (and usually in selfed flowers) bent pods are found, due, it is thought, to the accidental attachment of stigma to the anther filaments. Even when dead the filaments are very retentive and once the pod becomes bent it is seldom straightened by further growth.

When small seed types are used as females in crosses with large seeded forms the hybrid seeds sometimes have split seed coats because of the influence of the male on embryo size.

Pods of dwarf beans develop rapidly after fertilisation, those of the Canadian Wonder, Prince and Masterpiece cultivars becoming 'stringy' soon after reaching their full size. The improved cultivars of American introduction form a fleshy stringless pod which is circular in cross-section, and fibre is formed only when the seeds it contains are approaching full size. Seed development in the older cultivars tends to be more rapid, thus spoiling pod quality. In crosses between cultivars with the two pod types, the flatter Prince-type pod and the

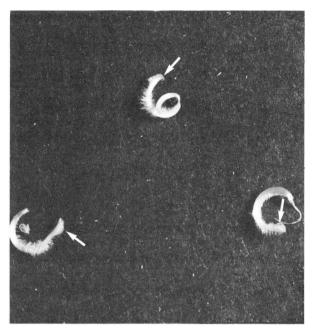

Plate 17. Stigmas of (left)
Runner bean – outward facing;
(right) Dwarf bean – inward
facing; (centre) F₁ hybrid
showing greater tendency to
inward facing than runner
bean.

Plates 18 and 19. 2 photographs
of bumble bees 'working'
runner bean flowers from the
left-hand side.

tendency towards early stringiness were each found to be almost completely
dominant in the F_1 generation. Coloured seed (many different colours exist) is
always dominant to white seed.

Runner Beans

Runner beans are of two main types – the indeterminate form of the dwarf bean
(*Phaseolus vulgaris*) which is most frequently referred to as the pole bean, and
the red, white or pink-flowered kidney bean (*Phaseolus multiflorus* or *coccineus*).
The first is merely a climbing form of the one just described and its breeding
system is therefore the same. Crosses between climbing and dwarf types,
however, give tall F_1 plants and a 3 tall : 1 dwarf segregation in F_2 – whichever
way the cross is made.

   Phaseolus coccineus has a mixed breeding system by which both selfed and
crossed seeds may be produced. The species is completely self-compatible and
the percentage crossing under natural conditions is directly related to insect
activity. Flowers do not normally trip themselves to cause pollen dispersal as do
those of broad beans but must be agitated by insects or wind action. Much self-
pollination occurs naturally since bees (particularly bumble bees) frequently
obtain nectar by biting the base of the petals as they do with broad beans, thus
failing to cross-pollinate the flowers. In the early part of the flowering season,
bumble bees are more likely to pollinate systematically and it is very noticeable
that they always 'work' the flowers from the left-hand wing petal – and so trigger
the action which allows cross-pollination. The keel petals and reproductive
organs of the runner beans are coiled like those of the dwarf form but the
stigmatic surface faces outwards rather than inwards and thus, probably,
prevents full self-fertilisation. It is interesting to speculate whether a consistently self-pollinating *Phaseolus coccineus* may be found, and if so, whether all its
flowers would possess only inward facing stigmas.

   Pod setting (especially on the lower branches) is variable and is thought to be
related to insect activity and weather conditions so that a self-fertilising runner
bean could prove extremely valuable by providing reliable and increased yields.
Because it is less likely that an outward facing stigma will be contaminated with

self pollen, crosses within the runner beans are usually more successful than those of the dwarf types and emasculation is unnecessary. If pollinating runner beans out of doors, and in spite of the fact that bees do not necessarily pollinate, the flower branch must be protected by an insect-proof bag shortly before any flower buds have opened. After making about four or five crosses the remaining buds should be pinched off and the bag removed after not more than four days. Outdoor pollinations should be made no later than the second week in August to be sure of a seed harvest.

When making crosses within any crop, individual plants should be selected and identified as parents. In runner bean, selection is made difficult by the confusion of twining stems but as long as the male parents are identified by labelling the 'pollen' branches, it will be possible to repeat pollinations with accuracy.

Interspecific Bean Crosses

Numerous bean species have been cultivated over a long period in South America, their centre of origin, with the result that there is considerable diversity of plant form and pod and seed type. Some species are fully cross-compatible while others have diverged cytologically to such an extent that fertilisation of one by the other is practically impossible.

TABLE 10 – INTER-SPECIFIC CROSSES IN PHASEOLUS

Species used in crosses	*Success*	*Worker*
Phaseolus vulgaris x Ph. coccineus Reciprocal cross	42.3% seed set 0.5% seed set	Rudorf
Ph. vulgaris x Ph. coccineus Reciprocal cross	up to 72.7% seed set up to 7.6% seed set	Thomas
Ph. vulgaris x Ph. coccineus Reciprocal cross	28.6 to 56.3% pod set 5.2 to 7.0% pod set	Kroh
Ph. vulgaris x Ph. coccineus Reciprocal cross	37% 11%	Coyne et. al.
Ph. vulgaris x Ph. dumosus	10 to 12%	Buishand
Ph. acutifolious (Tepary bean) x Ph. coccineus Reciprocal	1 hybrid with self sterile flowers NIL	Coyne
Ph. acutifolious x (Ph. Vulgaris x (Ph. vulgaris x Ph. coccineus))	2 hybrids (sterile)	Coyne
Ph. coccineus x Ph. Lunatus (Lima bean) Reciprocal and backcross	Some hybrids (sterile) NIL	Honma and Heeckt
Ph. vulgaris x Ph. acutifolious	4 hybrids after embryo culture	Honma
(Ph. vulgaris x Ph. coccineus) x Ph. vulgaris	46.6% recip. 54.6%	Smartt
(Ph. vulgaris x Ph. coccineus) x Ph. coccineus	24% recip. 19.6%	

Plate 20. Interspecific crossing
between dwarf and runner
bean. Healthy F₁ hybrids (rear).
BT dwarf (centre front). T
dwarfs (either side of B dwarf)
B dwarfs (centre on each side).

Inter-specific crossing may be desirable, and therefore worth the attempt, for a number of reasons; disease resistance, improvement of podding characteristics, alteration of seed size, colour or number etc. Table 10 shows the reactions to cross-pollinations of bean species obtained by a number of workers.

Phaseolus calcaratus, mungo, angularis, lunatus and *acutifolius* were largely incompatible in crosses with one another and with *Ph. vulgaris* and *coccineus* but showed evidence of partial compatibility by commencing the formation of pods which collapsed in the early stages of development. As will be appreciated from the above table the cross between the dwarf and runner bean has been made frequently by many more people than those listed, and with generally similar results.

The reasons for making the cross have ranged from a desire to increase flavour in dwarf bean pods, to decrease stringiness in the runner bean and to increase rooting potential in dwarf bean. All workers have found that the cross succeeds best when *phaseolus vulgaris* is used as the female parent, although the cultivar used as female has a pronounced effect on the vigour and appearance of the interspecific F₁ hybrid. Some F₁ hybrids tend to be unthrifty, showing chlorophyll deficiencies and retarded development of such severity that they appear to be diseased. Near normal flowers are nevertheless produced on these F₁'s and produce pollen which is as functional as that on unaffected plants. The unthrifty forms are recognisable in their genetic categories as B, T or BT dwarfs.

B dwarfs rarely survive beyond development of the first trifoliate leaf, T dwarfs are unthrifty, stippled with brown spots and may flower and survive for over a year but will not set seed. BT dwarfs are less healthy even than B dwarfs and are badly deformed as well as being completely stippled brown. Table 11 shows the results obtained by the author from crosses with different female cultivars.

91

TABLE 11

Appearance of F₁ plants resulting from crosses between Phaseolus vulgaris cultivars (females) and Phaseolus coccineus (male)

Female parent	Normal	'T' dwarfs	'B' dwarfs	'BT' dwarfs
Corneli			1	
Extender	1	3		
First and Best	14			
Golden Wax	4	2	1	
Golden Wonder	2			
Pencil Wax	5		1	
Prelude	3			
Prince	5	1		
Sari			1	
Slavia	5	1		
Topcrop	2	1		
Wade		4		
Widusa	5			3
Total numbers	46	12	4	3

The inheritance of the genes causing normal and various dwarf forms of F₁ hybrids has been elegantly deduced by Bemis and Kedar and is presented here as an example for genetical and practical interest.

The results were produced through the action of three alleles at two independent loci (positions) on the chromosome. Alleles at each locus may be v. vc. or c. with loci designated B and T. Thus at the B locus B^v is incompatible with B^c and produces B dwarfs. B^c is compatible with the other allele.

At the T locus alleles v and c are again incompatible with one another and produce T dwarfs. These are the chlorotic, genetically diseased types which, however, do flower. BT dwarfs are produced by incompatible combinations at each locus. The genotype of *Phaseolus vulgaris* would have alleles vc or v, usually in the homozygous state since it is an inbred species, while *Phaseolus coccineus* cultivars carry the allele c.

The genetic constitutions of the various forms are as follows:

Normal inter-specific F₁ hybrids T^{vc} T^{vc} B^{vc} B^{vc} or T^{vc} T^c B^{vc} B^c

T dwarf inter-specific F₁ hybrids T^v T^c B^{vc} B^c (incompatible combination at T locus)

B dwarf inter-specific F₁ hybrids T^{vc} T^c B^v B^c (incompatible combination at B locus)

BT dwarf inter-specific F₁ hybrids T^v T^c B^v B^c (incompatible combination at B and T loci)

Examination of pollen grains showed 91% fertility in *Ph. coccineus*, 77% in *Ph. vulgaris*, 34% in normal F₁ plants and 32% in T dwarfs. B and BT dwarfs did not flower.

Normal F₁ hybrids between the two species tend to have pink flowers of an intermediate size but the stigmatic region is only slightly more inward facing, suggesting greater dominance of the runner bean characteristic. In addition, the cotyledons of the germinating seedling occupy a position at soil level as compared with the hypogeal (below ground) position of the *Ph. coccineus* cotyledons and the epigeal cotyledons (about three inches above soil level) of the dwarf bean cultivars.

When normal F_1 interspecific hybrids were pollinated there were wide differences in seed-set depending upon the manner of pollination.

THE BREEDING OF
SPECIFIC CROPS

TABLE 12
Phaseolus vulgaris x Ph. coccineus

Results of self-pollination, mass-pollination and backcross-pollinations to F_1 plants.

Type of pollination	No. of pollns.	% successful pollns.	No. seeds obtained
F_1 plants			
Self-pollination	400	0.5	2
Mass-pollination	750	18.7	316
Backcross to			
F_1 plants			
Vulgaris as ♂	604	17.2	187
Coccineus as ♂	461	0.4	3

Examination of F_1 pollen grains showed 91% fertility.

Beetroot (Chenopodiaceae)

The beetroot is closely related to sugar beet, with which it is cross-compatible. It has the almost unique characteristic (in the vegetable kingdom) of being wind-pollinated like its related species spinach, and is therefore a very prolific pollen producer. Breeding work with this species should be carried out under pollen proof conditions employing filtered air and this need for extra refinements may be one of the reasons why the species has been largely neglected by plant breeders.

The most marked improvement in recent years has been the production of cultivars with resistance to bolting when sown early. This was achieved very simply by subjecting a large number of seedlings to long days (16 hours of daylight supplemented by artificial light from tungsten bulbs), selecting those which did not produce flowering heads from eight to ten weeks of treatment, and mass-pollinating the plants which grew on to produce high quality roots. Two well-known cultivars Avonearly and Boltardy were produced by this method and form early-maturing high-quality roots with a very low proportion of bolters.

The seed of beetroot is a cluster of true seeds forming a fruit which, when sown, will produce three and five seedlings in the same spot. This makes thinning difficult – especially on a field scale – and in order to avoid the inconvenience, and to save seed, attempts have been made to produce monogerm beet – those whose true seeds are produced singly. Monogerm sugar beet has been used commercially for a number of years but transfer of this character from sugar beet to red beet tends to lower the colour quality of the horticultural product. Nevertheless, satisfactory monogerm red beets are now available as a result of diligent crossing and selection.

Red beet cultivars may be spherical, flat-spherical, cylindrical or conical and the opportunities for producing new forms are many. Because of the normal method of pollination and the fact that flowers occur in groups close to the flowering stem it is almost impossible to emasculate or to ensure complete, controlled cross-pollination. Successful breeding of this crop is possible only if great care is taken to select the desired root shapes (coupled with foliage characters). Quality of each selected root can be assessed by cutting a vertical

93

wedge and replacing it afterwards. Selected roots should be grouped together, for flowering in the year after selection. If a large number of roots have been selected it is advisable to divide them into groups of not more than ten plants. These should be seeded together (under a fine muslin bag for example) in isolation from other groups.

Mass-pollinated seed will be collected separately from each group or possibly from single plants as for progeny-testing and sown separately. It is most likely that some group progenies will perform better than others and further selections should be made only from these.

Brassicas (Crucifereae)

This is the most popular and versatile group in the whole vegetable kingdom. Having its origin in the primitive wild cabbage – a rosetted leafy biennial/perennial – it has diversified over tens of human – and thousands of plant generations –, into six (or seven) distinct horticultural forms which are called 'botanical varieties'.

The species *Brassica oleracea* is divided into

var *acephala*   – *kale*
var *fimbriata*   – *curly kale*
var *botrytis*   – *cauliflower*
var *capitata*   – *cabbage*
var *gemmifera* – *Brussels sprout*
var *gongylodes* – *Kohl-rabi*
var *italica*   – *sprouting broccoli*

All are cross-compatible with one another, and when cross-fertilisation occurs between them the F1 hybrids normally appear intermediate in form between parents. As long as the female parent is known, the identity of the male parent can be deduced from an inspection of the seedling progenies. Table 13 lists the inheritance of characters which are mostly easily identified in hybrid seedlings.

TABLE 13
THE INHERITANCE OF VEGETATIVE CHARACTERS IN B. OLERACEA
SEEDLINGS (FROM FOUR TO EIGHT-LEAF STAGE)

Phenotype in F1

	dominant	recessive
Habit	reflexed	erect
Stem	tall	short
Bulb (of Kohl rabi)	present but small	absent
Leaf shape	circular	elongated
	petiolate	sessile (no stalk)
Leaf surface	bumpy	smooth
	waxy	glossy
Leaf edge	divided (as curly kale)	entire
	dentate (as Savoy cabbage)	
	divided	dentate
Colour	red or purple	green
Axillary buds	present (though minute)	absent

94 All botanical varieties bear the same basic breeding system and will therefore be

described as a single species where applicable. Crops will be taken independently under the present general heading, however, where individual requirements
and responses are considered.

Self-incompatibility

All types of *Brassica oleracea* possess a sporophytic self-incompatibility system
which tends to vary in strength according to the intensity of selection previously
applied to the crop-type or cultivar. The system (which encourages cross-
fertilisation and therefore heterozygosity throughout the population) is strong-
est in the more primitive crop types such as kale and weakest in the highly
selected and domesticated crops like summer-cauliflower. As a consequence,
self-fertilisation (inbreeding) of kale produces a marked decline in the vigour of
plants of the next generation while the selfed progeny of summer-cauliflower
(whose weak self-incompatibility system has not precluded self-fertilisation in
the past) show little or no inbreeding depression. The most common response to
inbreeding, in whatever species, is a decline in fertility, however, and when
measured as fecundity (the normal level of offspring production compared with
the potential level) cauliflower is found to suffer more than any other member of
Brassica oleracea.

Table 14 expresses the effects of the natural breeding system of *Brassica
oleracea* upon its component crop types, while from this table the best methods
of crop improvement may be surmised.

TABLE 14
GENERALISATIONS ON BREEDING SYSTEMS IN *BRASSICA OLERACEA*

Botanical variety	Potential seed set	Seed set when mass-pollinated	Seed set when selfed	Percent inbreeding depression in S_1 generation
		Expressed as percentage of potential		
giant kale	34 – 40	50 – 68%	11%	45%
curly kale	25 – 27	60%	20%	30%
kohl-rabi	24 – 26	49 – 60%	12 – 18%	17%
Brussels sprout	18 – 24	61 – 70%	11 – 41%	21%
sprouting broccoli	21 – 28	35 – 49%	9 – 10%	26%
cabbage	24 – 31	18 – 67%	3 – 22%	10%
winter cauliflower	20 – 30	28 – 62%	5 – 39%	29%
autumn cauliflower	22 – 34	29 – 59%	12 – 43%	24%
early summer cauliflower	22 – 32	16 – 31%	19 – 38%	None

The figures given in the above table are mean values from experimental
evidence but individual plants within any one crop may show extremes for self-
incompatibility or compatibility – and these, or their progeny, may respond to a
breeding technique different from that which is normally applied to the whole
crop. A breeding technique which has been devised on the basis of a high level of
self-incompatibility in cauliflower, Brussels sprout and cabbage crops for
example, would probably fail if the exceptional plants were selected.

Self-incompatible plants can be recognised by their response to pollination
when all pollen other than their own is excluded. If self-pollen is applied to the
open flower, truly self-incompatible plants will fail to form pods. Some wrong
deductions may be made initially since the ovary (style) appears healthy when
petals and sepals fall from the mature flower. Even at this early stage, however,

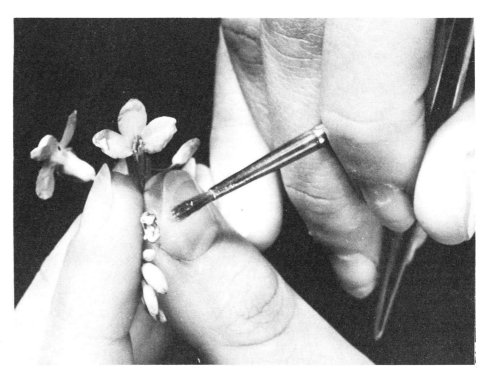

Plate 21. Bud-pollination of
Brussels sprouts.

slight projections should be visible where the ovules are swelling if self-fertilisation has occurred satisfactorily. If styles do not enlarge after sepal fall the self-pollination was incompatible. A minimum of five open flowers should be pollinated before assessments can be regarded as reliable. All too frequently there is some evidence of pod swelling but only one or two seeds may be produced per pod, and the plant is then considered to be almost self-incompatible.

When the self-incompatibility system is so intense that no seed is set by selfing open flowers, the breeder must resort to bud-pollination. Instead of applying pollen to the stigmas of mature flowers, buds are slit open from the base with forceps or dissecting needle, opening the apex of the bud sufficiently to see the stigma about two days before they would open normally, and are then pollinated with pollen from open flowers of the same plant. The self-incompatibility reaction is absent in juvenile flower buds and fertilisation of the ovules can therefore proceed unhindered. Success is very doubtful if buds are pollinated more than three days prior to flower maturity since they are then more susceptible to mechanical damage.

Cultivars or plants with almost complete self-incompatibility are most suited to a breeding programme for the production of F_1 hybrids, or, if they can be multiplied as clonal material (and most Brassicas are easily propagated vegetatively), to raising a synthetic cultivar. For either of these purposes a number of generations of inbreeding is essential in order to produce homozygous lines. The following details of individual crop responses illustrate that *Brassica oleracea* types conform to a general genetic pattern but this is modified to some extent with each crop.

(a) Curly kale

Two basic types exist, differing only in the height of stem. Little breeding work has been devoted to this crop largely because of its relative unpopularity (coarse leaves with strong taste and purgative action!) and improvements are most likely to be made by inbreeding for the eventual commercial production of F_1 hybrids.

96

(b) Cauliflower

This general heading should be divided into three crop classes, the early-summer-cauliflowers which behave as annuals, the autumn cauliflowers which mature for market in the same year as that in which they are sown (but cannot be classified as annuals because they do not flower and set seed within twelve months from sowing); and the winter-cauliflowers which are biennials and will not produce a head (curd) unless they have had sufficient cold stimulus through the winter.

All types produce their curds as a preliminary to flowering – the curd is, in fact, a huge unprotected growing point of incipient flower buds and only about 1/20 of the total area will eventually elongate and develop flowering tissue. The early summer forms are considered to have been derived from the autumn cauliflowers which in turn were probably selected out of the winter forms. Evolution in botanical terms regards perennial and biennial plant forms as primitive, the annual form is advanced. In addition, self-incompatibility tends to become progressively weakened as the annual habit develops (although in nature greater success is attributed to cross-fertilising types e.g. those with self-incompatibility) and this is a well established fact in the cauliflower. Figure 9 illustrates the probable relationship and development of each cauliflower type.

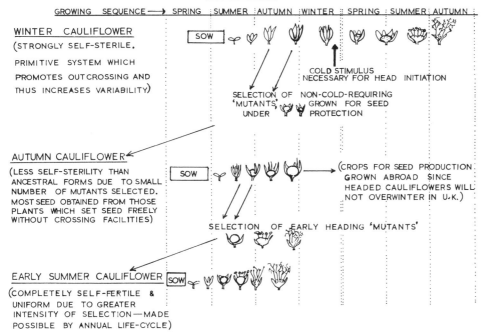

Fig 9. The evolution and relationship of three cauliflower types (summer, autumn, and winter).

Improvements and maintenance of quality in the cauliflowers have been generally slower and less successful than other members of *Brassica oleracea* mainly because of the difficulty of obtaining seed from selected plants. Individuals which are lifted from the field, potted and transferred to a glasshouse are effectively condemned to death, since the set-back in growth allows rapid colonisation of the delicate and unprotected 'curd' by disease organisms.

Many methods of vegetative propagation have been attempted ranging from curd cuttings (which root readily but die before commencing vegetative growth) to the more successful nutrient culture of plant tissue. No method of propagation can be considered entirely satisfactory, however, if it cannot be practised upon plants selected for quality under the appropriate growing conditions. The most successful technique appears to be that whereby selected

Plate 22. Beginning of vegetative propagation of autumn cauliflower. Plants decapitated and placed in sand in boxes to allow adventitious rooting. Photograph taken in December.

plants are decapitated in the field and allowed to remain for two or more weeks (as long as the weather is not too severe) to encourage callus formation over the cut surface. After this period plants are dug carefully, placed in a box or trough of coarse sand in such a manner that half of the roots are above and half below the surface. Watering is kept to a minimum, and high temperatures avoided. Within two weeks, adventitious roots should appear at the base of the stem and should be followed shortly by vegetative shoots – which may arise from the uncovered or covered roots, or from any part of the stem. Because of the years of selection for a single head or curd, cauliflowers lack axillary buds and vegetative tissue emerges in almost random positions.

The vegetative tissue will eventually be detached and propagated in the conventional way. Unfortunately, the delay in flowering after propagation usually means that a breeding programme is delayed for a year at the outset – but without this technique it would probably never get off the ground.

Winter cauliflower, which produce curds in spring, may flower successfully *in situ* but they will need to be protected from foreign pollen if critical breeding programmes are to be carried out. Winter cauliflowers tend to possess a more intense self-incompatibility mechanism than the other cauliflower types and isolation of single plants may therefore affect seed setting. Any self-incompatibility may, of course, be overcome by bud-self-pollination, as described previously. The December curding, winter cauliflowers will not survive a British winter if selected and left in the field and must therefore be propagated vegetatively.

Autumn cauliflowers are mature in the period August to early December and comprise two main types, Australian and Italian. The Australian types revolutionised the cauliflower industry from 1957 onwards by introducing uniformity and very high quality which was absent from Italian cultivars. Breeding work commenced with Italian Phenomenal types around 1930 in Australia and, because of the good climatic conditions, single plant selections were able to remain and set seed in the field in the position where they were grown – similar to some of our winter cauliflowers. It was something of a surprise to the Australians when the end products of their breeding programme proved to be so adapted to British growing conditions. The Italian cauliflowers have, even now, shown few improvements since British breeders have been frustrated by the difficulty of obtaining seed from selected plants. The situation should soon be rectified, using the new techniques of vegetative propagation, and the Italian types should provide characters such as upright growth, curd protection and frost hardiness which are not fully expressed in the Australian types.

98

The self-incompatibility reaction of autumn cauliflowers is less intense than that of the winter cauliflowers and self-pollination of mature flowers should always produce seed, although usually less than that resulting from mass-pollination.

Because of the incomplete self-incompatibility reaction of these two cauliflower types the chances of producing F_1 hybrid cultivars are remote since the percentage of *sibs* (a simple abbreviation for sister and brother plants) would probably be too high to guarantee uniformity and high yield of crop. Crosses between inbred lines do produce vigorous hybrids, however, and a method (such as using male-sterility) which reduces or prevents the appearance of sibs would have a distinct commercial value.

Early summer cauliflowers are totally unadapted to F_1 hybrid production since they are self-compatible and all cultivars are effectively pure lines. No inbreeding depression occurs following self-pollination and experiments have failed to point to any consistent yield advantage of F_1's over their parental inbreds. Inbreds and F_1's show very few differences in plant size and weight (and not always in favour of the hybrids) but the curds of F_1's, weighed separately from the leaves may be up to ten per cent heavier than the mean value of those of the inbred parents. This weight difference is not obvious in curd diameter, however, – the characteristic by which cauliflowers are marketed. In general, early summer cauliflowers are of such high quality that no breeding work is necessary, but new cultivars can best be produced by crossing followed by single plant selection of segregants in the F_2 and subsequent generations.

Cross-pollination should be followed by the selection of segregants in the autumn and winter types also, but in this case cross-pollination should be preceded by up to three generations of inbreeding in order to remove undesirable curd characteristics such as riceyness and bractedness. Selection for quality can never be relaxed if curd defects are to be removed since even after three generations of selection for perfect curds it has proved to be only too easy to select for, and restore, riceyness. As far as the cauliflower itself is concerned, a return to poor quality curds due to slack selection may serve as an evolutionary defence since the greater quantities of seed (and hence, the greatest chance of survival) are inevitably produced by the plants with curd defects. Good quality is inherited as a partial dominant, controlled by polygenes, and the genes controlling poorer quality are therefore ineffective until they attain a level of homozygosity.

Another polygenically controlled character is time of maturity, with earliness being largely dominant to lateness. Thus, the F_1 of a cross between the annual early summer cauliflowers and the winter cauliflowers will produce a curd before the onset of winter, though later than the summer cauliflower parent. The earlier the inter-crossing parent matures, the earlier will be the F_1. Plants of the segregating F_2 generations will cover almost the whole range of maturity between the two parents although reaching neither of the two extremes.

The dominance of the annual habit overcomes the need for a cold stimulus before curd production. All biennial Brassicas produce only vegetative growth in their first season and are unable to reach the flowering stage unless subjected to winter conditions.

The amount of cold stimulus required (measured as period and intensity) varies considerably according to crop type and cultivar, but in general those flowering in late autumn or very early spring require the least. The cold stimulus is effective only when plants have reached a certain stage of vegetative growth and, when this threshold value is attained, juvenile plants may be subjected to an artificial stimulus in order to speed up the breeding programme. Thus, for 99

Brussels sprouts, a plant with eight true leaves will flower quickly following a period of six weeks at a temperature below 4°C. No breeding programme should rely entirely upon artificial stimulation in the juvenile phase, however, since this could result in the production of a line with such a low cold requirement that it would bolt, curd, or flower prematurely and cause complete loss of crop.

(d) Brussels sprout

The great improvements in this crop have altered its whole characteristic from one which was highly variable, wasteful, or hand-picked for an average yield of 2½ to 3 tons per acre, to an extremely uniform, machine harvested, high yielding, no waste, crop averaging seven to ten tons per acre of high quality produce. The transformation has been brought about by the application of the basic breeding principles of intensive selection and inbreeding, with the eventual production of F_1 hybrids.

In spite of the resounding successes of F_1 hybrid Brussels sprout many problems remain, however, the greatest being those associated with the genetic techniques of seed production through self-incompatibility. Before producing F_1 hybrids, selected plants must be inbred for a number of generations and two lines which will intercross to produce F_1 hybrid seed are eventually grown together in a commercial field plot. Because of the effect of environment upon the self-incompatibility system of inbreds, however, some cross-pollination occurs between plants within inbred lines and a proportion of *sibs* will be present in the F_1 hybrid cultivar. Inbreeding in most *brassicas* tends to reduce plant vigour, sibs are merely products of the inbreeding process, and the yield of an F_1 hybrid is therefore reduced in a proportion corresponding to the amount of accidental self- (or sib-) pollination within each line.

The emphasis in contemporary sprout breeding is now towards the need to find inbred lines which are completely self-incompatible and will set no selfed seed however extreme the environment. These inbred lines will, of course, need to be reproduced by seed before field planting can take place and this is achieved by bud-self-pollination or by a method involving the use of chemicals. Details of F_1 hybrid production methods are given in the next section.

The most important characters for selection in the Brussels sprout crop are regularly spaced solid sprout buttons, erect stem, good leaf protection (although the leaves should readily fall away when sprouts are fully developed) and disease resistance, mainly to powdery mildew and botrytis.

Selection of plants with tight, high density, sprout buttons is essential since it has been shown that loose types succumb to internal browning (deterioration of the inner leaves) making them inedible, particularly following a period of cold weather. Type of plant and size of button are dictated by the breeding objective, whether for the fresh market or the processor and whether the crop is to be hand picked or machine harvested.

Whatever the objective, Brussels sprout cultivars are most quickly and effectively improved by a programme starting with inbreeding since this technique rapidly isolates good and bad lines. While inbreeding causes a reduction in vigour the maximum loss occurs in the first inbred generation (I_1 or S_1).

When plants are selected it is most convenient to make the necessary pollinations in a glasshouse but it is far from convenient to transfer whole plants, or even to house them. For this reason, and because only small quantities of seed of as many distinct genotypes as possible are required at the start of breeding programme, Brussels sprout selections are best propagated from cuttings and pollinated as small plants. The most easily propagated plant portion is the edible

Plate 23. Vegetative propagation of Brussels sprouts. Quartered buttons root and resist disease better than whole buttons.

button or sprout which may be propagated whole, in portions, or as leaflets. Whichever method is used (and whole button propagation is least successful) no propagation should take place until an adequate cold stimulus has been received by the whole plant. If by chance, a propagated button fails to flower it will still be receptive to a cold stimulus as described earlier and will then flower. By careful dissection, a medium sized (3cm diameter) button can be split into about twenty leaflets, each with its own axillary bud from which the inflorescence will eventually arise. After potting on, at least thirty flowers should develop on each plantlet, giving adequate seed for studying the next generation.

(d) Cabbage

Numerous forms and maturity types of cabbage are used as cultivars and the crop is available on the market throughout the year. Spring cabbages are normally sown in July or August and stand the winter as small plants to be cut as greens in the spring, or later as conical hearted cabbage. Summer cabbage are usually spherical when mature following a sowing in January or February under glass while winter cabbage mature through the colder months after being sown outdoors in April or May. Because selection has concentrated upon different seasonal and morphological characteristics, the breeding systems of each group tend to differ slightly from one another. Less inbreeding depression is exhibited by the spring and winter types indicating that cultivars may be produced by very close mating within each group, whereas the summer cabbage require larger numbers of plants to form the basis of a new cultivar.

Breeding techniques for all cabbage are the same as for other members of the *oleracea* tribe; inflorescences and flower buds differ slightly in shape from the Brussels sprout and cauliflowers; vegetative propagation is easily practised using axillary leaf buds which develop when the plant is decapitated.

Although the seasonal types are morphologically well defined there is no barrier to cross fertilisation between them and many new commercial forms may be produced by inter-crossing. One major genetic fault of cabbage exists mainly in the January King types and, in spite of years of selection, has still to be removed. This condition, known as *rosetting* results from the failure of leaves to overlap one another when forming the cabbage head.

Occasionally one or two outer leaves fully overlap and obscure the central cavity, but thumb pressure on the top of the 'head' can quickly reveal the rosetted plants – which should not be selected. The rosetting characteristic is polygenically inherited so that head quality is maintained most effectively by using material only from those lines which give solid heads upon inbreeding. 101

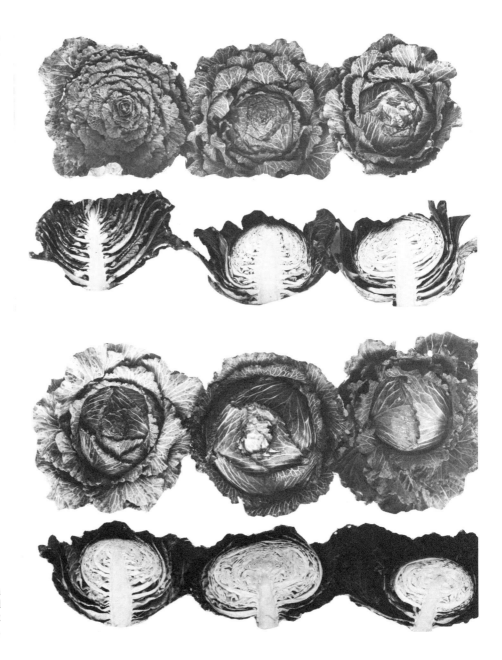

Plates 24 and 25. Rosetting in winter cabbage. 5 rosetted grades leading up to one perfect head.

Selection based upon the length of the central core of a cabbage should also eliminate rosettes from the population.

(e) Kohl-rabi

The breeding system of this botanical variety follows a similar pattern to that of the other *B. oleracea* but the self-incompatibility level is intermediate between that of sprouting broccoli and Brussels sprout. Very little selection for uniformity or quality has taken place in the past due largely to the difficulty of assessing 'roots' when planted for a seed crop. The spherical root is formed from a swollen stem to which leaf bases are attached and the conducting vessels which supply the leaves often form tough, inedible tissue. Although more intensive selection, coupled with controlled breeding, would probably have a marked effect upon quality and yield, the vegetable is so 'unfashionable' that even major improvements would probably fail to increase consumption.

For testing quality, fully mature bulbs should be examined for toughness, measured as thickness of vascular tissue and the outer skin or epidermal layer. A technique used by breeders of marrow-stem kale will provide rapid assessments of the thickness of tough (lignified) vascular tissue. A narrow wedge should be removed from the bulb and treated by immersing in a solution of *phloroglucin* which acts as a stain. The thickness of vascular tissue is a direct measure of toughness and will be indicated by the width of the pink zone. Bulbs with the narrowest layers should be chosen for future pollination (after ensuring that the cut area has been dusted with a fungicide).

Kohl rabi is biennial and flowering will therefore not occur until a few months following selection. It must be emphasised that qualitative and quantitative selection can be practised only upon bulbs of the same maturity. Undersized bulbs may be immature due to late germination or competition in the plant bed and should therefore not be considered for breeding work, while large bulbs with very narrow pink zones are especially valuable since their excess growth has not reduced edibility.

Pollination details are essentially the same as for the other Brassicas.

(f) Sprouting Broccoli

In some respects this crop may be regarded as a primitive form of cauliflower, from which the latter is, in fact, considered to be derived. Three basic types of sprouting broccoli are known, white, purple and green (or calabrese): the first two being sown and grown at the same period as winter cauliflower while the calabrese types (which are most popular with processing companies) are sown in spring and harvested in summer after a very short growing period. The calabrese types have been intensively selected and developed by American seed companies and research stations to the point where they show very high uniformity and quality, and it is only a matter of time before the white and purple types are similarly improved.

All sprouting broccoli possess a terminal head of incipient flower buds as well as axillary buds which each have their own terminal bud. The calabrese types have been modified to produce a large terminal bud capable of being mechanically harvested, and although the axillary buds remain, their development tends to be limited. Thus, selection has almost succeeded in producing the cauliflower habit, although in the cauliflower dominance of the terminal head is absolute, since axillary buds are completely absent.

Inbreeding of calabrese tends to depress plant vigour by ten to twenty per cent but it is of value in producing uniformity for synthesising the many F_1 hybrid cultivars.

The degree of self-incompatibility in sprouting broccoli is one of the highest in *B. oleracea* and the limitations to F_1 hybrid production are therefore not as great as for the other types. Nevertheless, mass-pollinated cultivars which have been subjected to strict selection appear to be almost as vigorous and uniform as F_1's and, since their seed production problems are less, this method of cultivar production is unlikely to be abandoned or neglected.

Common Factors in Brassica Oleracea Breeding

It is impossible to describe the best breeding technique for all *Brassica oleracea* types since each shows slight, but often significant, differences in response to a particular system. In addition, individual plants within a cultivar, and cultivars within types often exhibit anomalous behaviour and new cultivars may be developed by one or a number of systems.

If we consider uniformity and yield to be the main requirements, the methods most likely to produce or maintain improvements appear to be (a) F_1 hybrid   103 production in Brussels sprouts and curly kale, (b) the production of synthetic cultivars in summer cabbage, sprouting broccoli and winter cauliflower, (c) hybridisation with subsequent selection and maintenance by mass-pollination in spring cabbage, kohl rabi, autumn cauliflower (and probably sprouting broccoli) and (d) inbreeding or assortative mating, (i.e. crossing of very close relations) in early summer cauliflowers and winter cabbage – and possibly Brussels sprouts.

Carrot (Umbelliferae)

The major requirement in the carrot crop is generally considered to be increased uniformity. Much greater uniformity than hitherto has been obtained by improving growing techniques but the stresses below the soil surface associated with plant density, stones, uneven irrigation etc. are difficult to overcome completely. Because F_1 hybrids in general show the vigour and flexibility to cope with environmental changes most modern carrot breeding research is directed towards their development. Due to the fairly complex inheritance of male sterility (used for F_1 production) however, progress is rather slow and few assessments of the value of F_1 hybrid carrots on a commercial scale have been made.

Carrots are largely cross-pollinated (up to 95 per cent crossing has been found in the field) although some self-fertilisation may occur because of the proximity of flowers within the same corymb or flower head. Each flower develops anthers before the stigma is fully receptive (protandry) thus making self-fertilisation impossible within a single flower but the precautionary effect of nature is nullified by successional maturation of all other flowers. The initial stages of F_1 hybrid production in carrots, as in other crops, involve self-fertilisation to increase the *genetic homozygosity* and this is made possible by enclosing flower heads of single plants with pollinating insects (usually blowflies) within a muslin sleeve. Self-fertilisation may also be carried out by brush-pollination but is normally less successful as the brush rapidly becomes covered with a sticky exudate. Inbreeding was successfully used by Carlton & Peterson (1963) to establish separate lines of carrots with high and low sugar and dry matter content, but the loss of plant vigour was so marked that it was necessary to restore it by producing F_1 hybrids.

Since the flowers of carrot are very difficult to manipulate, flowers are cross-pollinated without emasculation. Although a small proportion of selfed seeds wll be produced these will probably be disregarded because of their poor vigour at germination and later. Probably the most successful technique for breeding carrots is the simple progeny test with which it is possible to identify good maternal lines and to combine them for seed production.

As far as can be seen at present, F_1 hybrids offer very few advantages in uniformity over other forms of cultivar, and continued maintenance by progeny testing offers the advantage of hybridity together with very stringent selections for correct morphological type.

Carrot roots, following selection for shape and colour, should be replanted into their flowering quarters where they will overwinter. Seed harvesting should be possible in the following August.

Carrots are badly affected by aphid attack in some seasons with the result that they may become diseased with the associated carrot-motley-dwarf virus. The production of cultivars with resistance to this disease – which in dry seasons may cause almost total crop failure – is probably the most urgent requirement in carrot breeding work, and any programme will probably involve the autumn king types which appear to offer most resistance. From the physiological, anatomical and nutritional point of view it is of major importance to produce a carrot of high carotene content and with a wide fleshy cortex. Both characters appear to be under a high degree of genetic control although high carotene content is not necessarily found in roots with the deepest colours. White carrot roots are occasionally found, the colour being inherited as a simple recessive.

Celery

Since this crop also belongs to the Umbelliferae, its flowers are formed in corymbs similar to those of the carrot. Each flower is protandrous, the styles being produced about six days after anther maturity (anthesis), but the effect of inbreeding – which is more common in this species – is less disastrous on plant vigour in subsequent generations. Emasculation is unnecessary for successful cross-pollinations and a very useful technique is described by Honma. Flowering of celery is induced in its first year of growth (normally it would take two years to flower, as for carrot) by giving plants a temperature of 18°C for three weeks and by raising temperatures subsequently.

When flowering starts, all but the outer three whorls of flowers on each corymb are removed and when the styles develop and become receptive, a male corymb, cut and placed in a test tube with water, is attached to the main stalk. Blowflies are introduced into the muslin sleeve surrounding the inflorescence and should pollinate successfully to produce a high proportion of hybrid seeds.

If light and dark green parents are used, the light green should be used as female parent; all hybrid seedlings will be *dark* green and any self-fertilised seedlings, being light green can be easily removed.

The major defects in celery cultivars are stringiness of the edible stalk, a tendency to early bolting and susceptibility to *Septoria apii* (late blight disease) which can be transmitted to new crops via the seed. While chemical controls for infected celery are well-known and efficient (particularly the Thiram soak treatment) attempts are being made to produce cultivars with a degree of in-built resistance. The disease, which causes brown spotting of the leaves and stalks, is very ubiquitous and no cultivars exhibit complete resistance. Tests may be made upon segregating seedlings from crosses by 'dunking' them in a spore suspension derived from infected plants and by growing them at high humidity and temperatures (*circa* 20°C to 25°C).

Physiological defects may be eliminated using various techniques which encourage defective types to show themselves. Segregating populations may be screened for bolting tendency by subjecting them to temperatures of about 8°C for five weeks, after the seedlings are six weeks old. The non-bolting seedlings should be used to form the basis of a non-bolting population. By using this technique even a very slow bolting American cultivar (Golden Plume) was shown to contain a surprisingly high figure of 60% plants with a bolting tendency.

Stringiness in celery stalks is, to some extent, inevitable as the strings comprise the conductive tissues which are essential for transporting water and nutrients to and from the leaves. Some tissues are more tender than others, however, and the degree of toughness can be measured with a tenderometer as used for peas. Since the tenderometer is an expensive item of equipment it is unlikely to be widely available and any reproducible cutting technique may be substituted. The important point is that stem sections should be submitted to 105 the same pressure with a tool of constant sharpness for every test. The plants with the lowest resistance should be chosen for further work – as long as they are also satisfactory in all other characteristics. American green celery is widely considered to be more crisp and tender than the self-blanching types.

When selected plants are removed from the field, great care should be taken not to damage the central growing point or cover it with soil, since the plants are very susceptible to disease once the smooth growing cycle is disturbed.

Chicory (Compositae)

Chicory appears to be gaining some ground as an accepted vegetable, particularly since the crop has shown its adaptability to easier and cheaper methods of culture. It is cross-compatible with endive and, because of its self-incompatibility, is easily cross-fertilised when used as the female parent. Endive, on the other hand is fully self-compatible and almost always self-fertilised. Interspecific hybrid plants tend to have a fairly low seed fertility, mainly due to the high percentage (over 50%) of non functional pollen grains. The F_2 generation illustrates that the blue flower of chicory is dominant to the mauve of endive. When cross-pollination of chicory is prevented there is some evidence that seeds may be formed apomictically i.e. by development due to stimulation (but not fertilisation) by their own pollen.

Some workers have shown the presence of self-compatibility in small numbers of individual plants. Bannerot and Cominck selected plants for high self-fertility and succeeded in inbreeding them and their progenies over five generations, by the end of which the level of self-fertility exceeded 90 per cent. In addition, the quality showed a marked increase although general vigour diminished in their experiments – contrary to those of others where self-incompatibility remained low but vigour was stable.

The improvement of chicory would appear to be best achieved either by cross-pollination of selected individuals or by selfing and improving quality where possible and ultimately re-crossing, pollination then being carried out without emasculation. Any plants which are re-selected for breeding work should be subjected to a short period of cold conditions to encourage the production of flowers. Late varieties tend to require a greater cold stimulus than the earlier maturing ones but it has been found that vernalisation at 1.5°C will induce bolting in all but the most resistant types. It seems possible to remove bolters after two or three generations of selection. As far as yield is concerned, plants with crinkly leaves have been found to weigh 25% more than smooth-leaved types, and core-length appears to be larger in plants with later maturity.

Cucumber

Because of their close relationships to cucumber, vegetable marrow, melons and courgettes will be included briefly under this heading. In spite of their morphological similarities, cucumber (*Cucumis sativus*) does not cross with marrow and squash (*Cucurbita pepo*), melon (*Cucumis melo*) or pumpkin (*Cucurbita moschata*), and intercrossing between the others does not occur except for the cross *C. moschata* x *C. pepo*.

After many years of experiment, Hayase in Japan found, when making the latter cross, that pollination was most successful with *C. moschata* as female at 7.0 a.m., using pollen from *C. pepo* stored at 10°C from 10.0 p.m. on the previous day. The reciprocal cross succeeded only when pollinations were made at 4.0

a.m. Perhaps many other 'incompatible' species crosses can be made success-fully with this type of shock treatment!

The cucumber and cucurbit species' main similarity is in the separate identity of male and female flowers upon the same plant (monoecy). Under normal circumstances the male flowers are produced first and are followed after a short interval by female and further male flowers. The female flowers can be identified by the presence of the ovary below the flower corolla and these may be pollinated by male flowers from the same or another plant. The number of seeds per fruit produced by self-fertilisation is usually lower than that from cross-fertilisation although inbred progenies do not necessarily lose vigour. The production of male flowers is favoured by long days with high light intensity and warm night temperatures although environment and/or chemicals may be used with effect to control the flower type. Two major genes Acr and G in the homozygous dominant condition produce gynaecious plants (i.e. bearing all female flowers), the homozygous recessive acr acr gg produces andromono-ecious types (all male or males and hermaphrodites) while Acr Acr gg gives hermaphrodite flowers and acr acr GG produces monoecious plants bearing both male and female flower types in sequence.

Cucumbers are able to form fruits parthenocarpically (i.e. without fertilis-ation of the female flower) but when fertilised they lose their tubular shape to become bulbous in the stigmatic region – where most of the seeds are formed – and are bitter to the taste. There is an obvious advantage in growing cucumber plants with a maximum number of female flowers while preventing fertilisation, and this is now done commercially by making use of the genetically gynaecious type.

Since cucumbers must be grown from seeds however, it is essential for the seed producer or plant breeder that male flowers should be produced for fertilisation purposes and this is now possible by applying giberellic acid at a given stage in the life cycle. Young plants respond better than old ones. At a dilution of approximately 1200 parts per million giberellic acid in water, repeated weekly spraying of the female plant will result in the production of sufficient male flowers to be used for pollination. Breeding of cucumber is best achieved under glass, and the highest seed set is obtained by pollination of the first female flowers to appear. Pollinations are made by removing part or whole of the female corolla and touching the stigma gently with the appropriate male anthers. Reasonable seed set may also be obtained by allowing the female flower to open normally, then inserting and leaving a complete set of anthers upon the stigmatic surface. Pollen vigour is best at approximately 80% humidity. Fruits should contain ripe seed about seven weeks after the date of fertilisation.

The outdoor species marrow, melon, etc. are usually fertilised in the same way, but in this case the female flowers or plants need good protection from pollinating insects if crossing is to be controlled. Because of insect pollination all fruits in a normal crop are full of seed at harvest time. Seedless melons are widely grown in the warmer counties though not as a result of parthenogenesis but of a genetic technique which produces triploid seeds. Triploid plants (derived from a 2x x 4x cross) produce seedless melons because chromosome maladjustments and misdivisions do not allow seed formation. In cucumber there is no requirement for triploids, and tetraploids (which are produced spontaneously at a rate between 1 in 5000 and 1 in 10,000) do not appear to possess any advantages over the conventional diploids.

So many workers have been involved in cucumber breeding that the inheritance of many commercial characteristics is known. Most current programmes are devoted to the continuation of resistance to powdery mildew

(*Erysiphe cichoracearum*) where the dominant gene imparts complete resistance or immunity. Other genes control characters as listed below (mostly as described by Poole 1944).

Dominant gene	*Recessive gene*
Spines on fruit	No spines
coarse spines	fine spines
tough skin	tender skin
warty	smooth
bitterness of fruit	non bitterness
cream flesh	white flesh
dull skin	glossy skin
resistance to cucumber mosaic	no resistance
resistance to scab	no resistance
indeterminate vine (trailing)	determinate (bushy)
open flowers	closed flowers (sterile)

F_1 hybrid cucumbers tend to bear greater numbers of fruits than conventional cultivars of pure lines and thus show the increased yield associated with heterosis. F_1 hybrid marrows of a genetically gynaecious constitution also produce many fruits which, when harvested at an immature stage are known as *courgettes*. This example illustrates the value of plants with female flowers – in contrast to their limitations in a crop such as asparagus.

It is perhaps appropriate at this point to re-emphasise the importance of studying all aspects of the commercial possibilities associated with varying breeding systems. Characteristics appearing to have little value at the present time may, by some thought and manipulation, prove the basis for new and valued techniques or production methods. In this context, male sterility (in some senses another form of gynaecy) was ignored as an embarrassment until only a few years ago while maleness or femaleness alone have already proved their worth.

Leeks (Liliaceae)

Very little can be drawn from breeding experience with this crop which, because of its freedom from disease, its regularly high yield, and ease of culture has required few improvements involving genetic theory.

Cultivars are extremely uniform and genetic variability is available only through crosses between the limited range of cultivars. The leek, *Allium porrum* is genetically non-compatible with the onion *Allium sativum*, a fact which is independent of its tetraploid constitution.

Since leeks show little morphological variation, the tetraploid segregation ratios from inter-cultivar crosses are almost impossible to define; any breeding work must therefore be based upon the production of identifiable lines through inbreeding or pair crossing. Leeks are completely self-compatible and crosses can be made only by saturation of the female plant umbels with pollen from the male parent (either by brush or blowflies), or by careful emasculation of a number of flowers after removal of all open flowers and most buds of the umbel – followed by cross-pollination and protection from other pollen or insects.

Because leeks form an almost 'perfect' species, however, the chances of producing great improvements for commercialisation must be rated as extremely low.

THE BREEDING OF
SPECIFIC CROPS

Plate 26. (left) Emasculated
lettuce flower (above).
Unemasculated flower (covered
with fluffy pollen) – below.

Plate 27 (right) Emasculation
of lettuce with water jet.

Lettuce (Compositae)

In some respects this crop has breeding characteristics in common with chicory
and endive, or even marigold. Its flower has a complete form and comprises up to
twenty florets, each with a basal ovary, which are combined in a capitulum or
sheath of sepals. Chicory and endive flowers are purple to mauve in colour but
those of lettuce are yellow. Lettuce is completely self-fertilised during elongation of the style through the cone of five joined anthers, where it picks up pollen
on stylar and stigmatic surfaces. All florets within a single capitulum open and
become self-fertilised over a period of a few hours, although development is not
precisely simultaneous. The capitulum never re-opens except to shed its seed,
each complete with its individual parachute (pappus) at maturity.

Because of the once-only opportunity for fertilisation on each flower, cross-
pollinations must be made in a very systematic manner. The abundant self-
pollen is removed by a thin, but vigorously applied, jet of water at a time when
the styles of the majority of florets are seen to have elongated. The droplet of
water remaining on the florets should be puffed away briskly so that the
capitulum will dry and be ready for pollination within a half hour. Pollinations
are made by removing an open capitulum from the male parent and pressing it
upon the emasculated flower. One male capitulum should successfully fertilise
about three females.

The need to observe a timetable for lettuce pollinations cannot be over-
emphasised since, if the developmental details are disregarded, the whole
emasculation and pollination procedure will be a complete waste of time. On
very bright warm mornings lettuce flowers can be ready for pollination at 7 a.m.
and may be closed four hours later. On dull mornings flowers may not be fully
open until 11 or 12 o'clock. Each pollinated flower should be identified by a label
which is best attached before making the pollination. Because several buds tend
to develop in a cluster, it is of prime importance to ensure (possibly after
removing the unwanted buds with forceps) that the label is tied only to the
pedicel of the pollinated flower.

At this stage it is important to emphasise that plants should be carefully
treated in order that they can reach the flowering stage. The closely folded heart
leaves may become diseased before bolting commences and, to successfully
produce a disease-free flowering stalk, all surplus heart leaves must be removed
about two to four weeks after the heart is first formed to allow free air
movement.

109

Lettuce is most closely related to, and is thought to be derived from, the wild species *Lactuca serriola* which occurs widely in Britain and the Continent, and from which lettuce (*L. sativa*) is considered to be derived. Like the cultivated lettuce, the wild species is normally self-fertilised and cross-pollination between the two is very unlikely even when plants are flowering adjacent to one another. Experiments have shown that lettuce can be naturally cross-fertilised by up to ten per cent, however, although more than one per cent is very unusual. Higher levels of crossing appear to be likely only in very late flowering crops when the population of hover flies is at its peak.

Other wild species, not indigenious to Britain, which are cross-compatible with *Lactuca sativa* are *L. virosa, L. salinga* and *L. altaica*. In spite of the wide morphological range the wild species appear to possess few characteristics apart from disease resistance, which could be transferred with advantage to the cultivated lettuce. All wild species form a prostrate rosette of linear or lobed leaves and show no tendency whatsoever towards heart production. One character – 'shattering' of the capitulum to give good seed dispersal – is ideally suited to the need of wild species but it would be disastrous if incorporated into a commercial seed crop. Inheritance of the 'shattering' character is through a single dominant gene – non shattering types as found in the cultivated lettuce which retain mature seed in the head, carry the double recessive.

Five distinct forms of cultivated lettuce are recognised, the heading butter-head, crisphead or cos types, and the chicken or stem and rosette types, all of which are completely cross-compatible. The reaction of heading types to different daylengths determines whether they are grown as winter or summer crops. Those maturing in long days are photoperiodically neutral while those which are normally grown through the winter will flower without hearting if sown as summer lettuce (long day lettuce). Plants which bolt in long days are genetically TT while the recessives (tt) are daylength neutral. Thus, a winter x summer lettuce F_1 will bolt early in summer after a spring sowing. Hearting is controlled by recessive gene kk, KK gives rosetted forms but recessive k is operative only when T is absent or is inactivated by short days.

When crosses are made between widely differing morphological types of cultivated lettuce the F_2 segregation presents a continuous range which defies classification. Lettuce forms are very quickly stabilised, however, and each F_3 progeny shows such reduced variability that the subsequent F_4 generation appears to comprise a series of almost pure lines.

Many shades of colour are found in lettuce species and cultivars, ranging from the very deep 'all over' red (except inside the heart) of *Continuity* through spotting or tingeing to dark or light green. Genes controlling each colour characteristic are subject to modification by polygenes but in general red is dominant to green, and dark green is dominant to light green – with good 3:1 ratios for basic colour expression in F_2.

Lettuce seed may be white or black in colour, black behaving as simple dominant and white as a recessive. Yellow seeded types have also been found but are no longer present amongst modern cultivars. Because black seeds cannot be seen on the ground after sowing, most breeders ensure that any new cultivars are of the white seeded type, even if some degree of backcrossing is involved. The seed coat is, of course, maternal tissue and all seed from a single plant will be of the same colour. Segregation for seed colour does not occur after a cross of white x black seeded cultivars until seed is produced on F_2 plants, three out of every four then producing black seed and one, white seed.

There is very little likelihood of the commercial production of F_1 hybrids due to the efficiency of the self-fertilising system, coupled with the fact that lettuce flowers do not appear to attract many insects – which would be needed for F_1 hybrid seed production. Various chemical methods have been used to induce male sterility so that cross-pollination would be facilitated but no chemical has proved reliable over all environmental conditions throughout the flowering period of the crop (up to six weeks). Genetic male sterility has been found as a combined effect of a dominant and a recessive gene, but the investigator appreciated that it was unlikely to be beneficial unless the degree of natural cross-pollination could be increased.

Lettuce diseases

Because lettuce crops are highly uniform all plants within a cultivar are equally susceptible to disease, and any group of diseased plants is very easily noticed. Three diseases occur commonly and much effort is being devoted towards increasing resistance. Tipburn is a physiological disorder affecting plants in the hearted condition and is most pronounced during irregular periods of high temperatures and fluctuating irrigation. Outer heart leaves may or may not be affected by the main symptom which is a browning of the leaf edges eventually causing a slimy deterioration of the inner leaf layers. No cultivar shows complete resistance but they may nevertheless be improved by selection of those plants from a segregating generation (F_2 or F_3) which retain the healthiest heart over the longest period. Continued selection for a high level of resistance will result in improved progenies as long as segregation is taking place i.e. up to the F_5 generation.

Downy mildew disease occurs widely in outdoor lettuces in the Autumn and is also produced by high humidity under glass. Resistance is controlled by a dominant gene with modifiers which tend to disrupt the expected 3:1 ratio of resistant to susceptible in F_2. At least ten strains of the fungus are known to exist and it is apparent that any resistance conferred by major genes will inevitably be overcome by the pathogen.

Lettuce mosaic virus is most troublesome in warm dry summers as it is spread by aphids from a source of infection within the crop or from weeds such as groundsel. When seedlings become infected they very seldom grow to full hearted maturity but remain in a dwarf rosetted condition. Plants infected at a later stage may prove unmarketable due to their small size, yellow mottling or tiny brown spotting. Resistance is higher within some cultivars than in others and is present in some *L. serriola* types, while one S. American cultivar Gallega, is currently providing resistance for a number of breeders. There is little doubt that in lettuce, continued selection for the healthiest plants amongst segregating breeding lines is one of the most effective means of producing extra resistance.

Onion (Liliaceae)

The first demonstration of the advantages of F_1 hybrid vigour in a horticultural crop was provided by the onion but, in spite of an almost ideal system of seed production, inherent pollination difficulties are such that F_1 hybrids form only a very small proportion of commercial crops. The advantages and difficulties are detailed in the next section.

The flowering head of onion is an umbel, forming a sphere of individual flowers on long pedicels. Pollination in the field is normally by insects which crawl over the flower head and transfer both self and foreign pollen. Thus, from a normally mass-pollinated crop both selfed and outcrossed seeds are produced in roughly equal proportions. Inbreeding causes some loss of vigour but any weak plants within a growing crop tend to be crowded out and excluded from the ultimate harvest. It will be appreciated, however, that a genetically uniform line where all plants are either hybrids or vigorous inbreds is bound to give a more satisfactory crop of evenly maturing bulbs.

Onion is a biennial and flowering occurs only when selected bulbs are replanted after winter storage. Selection can be practised over a number of stages – earliness of bulb ripening (when the leaves collapse at harvest time), shape, size and appearance of the bulb in store, and a final assessment for storage and disease resistance qualities when planting time returns.

Unless the object of the programme is to maintain an existing cultivar, selected plants should be self-pollinated. This is done in the field by enclosing the flowering heads within a muslin or nylon mesh sleeve. Porous cellophane bags may also be used but these are less weatherproof. Whatever the form of protection, sufficient support must be given to avoid putting strain upon the main flower stalk.

Inbreeding, as always, helps to show up particular genetic types and illustrates their importance to the future programme. Wide variations between inbred lines are to be expected although within-line variation will tend to be low since some level of inbreeding always occurs in the course of normal mass-pollination. It may be practicable to produce a cultivar by selecting only the bulbs from one inbred line. Success is more likely, however, if the best bulbs of the best lines (which conform to the desired shape and colour – size is not important at this stage) are selected and stored as separate lines, being replanted together when their storage qualities have been assessed. If any inbred line shows poor storage results all of its remaining healthy bulbs should be discarded. If they were included with those of the healthy lines, the fitness of the eventual mass-pollinated progeny would be correspondingly reduced.

Mass pollinations may be made in the field or under glass – as long as enough insects are present to achieve good pollination.

Cross pollinations are made either by enclosing the flower heads of both parents within the same muslin sleeve and introducing blowflies, or by hand-crossing preceded by emasculation. With the former technique, hybrid seeds will be produced in quantity upon each flower head but so will selfed seeds. This method is therefore used most efficiently when either or both of the parental lines can be identified by marker genes. Onion bulbs selected for crossing purposes are best grown in large pots so that they can be moved adjacent to those of other lines when flowering begins, and insect-proofing of heads should produce no difficulties. When new pollen plants which have not been planted in pots are to be used, the umbels from the new parent can be cut off with a short stalk, placed in a glass phial with water, and taped to the female flowering stalk. This technique (as already described for carrots) makes pollen available for the duration of the flowering period of the female umbel.

When more controlled crossing is necessary, the number of onion flowers within the umbel should be reduced by removing unwanted ones with forceps.

If three whorls of flowers are left, outer middle and inner, these will ripen successfully and cross pollinations may be made over an extended period to give a maximum chance of success. Each whorl should be emasculated in turn in the late bud or very young flower stage, (six anthers per flower), and pollinated when the next whorl is ready for emasculation. Pollen will be applied by brush from the flowers of the male parent. Stigmas of onion flowers should be receptive to pollen for at least five days after flowers first open.

Onion bulbs vary in colour and shape, the earlier strains tending to be flatter and the late maturing ones more spherical. Onion bulb sizes, shape and dimensions are inherited quantitively with flat partially dominant to globe –

which is itself genetically dominant to tall globe or torpedo shape. Bulb colour ranges from white, through yellow and brown to red and, in general, the disease resistance tends to increase with colour intensity. White bulbs are homozygous for I which inhibits pigment production – and these have been shown (by Jones et al. 1946) to be extremely susceptible to *Colletotrichum circinans* (onion smudge). Yellow or red bulbs (iirr or iiRR) were highly resistant. Similar gradients have been recorded for the association of bulb colour with resistance to *Botrytis allii* (neck rot – which usually occurs in storage).

Interspecific crosses have been made between bulb onion (*A. cepa*) and the Welsh onion *Allium fistulosum* which shows resistance to smut, pink root and thrips. Their F_1 hybrids bulb slightly, are perennial and self sterile. Backcrosses to either parent are successful, however, when the hybrid is used as the pollen parent. A natural, true breeding amphidiploid form was found by Jones (1942 J. Hered) but does not appear to have made much commercial impact.

Onion and shallot are quite cross-compatible.

Parsnip

This member of the *umbelliferae* is grown in only limited amounts outside of the British Isles and has been modified only slightly by breeding. What work has been done has been aimed at increasing the level of resistance to parsnip canker – a fungal disease which produces rotting areas of orange to black diseased tissue upon the shoulders of susceptible roots. Resistant cultivars are currently available and are being used as foundation material for improvements in root shape. Greater susceptibility to the disease is found in 'fen-type' soil than in mineral soils.

Parsnip flowers arise in corymbs, like the carrots, but although each flower is somewhat larger, emasculation and hand pollination are almost impossible. Flower heads are attractive to flies, ants and some butterflies, and cross-pollinations are best made by bagging heads of both parents together and introducing blowflies. Some self-fertilisation is inevitable but most seeds will be hybrid and, following a sowing in the next season, any selfs can be removed after comparison of the hybrid roots with the two parental types.

Screening for canker resistance is carried out on the lifted roots. These should be washed clean, a slice of the epidermis removed at the shoulder and a piece of agar containing a culture of canker (*Itersonilia*) applied to the cut surface. Roots should be kept cool and after 15 days they should show evidence of resistance or susceptibility. Resistance appears to be polygenic in inheritance and infection should therefore show a continuous range in intensity over the plant population.

After selections have been made for resistant roots of the desired shape they should either be stored in a sand clamp until growth starts again in February/March or planted in pots or soil and kept frost-free with straw covering, otherwise they may die from botrytis rots or dehydration.

Peppers (Solanaceae)

Most cultivars of pepper belong to the species *Capsicum annum* (the green, sweet pepper) and, with *C. frutescens* (red pepper) can be grown outside in temperate areas but under glass in Britain. The sweet pepper is becoming increasingly popular either in its green form or its riper red colour and, since cultural requirements are similar, it can be grown as easily as tomatoes. Flowers are produced at each leaf node, having a white corolla and blue to purple anthers, 113

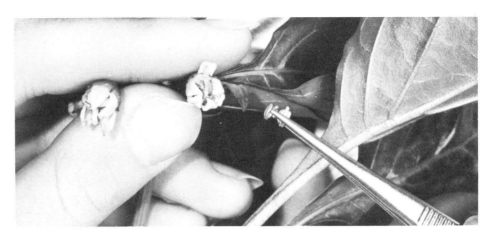

Plate 28. Emasculation of
Pepper flowers in the bud stage.

but otherwise with a morphological similarity to the tomato. The fruit contains tomato-type seeds but lacks the tomato flesh. The pungent flower of the red pepper types is due to the alkaloid *capsaicin* but the sweet or bell types are only slightly pungent by comparison. Pungent flavour is reported to be genetically dominant to sweet.

Although self-fertilisation has little deleterious effect in peppers except in some degree of yield reduction, flowers are not automatically self-fertilised to the same degree as those of tomatoes. Up to 16 per cent cross-pollination – by bees – has been found and some protection of the flowers is necessary after emasculation if genetic admixture is to be avoided. Anthesis (pollen shedding) occurs as the flower opens and controlled cross-pollination must therefore be preceded by emasculation in the bud stage. Stigmas are normally receptive at the late bud stage and pollen from the male parent can be applied successfully at time of emasculation. As long as sufficient pollen grains are transferred each pollination should give up to 200 seeds per fruit; these will be mature when fruit colour changes from green to brown or red.

The yield of F_1 hybrids grown outdoors in warmer climates may be, in some instances, over 100% better than the average of the parents – their superiority being most marked in years of unfavourable weather. Under the more controlled glasshouse environment, however, yield differences tend to be less pronounced.

Male sterility has been found and its inheritance studied but it appears to be too greatly influenced by modifying genes to have a constant value for producing F_1 hybrid seed. Pollen production of sterile plants occurred under cool conditions and, in general, the seed set on pollinated male sterile plants was only half that of normally pollinated cultivars.

Fig 10. Compatibility
relationships in *Capsicum*
species (Smith & Heiser 1958).
Key.
No viable crosses obtained
Crosses made possible only by
embryo culture
Poorly cross-fertile
Cross-compatible (Arrow
points towards female parent).

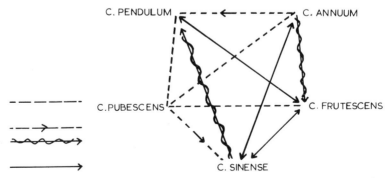

Botrytis, tobacco mosaic virus and wilt disease appear to have the greatest effect upon sweet peppers and their control may be possible by genetic means through introducing genes from other species. Smith and Heiser (1958)

114

produced a diagrammatic table of compatibility relationships (Figure 10) which illustrates the possibility of transferring characters from one species to another either directly or by 'bridging'.

'Bridging' through related species would ensure that a desirable character in *C. pubescens* for example, which could not be transferred directly to *C. annum* could be transmitted by using *C. sinense* as an alternative parent, – while ensuring the presence of the character by efficient screening techniques. Alternatively, *sinense* could be only the first step and the character could eventually be integrated into the *C. annuum* background through *frutescens*, *pendulum*, or both.

Peas (Papilionaceae)

Acreages sown to this crop in Britain are greater than the total for all other horticultural crops. This is a reflection both of its popularity as a green vegetable and of the ease with which it may be grown – in spite of having its fair share of fungal and insect pests. Earliness is related to the number of nodes (the point on the stem where the leaf is attached) which must be produced before the emergence of the first flowers. Early types produce their first flowers at about the eighth node while the later cultivars may not produce flowers until the sixteenth. Late flowering tends to be dominant to early but F_2's show a continuous maturity range.

Flowers, and therefore pods, may be produced singly, as doubles, trebles, or sometimes quadruples. For fresh picking in gardens the single podded types give a longer season while the concentrated podding of multipodded types is most suitable for mechanical harvesting. Round seeded types tend to be earlier than those with wrinkled seeds but they lack flavour since they contain approximately 46% starch (less sugar, therefore) compared with the 34% of the wrinkled seeded cultivars. When seeds dry off inside the pod or after removal from it, the wrinkled seeds assume their characteristic appearance because the seed contents (endosperm) contract to a greater degree than those of the round seeded types. Two other forms of surface wrinkling, 'dimpled' and 'indent', have been investigated but genes controlling these expressions behave differently from the classical mendelian dominance of round and recessiveness of wrinkled.

Purple pods may sometimes result from a cross between two green podded cultivars while purple x green results in a monogenic 3:1 ratio or a digenic 9:7 ratio in the F_2 generation.

Being self-fertilised, new pea cultivars can be produced only by hybridisation using essentially the same techniques as for sweet peas or broad beans. Anthers dehisce in the late bud stage and emasculation of flowers on the female plant should therefore be made when the flower bud is approximately the same length as the calyx. The ten orange anthers are exposed and removed by inserting forceps through the top of the bud to split the standard petal and to separate the wing and keel petals. Pollen of the male parent should be applied directly to the feathery stigmas using the protruding, pollen covered style of a freshly matured flower. Stigmas remain receptive for three days at 16°C. Cross-fertilised pods should not be allowed to ripen fully on the plant otherwise they may split and shed their seed.

Since Mendel's experiments on peas which started the whole subject of genetics, many new characters have been investigated. While none of the genetic experiments disprove Mendel's initial reasoning it is very apparent that confusion could arise if characters were not correctly classified. Thus, Mendel 115 showed that Tall was a simple dominant to short, but other workers have shown that the same result may be obtained by crossing a long internode type with a short internode type; that a gene causing flower sterility can also produce dwarfness; that crosses between dwarfs can also produce tall slender F_1's and that dwarfness can be produced by dominant genes. These complications (and others) have been found because peas have for long provided one of the most popular plant species for genetic studies throughout the world – and a descriptive work would probably exceed the Encyclopaedia Britannica in length.

'Rogue' plants, identified by their narrow petals, stipules and pointed leaflets, may be found in small proportions within some cultivars. Normal plants may produce rogues and an intermediate form, while rogues themselves breed true. In the cross normal x rogue, F_1 plants appear normal, but develop rogue characters as maturity increases – the character probably being produced by the activity of plasmagenes which were transferred through the pollen.

Although none of them have yet reached a commercial stage, fasciated peas have been used widely for breeding programmes in recent years, particularly for mechanically harvested types where their apical cluster of pods would have a distinct value. The shortened flowering period helps to overcome the ravages of the pea moth as well as producing simultaneous ripening. Fasciation (thickening of the stem because all flowers are carried to the plant apex) is inherited as a simple recessive although phenotypes are much affected by modifying genes.

Much interest is also being expressed in the 'leafless' pea forms, particularly for their use as commercial vining peas or, perhaps more suitably, as dried peas for packeting. Leafless peas grow tendrils in the place of leaflets and, in large groups, have the appearance of loose bundles of thin wire which cling together. Their value as green vining-peas is limited by the fact that pods lack the protection of a leafy canopy at maturity and therefore quickly lose their quality. For dried peas this produces an advantageous quick drying effect, however. Other genes and their alleles affect leaf form in different ways, having the genotypes shown below.

Leafless	(tendrils instead of leaflets)	afafTlTl
Acacia	(leaflets instead of tendrils – the plants thus collapsing for lack of support)	AfAftltl
Leafy	(minute leaflets instead of tendrils)	afaftltl
Normal	(conventional leaflets and tendrils)	AfAfTlTl

In addition to these leaf forms, the size of the stipule (two large leaflets in conventional cultivars at the junction of leaf stalk and main stem) is controlled by StSt (normal, large) and stst (small, straplike).

Perhaps the greatest need for improvement in peas is to increase the crop's standing ability by introducing a stiffened main stem. Unfortunately, none of the many cross-compatible 'wild' types, nor existing cultivars, appear to have overcome their natural trailing form and, until an exceptional mutant is found, the leafless forms due to their interlocking ability, have the least tendency to collapse.

Radish (Cruciferae)

Although radish flowers are similar to those of the cabbage tribe (except that their range of colours is much more extensive), the two genera have shown very

Plate 29. Variable leaf forms in
Pea. left to right: –
Normal AfAfTlTl
Leafless afafTlTl
Leafy afaftltl
Acacia AfAftltl.

little evidence of cross-compatibility. The morphological differences between the two forms are emphasised also in the pod types (radish being segmented and pithy, cabbage being pea-like) which indicates that genetic separation took place many generations ago. Radish shows degrees of self-incompatibility which vary between plants and between cultivars while most cultivars show uniformity for leaf size and type, but less uniformity for root form.

Most of the early cultivars were produced by mass-pollination of unselected roots which grew and produced flowers and seeds where they were originally sown. Today, however, selection intensities are applied and some inbreeding is carried out to improve basic material. The most important character for selection is solidity of the root – which should be maintained for a long period before the onset of pithiness.

Selection of good parental material can be easily made by first allowing roots of a normal cultivar to reach an overmature stage. These should then be dug up, their leaves (but not growing points) removed, and the bare roots immersed in a container of water. Roots which float (being pithy and full of air spaces) should be discarded and only the large sinkers retained for seed production. Small sinkers should not be retained since their small size may be an indication of immaturity and their solidity may be less positive genetically than phenotypically. Retained roots should be planted in a group and well-watered immediately. They should soon regenerate leaves and subsequent mass-pollination of the flowering group should give noticeable improvements in the root quality of the next generation. The most solid roots seem to be present in the white globe and long white cultivars.

Self-pollination is the quickest way of producing homozygosity and of studying the qualitative features of different lines – and it tends to have a dramatic effect with certain cultivars. Selfed progenies of individual plants may be better than or similar to the parent in both size, shape and colour while other progenies are minute even after only one generation's inbreeding. While radish is an ideal species for genetic demonstrations there is much evidence that great strides in breeding work can still be made.

Radish (*Raphanus sativus*) is completely cross-compatible with wild radish (*R. raphanistrum*) which grows as a common weed, particularly near the coast, and any outdoor pollinations should therefore be protected or isolated. The F_1 between the two species develops as a vigorous plant with a long stringy root. The wild species produces a woody seed pod (which is dominant in F_1) as compared to the more papery pod of the cultivated forms.

Red root colour is dominant to white with a 3:1 segregation in F_2 while the less common purple roots x red give the same result.

117

Spinach (Chenopodiaceae)

This species, which belongs to the same family as beetroot, resembles asparagus in its breeding system by having wholly male or female plants and also the intermediate, or monoecious, types which have both male and female flowers upon the same plant. As with beetroot, the ovules are fertilised by wind-blown pollen. The yield differences attributed to sex types in asparagus are less apparent in spinach where there was shown to be no difference in the weights of the first 15 leaves from male and female plants of a number of cultivars. The value of the different sex types in spinach appears therefore to be related mostly to F_1 hybrid production by utilising female lines in combination with known pollen parents. F_1 hybrid yields are known to exceed those of parental cultivars by up to twenty per cent.

For the production of F_1 hybrids the first essential is to produce inbred lines from which the ultimate parents will be chosen. Inbreeding is best achieved by the selection of good monoecious plants, each of which has a preponderance of female flowers but enough male flowers to allow effective pollination both for inbreeding and the later hybrid production.

Early sowings tend to result in higher proportions of female plants while more males are produced when growing conditions are less favourable or when temperatures are high (28°C). Thus, to ensure reliably female-type populations it is best to select for parent plants with the female habit *under conditions which encourage the production of male characteristics*. For local requirements it may not be worth while to engage in F_1 hybrid production and new cultivars may therefore be produced by mass-pollination or inbreeding alone – since lines lose little vigour – or by producing triploids. Monoecious tetraploid plants used as the female line give good sets of triploid seed when a dilpoid is used as the male parent and the resultant progeny should have the benefits of hybrid vigour.

Because the species is wind-pollinated it is difficult to be certain that all seeds of a cross were fertilised by the chosen male parent. Parent plants to be used as females should be protected from foreign pollen by a fine muslin sleeve until they are saturated by the appropriate pollen which has been collected in a test tube and shaken into the sleeve – which is then rapidly sealed.

Dark green leaf colour was found to be closely associated with late bolting – early bolting being a defect of most spinach cultivars. Dark leaved types tend also to be somewhat curled and to contain larger amounts of iron. The F_1 between smooth and savoy leaved types was intermediate.

Sweet Corn (Gramineae)

Thanks to the efforts of plant breeders throughout the world the degrees of cold tolerance, earliness of flowering and reduction of growing period of sweet corn cultivars have all been improved to such an extent that it is now regarded as a fairly common vegetable in Britain. Further improvements must be made, however, – the greatest requirement being good germination and seedling growth after an early spring sowing – before sweet corn can be regarded as a reliable crop in every year.

The basic difference between sweet corn and maize (which provides our morning corn flakes) is the sweet taste of the former – due to its sugary endosperm – while the endosperm of maize consists largely of starch. The F_1 hybrid cobs from crosses between sweet corn and maize are starchy since this character is controlled by a single major gene, sugary being recessive.

Sweet corn plants are monoecious, having separate female flowers (which

118

form cobs) and male 'tassels' which are borne at the apex of the plant. Two to six female flowers are produced in the axils of the leaves (depending upon the number of tillers or side shoots) and are identified by their silks. These are bundles of styles, each attached to a basal ovary which becomes the cob after fertilisation. The silks are produced a couple of days prior to the release of pollen from the male flowers of the tassel and are therefore fully receptive when pollen is shed and dispersed by the wind. The silks are, of course, liable to be pollinated by pollen from surrounding plants which have an earlier maturity and the effect of separation of the sexes is to encourage cross fertilisation. If continuous rain or overhead irrigation occurs during the normal pollination period a poor seed set is likely and the mature cobs will be mishapen and 'gappy'.

Mass-pollination of plants normally gives seed which, in the next generation, will produce a population with similar attributes of yield and quality. Most varietal improvements in sweet corn have been made by the production of F_1 hybrids however, since the time when maize was first exploited to show the benefits of controlled hybridisation. F_1 hybrids of sweet corn are particularly valuable for their uniformity as well as some increase in yield, and are relatively easy to produce.

Because sweet corn is naturally cross-pollinated, all plants are heterozygous to some degree and inbreeding is essential to obtain uniformity. The best plants in a population – using at least two cultivars – are selected on their morphological characters and are self-fertilised *in situ*. Selection can only be carried out before cob formation – or possibly after assessing the qualities of the first, immature, cob – since the selected plant must be given time to produce a self-fertilised cob. Self-fertilisation starts by bagging a female flower before the silk is extruded (being wind-pollinated, a cellophane bag, with its aperture sealed with a cotton wool plug, is therefore most protective). When the silk has reached its full length, the tassel of the same plant should be shaken inside to release pollen, after which the cellophane bag is closed again.

Seed of each self-pollination should be sown again the following year when further selection and selfing will be carried out. Inbreeding should continue for at least three generations, by which time inbreds should show considerable within-line uniformity and marked between-line difference.

For the production of F_1 hybrids an inbred line from one cultivar should then be cross-pollinated with an inbred from another cultivar. If inbred lines from the same cultivar are crossed to produce an F_1 (even though they may show great morphological differences) the resulting F_1 hybrid is unlikely to be as vigorous as one from crosses between cultivars.

While the uniformity of F_1 hybrid sweet corn is undeniable, it is very likely that overall yield can be equalled by good, mass-pollinated cultivars.

Tomatoes (Solanaceae)

Since they were first discovered in central and southern America, tomatoes have become as important a part of the diet as any other vegetable, and their popularity has prompted vast financial outlay on research. In spite of years of detailed work in breeding the crop however, the amount of genetic variability remains high and new and improved cultivars can be expected for decades ahead.

Tomato fruits vary widely in shape and colour but the general habit of plant growth is either indeterminate (those used as glasshouse tomatoes or staked outdoor types) – or determinate, producing the dwarf, outdoor tomato. 119

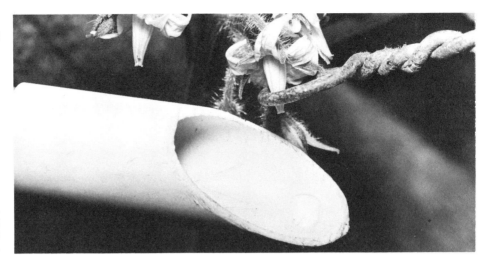

Plate 30. Collection of pollen
from 'male' parent using
electric bee to shake pollen into
plastic 'thumbnail'.

Indeterminate habit is dominant to determinate with a 3:1 ratio in F_2.

Although its wild ancestors were outbreeders, the cultivated tomato is always self-fertilised and no cross-fertilisation has been observed between adjacent plants of different, identifiable, cultivars when grown in temperate regions. In Equador up to 26% cross-fertilisation between recognised cultivars has been thought to be due to the presence of a particular native bee.

The five anthers of tomato flowers are joined together in the form of a cone around the long style and sufficient pollen is released directly on the surface of the stigma to produce well over 200 seeds per fruit. To make crosses, emasculation must be carried out in the bud stage about one or two days before the flower would open normally.

After a little practice the removal of the anthers should become a simple matter, although first attempts will almost inevitably result in breakage of the style. Anthers are removed as a group, with or without the surrounding corolla, by inserting forceps between the sepals to grip the base of the anthers and/or petals which are then removed by a firm but steady pull. If anthers seem reluctant to part company from a flower receptacle as a group it is advisable to remove a single one first by careful manipulation of the forceps. Following this the remaining four may be gripped firmly without any fear of damaging the style.

Pollen is best applied in experimental crosses by slitting the inside of the anthers of mature flowers of the male parent with the forceps in such a way that a small amount of pollen is collected at the tip of the forceps. This can then be lightly applied to the stigmatic surface and should be visible as a white covering. Forceps should be sterilised by dipping in alcohol or methylated spirits after each pollination – even if the same cross is to be repeated – so that a consistent routine becomes established. Pollen may be collected in larger amounts by inverting the mature flower and tapping pollen onto the thumbnail as for cyclamen. This is then applied directly to the stigma of the female plant.

Inexperienced operators frequently damage the ovary, though leaving the style intact, and their misdemeanours can be recognised later by the presence of one or two holes in the skin and flesh of the fruit as it matures.

Commercial hybridisation of tomatoes is a large scale industry and is described in detail in the next section.

Fruit shape is regarded as an important component of quality, particularly as higher prices are paid for the premium grades. The shape of multilocular fruits (those which comprise more than two septa or divisions, seen most easily when fruits are halved horizontally) tends to be less regular than that of the bilocular

THE BREEDING OF
SPECIFIC CROPS

Plate 31. Pollination of emasculated tomato flower by the 'thumbnail' technique – using a shaped plastic tube.

fruits; most breeders therefore concentrate their efforts on the bilocular types. Since the stigmatic scar on the mature fruit almost always reflects the number of loculi within, it appears that the right parents could be selected on the basis of stigmatic lobing at the flowering stage. In general, bilocular fruits also tend to have less air space – and thus higher quality.

The range of fruit characteristics is considerable and Table 15 details the type of inheritance for most of the types used in commerce or breeding.

TABLE 15
THE INHERITANCE OF FRUIT CHARACTERISTICS IN TOMATO

	Dominant	*Recessive*
Fruit size	small fruit	large fruit
(Fruit size in F_1's, F_2's and BC's approaches the geometric mean of parent cultivars)		
Fruit shape	round	oval
	oval	plum/pear
Locules	2–3 locules	over 3.5 locules
Fruit colour	red	yellow
Hairiness of fruit	hairy	smooth
Inflorescence (truss)	simple	compound

Earliness of fruiting is generally associated with earliness of flowering and, in glasshouse tomatoes, is a most important commercial character since the earliest home-grown fruits attract the highest prices. The ability to produce an abundance of pollen in poor light conditions with low temperatures is shown by cultivars such as Earlinorth, Puck, Fireball and Red Cloud (Daubeny) and leads to early fruit production in cold glasshouses. The advantages of earliness tends to be offset by a reduction in total yield and the best approach in breeding for improvements in both would appear to be selection for earliness only in segregating high yielding large-fruited breeding material. Greater progress is normally made in selecting for fruit size than for earliness and it is therefore best to first stabilise fruiting characters so that subsequent selection is unlikely to cause disruption.

Interspecific Relationships and their Importance for Producing Disease Resistance
The centre of origin of *Lycopersicon* (tomato) species is considered to lie in the narrow coastal region of S. America from the equator to 30° south. Here the primitive forms of our cultivated tomato species remain, as well as its related   121

wild species. Within these various species are found the invaluable genes which
continue to impart disease resistance to the evolved commercial types. Wild
species which have been used in programmes of disease resistance are listed in
Table 16.

TABLE 16

Species	Disease to which resistance is shown
1. *L. chilense*	tobacco mosaic
2. *L. glabratum*	red spider
3. *L. glandulosum*	corky root
4. *L. hirsutum*	*didymella* (brown stem rot), *fusarium* (wilt), tobacco mosaic
5. *L. peruvianum*	*alternaria*, bacterial spot, *cladosporium* (leaf mould), *fusarium*, *septoria*
6. *L. pimpinellifolium*	*cladosporium*, *colletotrichum* (brown root rot) *fusarium*, *septoria*

The cross *L. esculentum* x *L. hirsutum* can be made successfully if non-
emasculated flowers are pollinated about two days before maturity. Fertility is
low in the early generations but increases progressively with selection of the
more fertile progenies, or by backcrossing to the cultivated parent. The initial
cross may be more successful if growth hormone (*indolylbutyric* acid in its many
proprietary forms) is applied to the flower pedicel and calyx at the time of
pollination to prevent premature abscission, or shedding, of the flower. The
reciprocal cross is not successful. Backcrosses to *esculentum* and segregants give
a wide range of fruit colours which are absent from both parents.

The remaining species in the table are all cross-compatible with *L.
esculentum*, especially when the cultivated type is used as the female parent and,
with certain exceptions, are compatible with *L. glabratum* only when used as the
male parent. The relationships of *Lycopersicon* species and of a small number of
species from the related genus *Solanum* (the potato in all its species forms) are
such that the transfer of any disease resistance to the commercial types should
be attempted (where material is or can be made available). This can be done
either directly or by bridging from one species to another until the resistance
genes eventually reach their intended host.

Solanum species *lycopersicoides* and *penelli* are cross-compatible with *lycopersicon esculentum* although crosses involving the former produce a sterile F_1
hybrid, and this only after embryo culture. *Solanum pennellii* was perfectly
compatible when *L. esculentum* was used as the female parent.

Turnip

Although this vegetable belongs to the large *Brassica* family and bears similar
yellow (and occasionally white) flowers it does not cross readily with the
oleracea (cabbage) types and belongs to a separate species, *B. campestris*.

Various forms of this species exist, particularly leafy types, but the variation
within the bulbous garden turnip is very limited and there is litle scope for
improvement in plant form. The most likely improvements are those involving
quality and disease resistance of both leaves and root. Cultivars are normally
very susceptible to powdery mildew of the leaves and to pithiness of the roots, or
attacks by the cabbage rootfly larvae. Pollination techniques are similar to those
of the *oleracea* types while root quality can be improved by adopting the system
122 suggested for radish. Turnips show a high degree of self-incompatibility.

The swede (*Brassica napus*) has not been mentioned in its alphabetical sequence since it bears a direct relationship to the turnip. In general it forms a larger root than the turnip and is notable for its pink to orange-coloured flesh. Genetic variation within the species is limited and cultivars show good uniformity, probably coupled to the fact that self-compatibility is common. New cultivars are best produced by inbreeding or mass-pollination of the best roots.

The swede is an amphidiploid with 38 chromosomes and is known to be a natural hybrid between *Brassica campestris* (20 chromosomes) x *Brassica oleracea* (18 chromosomes). Neither of the ancestral types is known accurately, but it is thought that the cross occurred numerous times where the two species overlap in their natural habitat (from Western Europe to Eastern Asia). Man's directed selection through many hundreds of years has been responsible for stabilising the types we know today. The inter-specific class has been synthesised by a number of workers, although the result is not noticeably swede-like. Cross-incompatibility between the parent species is very marked and pollen-tubes tend to become distorted in the styles. Any successful fertilisation seems to result in the production of a sterile hybrid.

The various types of relationship between species and genera detailed in this section give a practical illustration of the theme which has, I hope, pervaded the whole sequence of crop descriptions. It underlines the great benefits to be gained in plant breeding by being genetically adventurous. Guide-lines to species relationships and compatible groupings are provided by chromosome atlases, and any crossing attempts should be based upon *similarities*; in basic chromosome number, within-family classifications, centres of origin of the various types, and common usage of ecological niches.

With this in mind, crosses should be made using

(a)   plants both as males and females.

(b)   a number of plants from any population (except for complete homozygotes) since their slight genetic variability will allow some to cross more easily than others.

(c)   bridging techniques of crossing through other species to transfer genes indirectly to the desired plant if there is no other way.

(d)   embryo culture techniques wherever there is a sign of initial cross-compatibility.

(e)   colchicine to double chromosome numbers of both parents before or after crossing so that cross-compatibility can be enhanced or to produce fertility in the hybrid.

(f)   any combination of methods. There is no excuse for *NOT* attempting a cross-pollination if there is a remote chance of success. Many species have evolved so recently in genetic terms that their affinity with other species can be close enough to give success on hybridisation.

Appendix 1
The Large-Scale Production
of F₁ Hybrids

Because of the research involved in selecting parents, testing progeny, assessing performance etc. prior to the commercialisation of an F_1 hybrid, seed costs are bound to be high. To cover these costs and to lower the cost of F_1 seed, systems of large-scale production have been devised (particularly in the USA), to such good effect that the continuous stream of reliable cultivars has generated greater and greater demand.

The importance of F_1 hybrids for increasing yield and uniformity is now well established and seed production techniques are becoming increasingly sophisticated. Nevertheless, the large scale techniques are merely an extension (often by mechanisation) of those practised experimentally with a small number of plants. On the small scale, in fact, F_1 hybrid lines of many crops which cannot be considered commercially feasible, can be produced in sufficient numbers to provide high yielding alternatives to the non-hybrids which are on offer in seedsmens catalogues. Thus, F_1 hybrid peas are unlikely ever to be marketed (a), because they are naturally self-pollinated and, even making use of male sterility, are visited to only a limited extent by pollinating insects; (b) because each pollination can produce a maximum of only ten to twelve seeds while half a million are needed to sow an acre of peas for consumption. The situation is similar for dwarf beans although they are visited more regularly by pollinating insects.

On a small scale, enough F_1 hybrid seed of peas can be produced by hand-pollination to grow a small garden plot and the increase in crop (to compensate for the labour involved in the crossing programme) should be of the order of 25 to 30 per cent.

The principles of F_1 hybrid production are similar for every crop since a programme must be started with a range of inbred lines from which the best combining pairs are chosen. Cross-pollination between inbred lines must then be conducted in such a manner that pollinations are made only between plants of unlike genotype and, for complete success, the flowering period of both inbreds should coincide. F_1 hybrid seed may be collected from one or both parents, depending on the system employed but, when the subsequent crop is grown, all plants should be identical, with the same morphological and physiological characteristics.

The ideal system for F_1 hybrid production is one which makes use of cytoplasmic male sterility as found in the onion – a genetic system which, because of its general reliability, is being sought in a wide range of plant material.

124

F₁ Hybrid Onions

(Produced by the use of Cytoplasmic male sterility). Within the onion crop some bulbs produce flowering heads with brown anthers which lack pollen. More often than not these heads are cytoplasmic male steriles Smsms, having the homozygous recessive male sterility gene(ms) within a sterile(S) cytoplasm. Fertile lines may have an F (fertile) or an S cytoplasm, but if the cytoplasm is sterile, fertility can only be expressed by a nuclear gene in the dominant (Ms) condition.

Thus: Male sterile   = Smsms
         Male fertile   = SMsMs or S Msms
                        FMsMs, F Msms or F msms

To produce F₁ hybrid seed, a male sterile plant (Smsms) must be pollinated by a male fertile plant, but before this stage is reached a programme of inbreeding is required to produce homozygosity of both the female and male parents.

Inbreeding of the female lines – involving the identification of male sterile and restorer plants

Male sterile plants are morphologically identifiable within a normal mass-pollinated cultivar. These are of little value, however, without a corresponding restorer (which should be of genetic constitution Fmsms). The cross Smsms x Fmsms will result in the production of Smsms seed since the S cytoplasm is perpetuated, giving rise to plants which are again male sterile.

The male sterile line is normally referred to as the A line while the B line is the restorer. Identification of the latter in a seeding onion crop is made by observing the behaviour of progeny from crosses between A line plants and male fertile test plants. In practice, a typical male sterile plant would produce up to eight flower heads each of which should be paired with a male-fertile head from separate adjacent plants.

Paired heads would be enclosed in a bag just prior to anthesis and pollination of line A by each suspected line B would be carried out by brush or by introducing blowflies into the bag. The arrangement (before bagging) would be as illustrated diagrammatically in Fig. 11.

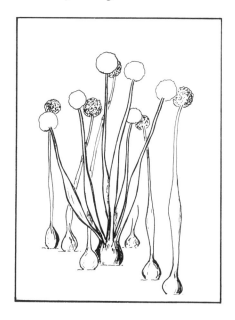

Fig 11. Pairing of male-sterile flower heads with separate male-fertile onion flower heads in order to identify 'restorer' plants. Each pair of flowers will be enclosed within an insect-proof bag.
'Restorer' test plants will normally be multi-headed, as male-sterile plant.

Seed from each umbel of a pair cross would be harvested separaately but identified by a cross reference. Thus, seed from the male sterile umbel would be ♀1 x ♂1 and seed from the male fertile umbel (i.e. selfed seed, since there was no other pollen) would be ♂1. Similarly, seed of the second pair cross would be ♀1 x ♂2 and ♂2.

In the following year, each seed sample would be sown separately. Thus, from our diagram, 12 lines of seed would be sown, the bulbs which they produce then stored over winter and replanted in the following season to give flower heads.

In the search for a 'B' line the types of flower heads produced should give an immediate indication of success or otherwise. Progeny of the selfed male plants would probably be completely male fertile within lines, although some selfed lines could show a 3:1 segregation of male fertile: male sterile plants. The latter situation is possible only if the parent plant was genetically SMsms; all other male parents would be homozygous MsMs, msms, or heterozygous Msms with fertile(F) cytoplasm. Table 17 gives the possible genotypes for male parents, and the types of progeny to be expected in crosses between them and male sterile plants. While the table illustrates the whole genetic picture, in practice the only male parents retained for breeding work would be those producing all male-sterile plants.

TABLE 17

Genetic constitution of parents and progeny for identification of male-fertile restorer genotypes.

Female parent	Male parent		F_1 progeny of cross
Smsms	(i)	SMsMs	SMsms (All plants fertile)
	(ii)	SMsms	1SMsms : 1Smsms (50% plants sterile)
	(iii)	FMsMs	SMsms (All plants fertile)
	(iv)	FMsms	1SMsms : 1Smsms (50% plants sterile)
	(v)	Fmsms	Smsms (All plants sterile)

If situation (v) occurred, the B line restorer would have been found immediately and further work would be confined to selection of the best bulbs of the male line. These would be mass-pollinated together at flowering time and also allowed to cross with male sterile bulbs of the 'A' line. Seed obtained would again be of genotype Smsms from the female, and Fmsms from the male. As the selection and crossing programme continues, so, inevitably, the A and B lines become genetically more similar for other morphological characters and, effectively, inbred.

For situation (ii) in Table 17 the original male parent shows exactly the same type of segregation as that in situation (iv). At this stage however the true genetic identity of male parents will not be known. Male parent (ii) is of no value in a hybridisation programme because of its cytoplasm but (iv) can be selected to produce true restorer 'B' line plants Fmsms and should therefore be retained.

If we assume that situation (v) did not occur to give us a 'B' line immediately we should be forced to obtain our 'B' from one or other of the two segregating parents and each would therefore need to be correctly identified. To do this we need to grow the selfed seed obtained from each fertile male and study segregation ratios of male fertile to male sterile. The S_1 of the male parent in situation (ii) will give a 3:1 segregation of male fertile to male sterile i.e. 1SMsMs, 2SMsms, 1Smsms. Although the *nuclear* segregation for the S_1 of (iv) will be exactly the same, no male sterile plants will appear because of the presence of the F (fertile) cytoplasm. Instead of discarding the whole S_1 progeny of male parent (ii) immediately, the male sterile plants (that is, one quarter of the segregating progeny) should be used in crosses with the S_1's of (iv) so that the restorer (B line) male fertile plants can be isolated from the other male fertiles.

This whole sequence is possibly easier to assimilate by seeing it in diagrammatic form.

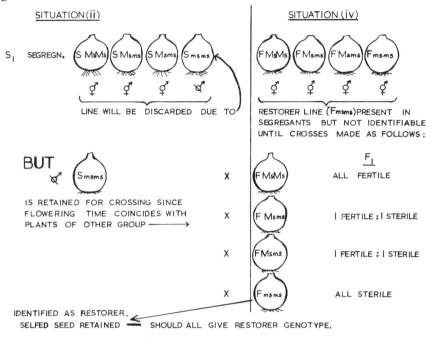

Fig 12. The identification and isolation of restorer (B line) genotypes of onion in the progenies of heterozygous male plants.

The Frequency of Male Sterility

Cytoplasmic male sterility occurs widely in onion cultivars although the frequencies vary. The nuclear gene *ms* tends to occur at a much higher frequency than the cytoplasmic male sterility factor S, 95 per cent to one per cent respectively for example, in the cultivar Rijnsburger; male sterile plants (having the correct combination of S and msms) have been found at a frequency of approximately three per thousand plants in this cultivar.

Related cultivars showed a frequency of up to 17 male sterile plants in a thousand while other, unrelated, cultivars are known to exhibit far higher frequencies of male sterile plants. In general, a reasonable expectation is up to five per cent male sterile plants, thus indicating that starting an F_1 hybrid breeding programme should not be too difficult.

Field Production of F_1 Hybrid Onions

Because of the limited flowering period of the onion crop it is essential that any promising experimental F_1 hybrid should first be produced on a small scale in the field in order to check that the two parent lines (i.e. the A and C lines) flower simultaneously. Some small allowance can be made for earlier flowering in the male lines *but under no circumstances should commercial production be considered if the female line is the first to flower*. This is because the F_1 seed yield (taken only from the female A line) will be reduced in direct proportion to the number of days when pollen is unavailable. If coincident flowering is impossible for the selected F_1 hybrid combination, further combinations should be considered until parents match one another in flowering time and period. As with all generalisations however, there may be exceptions and, if an F_1 hybrid is of such high value that customers are prepared to meet the higher seed costs resulting from reduced seed yields, then some lack of coincidence in flowering period could be acceptable.

Seed of the A line should be produced by interplanting rows (usually three or four) of bulbs with a single row of the B line from which seed will also be harvested (separately). Since both lines will be genetically similar and considerably inbred, the number of flowering heads per plant will probably be between two and three, giving roughly eight to ten grams of seed per plant. At the same time seed of the male parent to be used in hybridisation (another inbred or a uniform cultivar with full fertility and referred to as the 'C' line) should be raised in another isolated area. After this seed-raising programme the A line and C line seed should be sown to raise the requisite amount of bulbs – three to four times as many A's as C's. Bulbs of each line will be stored separately over winter and selected on the basis of their storage ability.

In the spring, transplanting of the bulbs will be carried out according to the most satisfactory inter-planting system but usually related to the three or four to one requirement – and assuming good pollen production by the C line.

When flowering has finished and before seed heads ripen, all C line flowering stalks should be removed in order to avoid confusion when the ripe seed of the A line is ready for harvest. On a small scale, C line heads should be left until maturity and harvested to save seed for another generation. On the large-scale, however, this practice would be too dangerous since admixture could occur because of adjacent flower stalks. Thus, commercially, seed of the C line must always be raised separately in isolation.

Having removed the C line, all seed in the field should now be borne only by A line plants – and will all be of F_1 hybrid constitution. This seed should produce high yielding, very uniform, early ripening commercial crops.

Production of F_1 Hybrid Brassicas

No cytoplasmic male-sterility system has been used commercially to date in the *Brassica oleracea* group, although it has been introduced into calabrese sprouting broccoli from crosses with wild mustard and nearly all F_1 hybrid cultivars are produced by the self-incompatibility method. Although the sporophytic system of incompatibility is operative within the species, the normal commercial tendency is to use it more as a gametophytic system since little regard is paid to dominance, interaction etc. of S alleles within the same line. The advantages of a sporophytic type of incompatibility are appreciated and used for the production of selfed seed, however, this being generally impossible with gametophytic self-incompatibility.

Since the older brassica cultivars are largely heterozygous because of random cross-pollination, any programme for the production of F_1 hybrids must be preceded by the selection and inbreeding of desirable plants and lines in order to increase homozygosity.

Although selection is based upon morphological characters, after one generation's inbreeding many of the parental characteristics may not be so obvious. Be this as it may, inbreeding should continue for two or three generations until lines are easily distinguishable from one another. As well as selfing plants by bud pollination, open flowers may also be self-pollinated but should be identifiable by label. A comparison of the seed set between the 'open flower selfs' and 'bud selfs' should give evidence of the degree of self-incompatibility appropriate to the particular plant. Self-incompatibility may also be assessed (earlier in the pollination programme), by the use of an ultra violet fluorescent microscope. The basic details of this technique are well recorded elsewhere but, in brief, open flowers of *Brassica* are self-pollinated and

128

their styles collected and fixed in solution about 12 hours later. The stigmatic area and the upper part of the style are subsequently squashed and examined on a microscope slide. Self-compatible pollinations will show a 'rope' of fluorescent pollen tubes filling the neck of the style while self-incompatible plants should show aborted pollen grains on the stigma but no extended pollen tubes. Semi-compatible pollinations can be identified by the variable number of pollen tubes.

Field production of F_1 hybrids by the self-incompatibility system has so far been practised only with inbreds which have a very slight degree of self-compatibility – which allows them to set small amounts of self seed when grown in isolation. Such inbred lines would have been combined experimentally in the early inbred generations in order to identify the best hybrid combination and to check that they are fully cross-compatible. In *Brassicas* it is less important to ensure coincident flowering than for onions because the flowering period is more prolonged and each individual flower has a longer life. Nevertheless, it is important to select parents with as great a coincidence of flowering as possible otherwise some self-pollination is bound to occur.

Raising Inbred Seed

Inbreds at the S_5 generation and later are normally used to produce commercial F_1 hybrid seed. Inbred seed is normally raised under glass by hand or by blowfly or bee pollination. Blowflies are efficient for inbreds or for hybrid seed production inside polythene houses.

Alternative methods have been used in an effort to increase the amount of seed set by inbreds since their general loss of vigour and fecundity, coupled with the necessarily high levels of self-incompatibility, combine adversely from an economic point of view. 'Thermally aided pollination' (TAP) was introduced by H. Roggen and H. van Dyk using, in effect, a tiny soldering iron on open flowers for two seconds while self-pollinations were being made. At temperatures of 70 to 80°C some inbred lines of Brussels sprout and white cabbage responded by giving seed yields of a high enough order to encourage breeders to use the technique commercially. Seed yields of inbreds have been increased also by high humidity and by saturating the glasshouse atmosphere with carbon dioxide to a concentration of 4.5 per cent.

If selfed seed is produced by hand (bud) pollination, the practical limitations impose a further limit on the ultimate quantity of F_1 hybrid seed. In Brussels sprouts one person is (theoretically) capable of bud selfing about 4,000 flowers a day – giving an average of five seeds per pod. As the flowering period should last about three or four weeks under glass the total production by this same person (assuming a five-day week) would be

$$\frac{4,000 \times 5 \times 20}{8,000} \text{ (seeds per ounce)} = 50 \text{ ounces.}$$

At a planting rate of two ounces seed per acre one person could therefore, produce enough seed to plant 25 acres of one inbred and this, with 25 acres worth produced by a colleague could produce up to 7½ tons of F_1 hybrid seed. Unfortunately, in practice the limitations of glasshouse space, and unthriftiness of inbred plants, tend to reduce seed quantities – even when more pollinations are available and it seldom appears possible to raise more than 1½ tons of seed of any hybrid regardless of initial pollinations.

If selfed seed is produced by open pollination in the field instead of under glass the quantities are likely to be higher, in spite of the limitations imposed by the self-incompatibility system. This technique is vulnerable, however, because of the danger of foreign pollen from neighbouring seeding crops, or even single plants. The basis of F_1 hybrid production by self-incompatibility is that foreign pollen (i.e. that of the second inbred line) is better able to fertilise ovules than self-pollen, and rigorous inspection of areas surrounding an inbred line is vital to ensure that there is no chance of cross contamination.

However it is produced, inbred seed of both parents should be sown in the right proportions in order to raise the plants which will eventually flower. Sowings should be made into seed blocks or directly into the field with a precision drill order to avoid wastage.

Sowing the Inbred Parent Material

When F_1 hybrid seed is to be obtained from one inbred only, one row of the 'Male' inbred is usually sufficient to pollinate a block of four rows of the seed bearing inbred. If the F_1 hybrid seed is to be harvested in bulk from both inbreds, however, the seed of both parents can be mixed before sowing. This will provide a completely random stand of two identifiable types and will aid inter-pollination later.

Decisions on the role of each inbred can only be made as a result of experience in their development. Thus, if one line is liable to give large quantities of selfed seed it should be used only as a male parent and no seed should be harvested from it after its use in hybrid production. If, on the other hand, both inbreds were equally self-incompatible they would be grown in similar quantities (mixed as above or in alternate rows) and seed harvested in bulk. If, in this latter situation, however, one inbred was a very good and the other a very poor seed producer when crossed, it would probably be better to use only one row of the poor seed producer to every three or four of the other – all seed would be harvested in bulk but the yields would be very much higher.

All seed obtained from the F_1 hybrid production plots would be sold, although a check on sib percentages (the amount of crossing between sister plants – i.e. equivalent to selfing) should first be made.

The Importance of Pollinators in F_1 Hybrid Brassica Seed Production

The inbred lines of *brassica* used for F_1 hybrid production in the field rely upon bumble and honey bees for pollination and each inbred should, ideally, produce large quantities of pollen. Although the result of inbreeding is normally seen as a loss of vigour, the greatest adverse effect is severe reduction in fertility (fecundity). Lower fertility is exhibited as less abundant pollen, smaller numbers of ovules or less successful fertilisation, and the seed yields of inbreds (even when crossed together to produce F_1 hybrid seeds) is affected accordingly.

When flowering of inbreds is not simultaneous, pollinating insects will be confined to one line only. Because of the self-incompatibility system, however, fertilisation should not occur. In theory, where flowering of inbreds is completely coincidental and each is present in equal proportions, all seed should be the result of cross-fertilisation. Certain factors can operate to upset the ideal system however, and a small but variable proportion of inbred seed is usually contained in the final 'F_1 hybrid' product. Inbreds have probably been selected on the basis of slight self-compatibility in order to facilitate the raising of seed and some selfed seed will probably be set when flowering of one or other of the inbreds is out of phase.

Insects visiting a flowering crop tend to pollinate a number of flowers on one plant before moving to another. Although the insect may previously have visited a plant of the alternative inbred line, by the time a few flowers have been pollinated any 'cross' pollen will have become diluted with 'self' pollen so that self-pollination is more likely to occur.

Any variation from the alternate row or mixed sowing systems is likely to reduce cross-fertilisation and it is therefore best to use two inbreds whose seed is bulk-harvested rather than to pollinate (and harvest) a number of female rows with a single row of non-harvestable male.

Studies of bee behaviour show that preference for certain plants or inbred lines may greatly influence the yield of true hybrid seed. Bees tend either to develop a taste for a particular line or will concentrate their visits to the inbred line upon which they first alight. Visits between lines are often very casual, and hybrid seed may sometimes appear to be produced by chance. It has been suggested that the alternate-row arrangement of inbred lines (below) leads to a greater likelihood of self-pollination as bees work up and down, rather than back and fore between, the rows.

```
Lines   A   B   A   B   A
        A   B   A   B   A
        A   B   A   B   A
        A   B   A   B   A
        A   B   A   B   A
        A   B   A   B   A
        A   B   A   B   A
        A   B   A   B   A
```

As an alternative, interplanting of inbreds within each row is, at first sight, more likely to encourage cross-pollination but, to a bee, this system is no different from the other one since the rows now run diagonally!

```
e.g.    A   B   A   B   A
        B   A   B   A   B
        A   B   A   B   A
        B   A   B   A   B
        A   B   A   B   A
        B   A   B   A   B
        A   B   A   B   A
        B   A   B   A   B
```

The Production of F₁ Hybrids Using Male Sterility

While cross-pollination between two lines is seldom complete, the above situation is exacerbated by the inconsistent and variable proportions of sibs within a so-called F_1 hybrid cultivar. Sibs are usually crowded out during growth by their more vigorous hybrid relations, but close checking in some commercial crops can reveal up to eight per cent crop loss due to their presence. When hybrids are produced from male sterile plants, no sibs will be present since any male sterile flowers which do not receive pollen from the pollinator line will fail to set seed. In this sense the male sterility system has great advantages, but is seldom used commercially because of the limitations in identification of the male sterile plants. Only the recessive gene for male sterility has been widely recorded.

To use this type of male sterility on a commercial scale, male sterile plants must first be produced in large numbers out of the cross msms (male sterile) x Msms (male fertile heterozygote). From the seed, 50 per cent of the plants should be male sterile and 50 per cent male fertile – the normal backcross ratio. All cytoplasm is of the fertile (F) type and there is consequently no chance of obtaining higher proportions of male sterile plants. By previous repeated selfing of heterozygous *Msms* plants the material used to produce *msms* seed on a commercial scale would be genetically and phenotypically uniform. Plants from the male sterile inbred line would be interplanted with a male fertile inbred which had already proved to combine well.

The drawback to hybrid production by this method is apparent at the flowering stage since one half of the plants of the female line will be male fertile and must be removed as soon as they can be identified through the appearance of the first flowers. On a field scale such removal is totally impossible but on a minor scale (up to 200 male fertile plants) it is worth consideration.

Apart from the physical inconvenience, however, the planted area will now be only two thirds (or thereabouts) occupied and further wastage will occur at harvest time because F_1 hybrid seed will be collected only from the male sterile plants.

For supplying quantities of up to 6 or 8lbs of F_1 hybrid seed the nuclear male sterility method is to be recommended and should be possible on an area of 250 square yards as follows:

400 plants ex 'backcross' grown to give 200 male sterile plants. 100 pollinator plants grown.

400 plants @ 2ft x 2ft and 100 plants @ 2ft x 3ft = 2100sq.ft.

to give: 200 seeding plants @ ½oz seed per plant = 100oz seed

Above this requirement there seems to be no present alternative to using the self-incompatibility system and accepting contamination from some sibs.

The two systems involving the use of nuclear (as for Brassicas) and cytoplasmic (as for onions) male sterility are compared in Figure 13.

One way of overcoming the difficulty of distinguishing male sterile from male fertile plants is to use a marker gene which is linked to one or other of the genotypes. If present in the juvenile plant stage, removal of the unwanted types can be done early without difficulty but unfortunately, no such marker gene (linked to that for male sterility) has yet been reported.

F_1 Hybrid Marigolds

Until very recently, F_1 hybrid marigolds have been produced exclusively in the USA, mainly in the open in California, relying upon insect pollinators. The two main systems of production both involve the use of male sterile lines either as the 'apetalous' (and stamenless) form or the true double form which produces no anthers in the central part of the flower. In Britain, the apetalous male-sterile form is used because of its greater reliability, and is pollinated manually under glass.

The seed which will give rise to male-sterile plants is produced by pollinating male-steriles of an inbred line with male fertiles which appear within the same line. These male-fertiles act as 'restorers' of varying efficiencies. Single male-fertile plants within a predominantly male-sterile line may, in crosses with the male-sterile inbreds give offspring where only one or two per cent are male

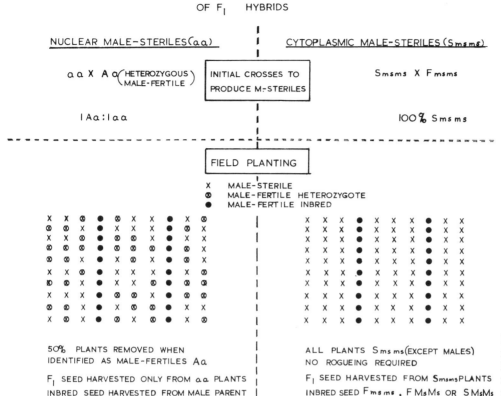

THE PRACTICAL USE OF MALE-STERILITY FOR THE FIELD PRODUCTION OF F₁ HYBRIDS

NUCLEAR MALE-STERILES (aa)   CYTOPLASMIC MALE-STERILES (Smsms)

aa X A a (HETEROZYGOUS MALE-FERTILE) | INITIAL CROSSES TO PRODUCE M-STERILES | Smsms X Fmsms

1 Aa : 1 aa   100 % Smsms

FIELD PLANTING

X   MALE-STERILE
⊗   MALE-FERTILE HETEROZYGOTE
●   MALE-FERTILE INBRED

50% PLANTS REMOVED WHEN IDENTIFIED AS MALE-FERTILES Aa

F₁ SEED HARVESTED ONLY FROM aa PLANTS
INBRED SEED HARVESTED FROM MALE PARENT

ALL PLANTS Smsms (EXCEPT MALES) NO ROGUEING REQUIRED

F₁ SEED HARVESTED FROM Smsms PLANTS
INBRED SEED Fmsms, FMsMs OR SMsMs

Fig 13. The application of nuclear male-sterility (as in Brassicas) and cytoplasmic male-sterility (as in Onions) for the production of F₁ hybrids.

sterile. Other single plants have given offspring with up to 50 per cent male sterile plants but so far, in Britain, no inter-line cross has produced more than this. For this reason, the commercial seed producing crop must be rogued heavily to remove male-fertiles before plants (raised in pots) are transferred to their final seeding positions – this being easily accomplished by noting bud shape.

The number of rows of male-sterile to those of the inbred male-fertile parent is largely dependent upon the width of the glasshouse where the seed crop is to be raised, but a ratio of three to one is probably the optimum. Male parents should be sown about two weeks before the females in order to provide an adequate pollen supply as the first male-sterile flower opens. If the male parent flowers too early, the first flowers can be removed since this encourages new vegetative and bud growth. It is most common for the male-fertile line to be more uniform in habit than the male-sterile and removal of any off-types should be straightforward. Any variation within the female (male-sterile) is usually masked in the F₁ generation. Pollination of male-sterile plants is achieved by taking flowers from male plants, inverting and twisting them lightly over the stigmatic surface of the female. Each male-sterile 'flower' bears up to 300 styles which mature over a period of two to three weeks and pollinations should therefore be repeated at least twice a week. In practice, on a large scale, male flowers would be constantly picked and used as pollinators over all open male-sterile flowers so that repeat pollinations would be made as a matter of course.

If pollen supply becomes short, the blooms removed from male plants can be stood in water until the next pollination period by which time their immature anthers will again be shedding further pollen. With a good pollen-parent, one detached flower should pollinate five or six male-sterile flowers. A more sophisticated method involves collecting pollen from the male parents through a   133

Plate 32. Commercial
production of F₁ hybrid
marigolds using an African
marigold male sterile as female
(tall plants) and a French
marigold as male parent.
Selfed seed set on 'male' parent
can be used as a pure-line
cultivar.

vacuum pump. Pollen, deposited in a glass tube, can then be 'dusted' on to the male-steriles.

Seed from the male-steriles should be harvested in its capitulum as it ripens (usually six to eight weeks after the first pollination). Only the black seeds (as compared with the grey or light brown) within the capitulum will be viable and should all produce perfectly formed F₁ plants.

F₁ Hybrid Petunias

Although petunias have a straightforward incompatibility system (of the gametophytic type) F₁ hybrids are produced commercially by hand-pollination rather than by insects. This is economic because of the fact that each single pollination results in the production of hundreds of seeds. The gametophytic system is basically reliable and easy to manipulate in the field – F₁ hybrid seed being produced on each inbred line – but there are obviously good commercial reasons for preferring to raise F₁ hybrid seed under controlled glasshouse conditions.

F₁ hybrid production is always preceded by inbreeding – the gametophytic incompatibility being overcome by bud self-pollination. Thus, a large population of plants which will not self or cross fertilise each other may be built up. Plants of one inbred line can be pollinated, without emasculation, by plants of another inbred line which carry a different S allele; the reciprocal cross can also be made and large quantities of seed should be produced.

Another system can be used which does not require much intensive inbreeding throughout the programme. Although easier at the outset, it makes greater demands on labour when F₁ hybrid seed is being produced, however.

A group of up to about eight selected plants can be mass pollinated, and the process repeated with smaller numbers for three to four generations until a very uniform line is produced. This is a fairly loose form of inbreeding or brother-sister mating in order to establish uniformity with no loss of vigour and no self-incompatibility.

From this point, F_1 hybrid seed is produced by crossing two such lines after emasculation of the female plants in the bud stage. Emasculation and pollination of large numbers of buds can be carried out rapidly at a rate of at least five or six buds per minute giving over 1000 seeds.

It is not known which of the two methods is used most widely in commerce, but choice of one or the other is probably related to local circumstances and to the reliability of the incompatibility system throughout the pollinating season.

F_1 Hybrid Tomatoes

F_1 hybrid tomatoes are considered to be most satisfactory for the more specialised growing techniques of glasshouse production rather than for the less-demanding outdoor cultivars. Tomato cultivars, other than F_1's, are pure lines and quite homozygous so that seeds of uniform F_1 hybrids can be obtained straight away from pair-crosses without inbreeding the parents.

Commercial production of tomato seed is undertaken when particular pair-cross combinations have produced a high value test hybrid. During the testing period, records should have been taken to indicate which parent was the biggest seed producer and which the most prolific pollen parent. If one of the two parents was top for both characters it would probably be best used as the pollen parent for F_1 hybrid production since a slightly lower seed set is preferable to incomplete pollination (due to lack of pollen) which would after all, result in a low seed set.

Crosses to produce F_1 hybrid seed are normally made in one direction only, using four or five times as many plants as females than as males. Apart from allowing a small quantity of fruit to be set to maintain the male parent for future use, the only fruit to be harvested will be that from the female parent, containing F_1 hybrid seed. In addition, a small number of female line plants must be set aside for selfing.

Flowers of the female line must be emasculated in the bud stage as described earlier. Stigmas are immediately receptive and should be covered with pollen as soon as they are exposed after emasculation. Although results vary, 100lbs of ripe fruit should produce approximately 4oz seed – which is cleaned as described in Appendix 4.

Because of the large-scale production of F_1 hybrid tomatoes, mechanical aids are used whenever possible. Pollen is collected with a battery-powered electric 'bee' whose effect is to shake pollen from the anthers of the male parent into a receptacle – either a glass tube attached to the 'bee' or into a thumbnail receptacle worn on the operator's third finger. Pollen is applied to the female flower either by brush from the pollen supply in the glass tube or directly, by inverting the emasculated flower over the 'thumbnail'.

One of the major reasons for the success of F_1 hybrid glasshouse tomatoes is the introduction of disease resistance. Resistance to most diseases which affect the normal glasshouse crop is controlled by dominant genes, so as long as one of the parents of an F_1 hybrid shows resistance to specific diseases the other may be completely susceptible. It is important that the resistant line should be used as female because an occasional self-pollination (due to inefficient emasculation or 'missing' a flower with a cross-pollination) would still produce resistant plants in the general F_1 hybrid population.

If the susceptible parent was used as female, an accidental self-pollination would result in the presence of a number of susceptible (supposedly) F_1 plants and would undermine the value of the cultivar.

135

F₁ Hybrid Sweetcorn

Techniques used for the commercial production of F₁ hybrid maize are equally applicable to sweet corn. Cytoplasmic male-sterility similar to that described for onions is found and used with both crops but this system tends to take second place to that which has been practised for 50 years or so. With the older commercial system, advantage is taken of the fact that male (tassel) and female (silk) flowers are borne on separate parts of the plant and can therefore be treated independently. During the inbreeding programme which precedes F₁ production, plants would have been self-pollinated by inserting parts of the tassel into the selfing bag covering the female flower until such time as the silks become brown and non-receptive. Final multiplication of inbred lines would be by mass-pollination of the S₄ and S₅ generation plants.

For F₁ hybrid production the inbred line capable of yielding most seeds would be grown in groups of four or five consecutive rows separated by a single (or occasionally double) row of the inbred line to be used as male. When plants reach maturity, but before pollen is shed, the tassels of the female line are removed so that fertilisation is possible only with pollen from the male. Female silks are fully receptive about four days after the first pollen is shed from tassels of the same plants and the choice of male line should therefore be directed towards one which is slightly later than the female. Pollen is carried by the wind to lodge within the clustered 'silks'.

No overhead irrigation should be given when pollen is being produced since this restricts pollen dispersal and activity, and half filled cobs will be produced on the female lines.

F₁ hybrid seed is first harvested from the mature cobs of the female line – usually one cob i.e. up to 3 or 400 seeds per plant, – and this is followed by a second harvest from the male line. Here, cobs will have formed in exactly the same way, but each will contain inbred seed since the only pollen available would have been from brother plants of the same line.

Inbred seed of the female line will not be available from this crop but may have been produced elsewhere by reversing the parental roles in producing the same or another F₁ hybrid. Alternatively the inbred could be multiplied by mass-pollination in an isolated area.

In order to raise the large quantities of seed needed to satisfy the demand for F₁ hybrids, the inbred parents should be good seed producers. One of the effects of inbreeding, however, is to lower the seed production potential and, to overcome this defect, American breeders have developed a 'double-cross' system in which the hybrid from a pair cross is pollinated by a hybrid from another pair-cross. Naturally, this entails extra involvement in the de-tasseling process and the cytoplasmic system of inducing male-sterility has therefore been welcomed and used widely.

As with onions, a male-sterile line will be of genetic constitution Smsms and a cross with the fertile line Fmsms will produce male-sterile F1 AxB. If the other pair cross CxD comprises fertile Fmsms lines (de-tasseling essential for this cross), the double cross (A x B) x (C x D) will produce only male-sterile plants. For production of the commercial crop, seed of this double cross is mixed or blended with a smaller amount of seed from the identical cross (A x B) x (C x D) which is fully fertile FMsMs, having been inbred in parallel with the male sterile lines. In the field the randomly placed male fertile plants will provide adequate pollen for a normal crop of seed on all plants.

The cytoplasmic system fell out of favour in the early 1970's when much of
the maize was decimated by Southern Corn Blight (Helminthosporium). This

epidemic was attributable to the fact that the majority of F_1 hybrid cultivars had been produced from cytoplasmically male-sterile material from the same source and the breakdown in resistance was therefore universal. Fortunately, reserve material was available for subsequent years but the warnings against using a narrow genetic base in any breeding programme were very forcibly presented.

Ensuring Pure F_1 Hybrid Seed

Because of the extra research, effort, and cost involved in producing F_1 hybrids it is imperative that every precaution should be taken to ensure that no genetic or mechanical admixture of seed or plants occurs at any part of the process. The first essential requirement is that each line contributing to the F_1 hybrid should be produced in complete isolation – either spatial or physical – from every other. In the field this means separation by approximately 1000 yards between lines of *Brassica*, 400 yards between onions and, because its pollen is windborne, well over a mile between sweetcorn plots.

The second requirement is that inbreeding should be carried out long enough to produce complete phenotype uniformity.

Thirdly, and this is basic to the production of sufficient quantities of F_1 hybrid seed, male and female lines must be chosen for their flowering coincidence.

The fourth point, which is every bit as important to a successful programme, is that no confusion in identification of seed stocks should be possible during seed harvest or threshing.

When these various requirements are allied to the importance of choosing two parents which together form a good hybrid it can be appreciated that successful F_1 hybrid production is very much more than a matter of chance.

Other F_1 Hybrids

Numerous horticultural crops and species – which are not yet commercially available as F_1 hybrids, are nevertheless being developed experimentally. While the principles of F_1 hybrid production are basically similar, the limitations to the ultimate range of crops lie in the economics of the production system (how many seeds per single pollination, how much time and labour will be involved in emasculation, etc.).

In the flower crops, the following species appear to hold commercial promise as F_1 hybrids for both seed-raiser and for the nurseryman who sells the F_1 hybrid plants or seed:

Ageratum; produced by field pollination, making use of its variable self-incompatibility system, but liable to considerable *sib* contamination.

Anemone; hand-pollination under glass, taking advantage of protogyny.

Cyclamen and Exacum; raised by hand-pollination under glass, mostly without emasculation.

Primula; Pin x Thrum, thus obviating the need for emasculation. Under glass, three parents can be used to produce three F_1 hybrids (a) A pin x B thrum, (b) B pin x C thrum and (c) C pin x A thrum.

Wallflower; field-pollination using genetic male-sterility with 50% roguing in the flowering crop.

In addition, species such as poppy, aquilegia and some compositae have the potential for hybrid production, though possibly not the market appeal.

In contrast to the flowers, the number of F_1 hybrid vegetable species is 137 unlikely to show any marked increase. This is because the floral or fruiting parts of vegetables are not eaten (tomato and artichoke excepted) and the enlargement of vegetative tissues, which may result from F_1 hybrid vigour, is not always desirable. Although genetically possible, F_1 hybrid beetroot has not so far been produced, mainly because root sizes and uniformity are satisfactory at present. Cabbage F_1's now have a large share of the market, but the earliest hybrids were very unpopular because of their huge head size. Their present value is based upon their reliability, uniformity and predictable harvest period.

The Use of Clones in the Production of F_1 Hybrids

Vegetative propagation is possible in more crops than is generally appreciated. Even annual forms of flowers and vegetables such as antirrhinum, marigold, salvia and lettuce which are considered intractable, can be easily rooted. For F_1 hybrid production, any means of increasing the numbers of inbred parent plants is of value yet few, if any, F_1 hybrid programmes have clonal propagation as part of their system.

The reasons appear to be (a) that inbred plants are usually less vigorous and produce only a small amount of vegetative tissue which can be detached for propagation, (b) the detached portions are too weak to root quickly and so avoid disease infection, (c) propagants root and develop over a long period with the result that plants to be used in the field are irregular in size and flower erratically, (d) debilitating diseases are transmitted most easily through vegetative propagation.

In spite of the limitations, there could occasionally be a real advantage in creating inbred clones, particularly for small-scale F_1 hybrid production. Maintenance of highly self-incompatible inbred lines or of genetically male-sterile material in *Brassicas* are two examples where it should be possible to capitalise on the genetic research which has isolated the right types.

Appendix 2

Gene Specialisations

Modifying Genes

Genes which have small effects by themselves, may nevertheless influence the expression of major genes. In this respect the dominant major gene controlling the resistance of lettuce to downy mildew gives complete resistance in the F_1 generation, with a 3:1 F_2 segregation in some crosses. In crosses with some susceptible parents, however, the resistance is less well defined due to the presence of genes which modify the reaction, and lower numbers of resistant plants are obtained.

In circumstances when the susceptible parents were always used as females, it could be postulated that the cytoplasm was producing an effect, but the inheritance of lettuce mildew resistance is similar in progenies from the same cross whichever way it is made. In other instances, such as the inheritance of perfume in cyclamen when it is essential to obtain accurate genetic information, it is often necessary to make a series of crosses (and their reciprocals) using one common parent with several alternative partners. This is in order to establish the effect of modifiers and to show that variation was not environmentally induced.

Modifying genes also have a marked effect upon another group of major genes, those which control male sterility, and are widespread through many species.

Pleiotropic Genes

Genes whose activity affects more than one character in an organism are said to be pleiotropic and show their presence as dominants through a group of associated characters. The whole character-group is either missing or altered in appearance when the pleiotropic gene is present in the recessive state.

Easily indentified characters such as the colouration of Broad Bean flowers and plant parts illustrate the functioning of a pleiotropic gene, but those involved in metabolism or enzyme production, for example, are less easily defined and can confuse the distinction between modifying and pleiotropic polygenes.

Linked Genes

Linkage between genes is much easier to recognise than the effect of modifiers, although the degree of linkage is less easy to define. Large numbers of genes are present on any chromosome, and although chromosome segments (as chromatids) break and rejoin at cell meiosis, genes closely adjacent to one another on a particular chromosome will tend to remain together.

The only genes which will always segregate independently are those on different chromosomes. Alleles of a particular gene (e.g. Round 'R' and wrinkled 'r' seed types in peas) will always be present on separate chromosomes of a pair. Genes which are carried upon the same chromosome will segregate only if they are far enough apart for crossing over to take place between them. Thus, large groups or blocks of genes will often be inherited together – so that in the segregating (F_2) generation parental combinations are most likely to be excessive, and recombinations deficient.

Linked genes may exist in valuable or useless combinations but evolutionary processes will favour desirable combinations and these will have been inherited and transmitted as gene blocks over many generations. Not all nature's linkages are desirable from the cultural standpoint, however, and plant breeders frequently attempt to overcome unwanted linkage combinations by making extra numbers of crosses. Segregating progenies are later checked to see whether linkage of characters has or has not been broken. Characters for which selection is being practised are frequently associated with other minor (and possibly unwanted) effects due to gene linkage – the whole result being termed a 'correlated response'.

Evidence of well-defined linkages is found in the tomato Marglobe which is of normal height and has round fruit. Both characters are dominant to the extreme tallness and oblong fruit of Louisiana Slicer. Segregation in the F_2 generation from a cross showed an excess of parental combinations. Instead of finding three out of 16 normal height with oblong fruit and another three extremely tall with round fruit as would be expected in the recombined F_2 progenies (i.e. 37.5 per cent of the population), the recombined genes showed up in only 21.5 per cent of the F_2 population and the parental forms comprised over 13/16 of the population (actually 78.5 per cent) instead of 9 + 1.

In African marigolds the gene for lack of petals (apetaly) is very tightly linked to that for male-sterility but, as already discussed, this linkage has proved to be of high commercial value.

Mutant Genes

The combined activity of the whole gene complement is responsible for the external appearance of all parts of a plant. Occasionally, non-typical or unexpected forms may be observed amongst a conventional population or may be revealed in the course of critical genetic experiments. The new forms are frequently the result of a spontaneous change in the gene which, having appeared may then be retained or removed from the population according to the current aims of the plant breeder.

Such mutant genes are frequently deleterious since they are unadapted to their local environment – even at plant cell level – and have probably occurred and been discarded in earlier generations. Not all gene mutations are harmful, however, since they provide the necessary variability for greater adaptation and evolution. Even if mutant genes prove to be harmful they are unlikely to be removed completely from the population because most appear in recessive form and can be identified only when present in the plant in the homozygous condition. Great numbers of recessive mutants must therefore exist unnoticed in heterozygous state.

The value of mutant genes in horticultural plant breeding lies mainly through the increase of novelty flower forms such as variegated Aylssum and butterfly and Penstemon-flowered antirrhinums. Mutant genes have also been utilised in vegetables (the 'suppressed lateral' mutant gene in tomato which overcomes the need for side-shoot removal), but in most cases they offer little advantage.

Marker Genes

Marker genes are usually major genes which are recognisable by their phenotypic expression and may be dominant or recessive. See table 2, page 10. They have a particular value in genetic studies as well as for varietal identification. Their main purpose lies in aiding the identification of cultivars, in showing the degree of contamination within cultivars, or the success with which crosses have been made. When dominant, they are best used as male parents in crosses so that true hybrids can be identified in a mixed progeny of selfs and hybrids. Conversely, plants with homozygous recessive marker genes are used as females in crosses in order that self-fertilised plants may be identified in the progeny by the presence of the 'marker' character. Any hybrid plant will have a phenotype other than that of the selfed plants.

Marker genes are a valuable tool for the identification of F_1 hybrids in commercial production, particularly when the 'marker' character can be identified in the plant's juvenile stage. Although the genes may be operative at any stage of the plant's life cycle, their value as marker genes diminishes as the plant becomes more mature because other characteristics can then also be identified. They are especially useful for assessing the amount of natural cross-fertilisation in crops where the breeding system is unknown, or to act as indicators of genetic contamination when groups of individuals have been seeded in an isolated outdoor area. Marker genes controlling flower and leaf colour (dark colours usually being dominant to light) are among the most common.

Complementary Genes

Some marker genes can be identified by the different plant form which they produce when they act together. Thus, two glossy-leaved Brussels sprout lines may produce normal plants with glaucous (or waxy) foliage when crossed, since each gene complements the other one. This type of marker gene effect is less common than the dominant – recessive situation, however.

Complementary genes together produce characters different from those present in either parent, usually by combining separate dominant genes. Purple sweet peas are produced from crosses between two white flowered types when the two genes affecting flower colour are on different chromosomes. In general, genes are considered to be complementary when their effects are easily demonstrable – usually due to major gene effects. At the polygenic level complementary behaviour is less easy to recognise, since there tends to be a range of 'in-between' characteristics. The interaction of some sets of genes with others, however, often gives hybrids with greatly enhanced values over those expected from the combination of parents, notably in total yield.

Complementary dominant genes in *Rudbeckia* give a purple-flowered F_1 from a cross between two yellow-flowered parents.

CCrr (yellow) x ccRR (yellow) give rise to CcRr (purple) while the F_2 segregation gives 9 purple : 7 yellow as shown below.

9CcRr (purple) : 7 yellow. { (3CCrr) + (3ccRR) + (1ccrr) }   141

Other Segregations Involving Two Major Genes

In *Antirrhinum* a cross between yellow and white flowered types can result in a 9:3:4 F_2 segregation as follows:

YYww (yellow) x yyWW (white)
F_1 YyWw (red)
F_2 9 YyWw (red) : 2 YYww (yellow) : 4 white (3yW and 1 yw)

A 12:3:1 ratio may be found when one gene is epistatic to another, yet is not completely dominant. In squashes (*Cucurbita pepo*) yellow fruit colour is recessive to white but dominant to green. White is dominant to both. Therefore the cross WWYY (white) x wwyy (green) produces a white F_1 WwYy.

The F_2 segregates to give 12 white (9WY and 3Wy) : 3 yellow (wY) : 1 green (wy).

13:3 ratios result when distinctions between AB, Ab + ab are impossible – due normally to the presence of a dominant gene which inhibits expression of the other.

When *duplicate* dominant genes are in operation, each produces the same effect as the other and only the double recessive homozygote is able to give a different expression. An F_2 segregation of 15:1 may be regarded as the result of interaction between duplicate genes unless the population under survey was so small that the result was suspect.

Appendix 3

Plant Breeding Mathematics

To assess the value of a single or a number of potential cultivars it is necessary to be able to compare them with other existing commercial types and to measure their degrees of difference in a reliable way. While a cultivar may perform well or appear perfect in the field, the only true criteria of its value is its performance in well planned trials which allow statistical analysis of the features which affect its commercial success.

Statistical analysis can be used to assess the field performance of new cultivars, the value of parent lines for producing F_1 hybrids, the potential of F_1 hybrids to produce good segregating lines, the relationship between cultivars and certain cultural treatments, the types of progeny to be expected from certain crosses, the association between one character and another, and many other genetic effects which are capable of mathematical interpretation.

This section should not be regarded as a lesson in statistics or mathematical theory, but rather as a demonstration of the value of statistics as an aid to the basic principle of plant breeding, – selection.

Chi Squared

In the early stages of any breeding programme, especially when crosses have been made, it is necessary to understand the genetic inheritance of particular characters – or, if the mode of inheritance is already known – to check whether the present material is behaving in the expected manner.

The simplest case is that of monogenic inheritance when plants differ from one another only by the expression of a single character. Thus, pea seeds may be either round or wrinkled. We know from section 2 that the F_1 generation from a cross between parents which breed true for these characters will give round seeds only, while in the F_2 generation three seeds will be round and one wrinkled, although this ratio can only be expected if a reasonable number of pods are examined. The ratios are similar for tallness and dwarfness since these characters are inherited in like manner. If the two characters are combined in each parent we expect the F_2 ratio to be 9 tall round : 3 tall wrinkled : 3 dwarf round : 1 dwarf wrinkled – but in the case of distorted ratios a satisfactory check can be made only by using the χ^2 test: The object of this test is to see whether the observed ratios do, in fact, correspond to the expected one and thus to indicate the reliability of the results as an expression of the χ^2 table (Appendix 5).

The table uses the expression 'Degrees of freedom' simply as a guide to the correct row of figures and is one less than the number of observed categories. For 143 a monogenic ratio e.g. $72 : 82$ the degrees of freedom are 1, while for a digenic ratio e.g. $270 : 97 : 85 : 26$: there are three degrees of freedom (i.e. one less than two and four categories respectively).

In the pea example we could find that 240 seeds from F_2 plants comprised 187 round seeded and 53 wrinkled. Knowing that round seeded is inherited as a simple dominant, we should have obtained a ratio of $180 : 60$ and, since there is some divergence, the validity of our population results must be tested by $\chi 2$ as follows:

$$\chi^2 = \frac{(\text{observed} - \text{expected})^2}{\text{expected}}$$

a 3:1 ratio (i.e. 180:60) was expected while the observed ratio was 187:53

$$\chi^2 \text{ (for 1 d.f.)} = \frac{(187 - 180)^2}{180} + \frac{(53 - 60)^2}{60} = \frac{49}{180} + \frac{49}{60}$$

$$\chi^2 \text{ (1 d.f.)} = 1.09$$

From the 1 d.f. column in the χ^2 table our result lies between column headings 0.50 and 0.10 which indicates that there is a 10 to 50 per cent chance that our result represents a 3:1 ratio. If the observed figures were closer to the expected 180:60 the χ^2 table would indicate a greater likelihood that the result we obtained was truly representative of a 3:1 ratio.

If we obtained the following figures in the F_2 of a cross between tall round seeded x dwarf wrinkled seeded peas,

590 tall round: 184 tall wrinkled: 190 dwarf round: 60 dwarf wrinkled, χ^2 would be based upon a 9:3:3:1 ratio to give:

$$\frac{(590-576)^2}{576} + \frac{(184-192)^2}{192} + \frac{(190-192)^2}{192} + \frac{(60-64)^2}{64}$$

$$\chi^2 \text{ (3 d.f.)} = .34 + .33 + .02 + .25 = 0.94$$

In the χ^2 table .94 (for three degrees of freedom) lies between column headings .50 and .90 which tells us that the figures obtained are likely to have an (approximately) 80 per cent chance of conforming to a 9:3:3:1 ratio – showing that characters are most likely to be under the control of two major genes.

Occasionally, results which appear roughly to correspond to the expected ratios, diverge from them to such an extent and in such a regular manner (after analysing a few progenies) that linkage of one character with another may be implicated. Genes are very frequently 'linked' in the parental combinations in which they were originally used.

Thus tall round seeded x dwarf wrinkled seeded could produce an F_2 result of 100:15:15:30 where the recombined genotypes tall wrinkled and dwarf round were deficient. Linkage can be suggested from the results of an χ^2 test, so that this present example would give us:

$$\chi^2 = \frac{(100-90)^2}{90} + \frac{(30-15)^2}{30} + \frac{(30-15)^2}{30} + \frac{(30-10)^2}{10} = 42.6 \text{ for 3 d.f.}$$

From the χ^2 table it can be seen that there is less than one chance in a thousand that this ratio is a true example of digenic inheritance and, with this fact established, the observed figures would suggest linkage of the parent gene combinations.

Other statistical methods can be used for the detection of gene linkage but the versatility of the χ^2 test is self evident.

Determining Population Sizes for Identifying Major Genes

A rapid statistical technique has been devised by Mainlane (1951) to dictate the size of populations necessary in order to find certain genotypes when the inheritance of the appropriate genes is known.

The general formulae for a 99:1 chance of finding the appropriate genotypes and a 95 per cent chance are (The expected proportion relative to 1, + 0.5) x 4.6 and (The expected proportion relative to 1, + 0.5) x 3.0 respectively.

Thus, if a 3:1 ratio in F_2 is expected, the number of plants to be grown in order to be 99 per cent certain of finding one recessive = (3+0.5) x 4.6 = 16.

If the recessive genotype from a digenic F_2 segregation is to be identified with a 95 per cent level of certainty, the population size must be at least (15+0.5) x 3.0 = 47.

As long as the proportion expected in the result is related to 1, the formula may be used to calculate sizes of populations for any circumstances.

In lettuce, for example the disease lettuce mosaic is transmitted by a virus from an infected parent plant through approximately 2.5 per cent of its seed. In order to know whether a parent plant was infected (because the disease is not always easily identifiable) or whether an infected parent plant showed a different level of transmission from the general average, enough seedlings should be grown to ensure that at least a single infected one is present. For a 2.5 infection level (or 39:1), (39.0 + 0.5) x 4.6 = 182 plants should be grown to have a .01 probability that at least one infected seedling would be found.

If only 0.5% transmission was expected, more plants would need to be grown; in fact, (199 + 0.5) x 4.6 = 918 plants.

Detection of Polygenic Effects

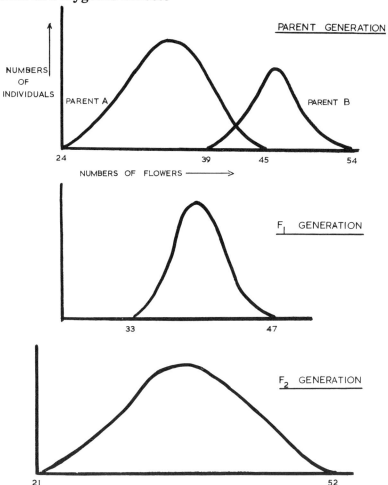

Fig 14. Theoretical representation for flower number in salpiglossis where parent A has a range of 24 to 45. and parent B 39 to 54; F_1 range = 33 to 47 and F_2 range = 21 to 52.

The χ^2 test can be used to reveal conformity (or otherwise) to expected ratios, and assesses on an extended basis, any departure from a general situation. Polygenes with their small effects, on the other hand are usually impossible to fit into a prescribed pattern but nevertheless possess dominant or recessive effects which must be identified if they are to be used sensibly in the breeding programme.

Polygenic effects can be analysed only when presented numerically, and usually on a fairly large population of plants. As an aid to analysis they may be produced graphically in a similar way to that shown in Figure 14.

Analysis of polygenic effects is based upon the relationship of the population to its mean or average and can be accurately assessed only by using a calculator. Thus, for our theoretical salpiglossis population the individual plant figure would be squared, totalled, and the mean figure calculated as, for example, where 'n' = number of flowers borne by an individual plant.

	n	n^2
	10	100
	20	400
	30	900
	25	625
	27	729
mean	$\dfrac{112}{5}$	$\dfrac{2754}{5}$

The mean value of this small, theoretical population is 22.4 while the *variance* (the mean of n^2) is 550.8 and, by a further calculation, is reduced to a term known as the standard error. This is applied to the mean value to indicate its reliability as a characteristic of the population.

$$\text{In this example standard error} = \sqrt{\frac{550.8}{n-1}} = \sqrt{\frac{550.8}{4}} = 11.1$$

and the population mean is therefore 22.4 ± 11.1. Although the mean value is 22.4 it may be 22.4 − 11.1 = 11.3, or 22.4 + 11.1 = 33.5, and therefore subject to a large 'error'. In practice the 'error' value of a small population is almost certain to be higher relative to the mean, than that for a large population. If the mean of another population was also 22.4 with a much lower standard error it would be concluded that the mean of the latter was more representative of its population than the former was for its own population. A further conclusion may also be derived – that the second population was considerably more uniform (i.e. showed less variability) than the former and was therefore more stable polygenically.

Graphically, the two populations would probably be represented as:

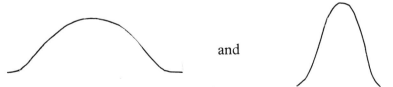

and

Quantitative measurements and analyses such as these have been used (notably by E.M. East in 1916) to show that control of polygenes as well as major genes is exercised by the nucleus. Where major genes cannot be identified as such, however, the variability of parental lines can be measured graphically as frequency distributions, or numerically as means and standard errors.

When the F_1 hybrid is examined quantitatively it should show no greater variability than the most variable of the two parents. In the F_2 generation, however, maximum segregation of polygenes should occur, as would happen with major mendelian genes. Selection and selfing of several individuals from the whole F_2 range should produce a number of F_3 families which differ widely in their mean values. They will probably also differ between one another in their range of variabilities but none of them, nor of succeeding generations, should show a higher degree of variability than that of the F_2 from which they were derived.

If inbreeding (or close brother-sister mating) is continued to produce F_4 progenies, these should again be less variable than their particular F_3's – as measured above. Such reductions in variability (or, conversely, increases in genetic uniformity) may be less obvious in later generations due to the influence of non genetic factors.

Characters – especially quantitative – which are controlled by polygenes, are often very sensitive to environmental conditions and the distinction between heritable and non-heritable (environmental) expression is often difficult to assess. Numerous statistical methods have been devised to measure these and other small effects (see bibliography), but the dependability of genetic control is most commonly assessed through the relationship between one generation and another, or one character and another, as elaborated below.

Relationship of One Character to Another

The Coefficient of Correlation
Relationships between various characters are sometimes obvious but at other times may be more difficult to recognise. The mean character value of a series of

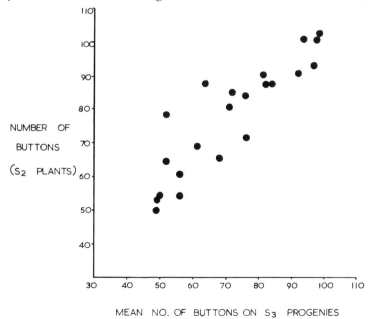

Fig 15. Relationship (correlation) of parents and progenies for 'button' number in Brussels sprout.

parent plants and their progenies should show some degree of relationship, while within individual plants one character may modify or control the expression of another. If related characters for each individual are plotted against each other on a graph, the degree of relationship (i.e. strength of genetic control) will be indicated by the appearance of the resultant dotted line. Whether the line is approximately straight or not, calculation of the correlation coefficient will indicate the statistical value of the relationship (r) which will fall between 0 (no relationship) and 1 (complete).

As an example, we may plot the number of sprout buttons on S_2 Brussels sprout plants against the mean number of buttons on their respective S_3 progenies as listed below, giving a result as presented in Figure 15.

$S_2 (= x)$	$S_3 (= y)$
50	49
53	49
54	50
54	56
61	56
65	53
66	68
69	61
72	76
78	52
81	71
85	76
86	72
88	63
88	82
88	84
91	81
92	92
94	96
102	93
102	97
103	198
1722	1575

Calculation of the correlation coefficient (r) follows the formula (Σ = the sum of)

$$\frac{\Sigma\,(x - \bar{x})\,(y - \bar{y})}{\sqrt{(x - \bar{x})^2\,(y - \bar{y})^2}}$$

by the following mechanical procedure.

1) Each figure in column x is multiplied by its related figure in column y e.g. 50 x 49, this result then being added to the product of the next pair (53 x 49) and so on until all pairs have been multiplied together and totalled. From the calculated figure (128745 in this example) is deducted the *correlation factor* which is the true total of the x column multiplied by the total of the y column and then divided by the number of pairs of figures (22 in our example) to give 123279.5.

The 'sum of products' now becomes 128745 − 123279.5 = 5465.5

2) The 'sum of squares' for column x is calculated by squaring each figure in 148 the x column and adding it to the square of each subsequent figure. From the

total sum of squares the correction factor is deducted – this being obtained by squaring the proper column total (1722) and dividing it by the number of individuals. This calculation gives

$$140884 - \left(\frac{2965284}{22}\right) = 6098.4$$

3) The 'sum of squares for column y is calculated in the same way as for x, giving the answer 6105.3

4) The results for x and y (the corrected sums of squares, to use the appropriate term) should now be multiplied together, their total reduced to the square root form, and this divided into the figure for sums of products obtained in calculation (1).

The final part of the mathematics thus becomes

$$\frac{5465.5}{\sqrt{37232561.52}}$$

$$= \frac{5465.5}{6101.8} = 0.896$$

5) The final result 0.896 is now referred to the table for 'r' (Appendix 5) by consulting the row for 20 degrees of freedom. Degrees of freedom are two less than the number of pairs of observations since the *two* constants x and y have been fitted to the data.

In the table of 'r' the highest figure against 20 d.f. is .652, in the column 0.001. If our result was .652 or thereabouts it would mean that the correlation between the recorded observations was of a very high order and likely to be shown against 999 times out of 1000. Because our final figure was higher even than .652 there is greater evidence of a true correlation between the series of paired observations. If on the other hand, our value for 'r' was at the opposite side of the table (e.g. .360) the heading of the column indicates that there is a 0.10 probability (or 1 in 10 chances) of obtaining such a value for 'r' without the presence of any correlation. We could not assume therefore a true relationship between the paired observations.

A further series of calculations may be applied in order to predict the likely value of 'y' when 'x' is a known quantity (regression analysis) or to estimate the 'heritability' of particular characters. While the extra information is valuable, the statistics become rather too complex for this section and are best studied by reference to the bibliographical list. A knowledge of the statistics of heritability is particularly worthy of extra study since it can be used to indicate which parts of a breeding programme are most responsive genetically.

Diallel Analysis

In order to find the best parental combinations for the production of F_1 hybrids, it is desirable to cross together as many pairs of inbred lines as possible. The expressions of hybrid vigour are usually the result of unique combinations of polygenes which can only be reproduced by repeating the original cross and for this reason, parent plants must be homozygous.

Because of the great number of inbred lines involved in a hybridisation programme, it is imperative that the maximum amount of information about parents and their respective hybrids should be obtained at an early stage, so that any extension of the programme can include only the most desirable lines.

Using the diallel technique, inbred lines are crossed with one another in all   149 possible combinations – but usually excluding reciprocal crosses – and, after field recording of the performance of parents and F_1 hybrids – the results are presented as in Table 18.

TABLE 18
DIALLEL TABLE OF YIELD RESULTS FOR 8 INBRED LINES AND THEIR F_1 HYBRIDS

	1	2	3	4	5	6	7	8	Totals for F_1's with common parent
1	24.2	19.3	26.1	22.0	37.7	23.1	26.5	30.3	209.2
2		15.6	25.1	20.4	34.6	18.9	25.2	29.1	188.2
3			30.6	25.8	43.7	24.0	29.8	31.3	236.4
4				21.9	23.7	20.2	25.6	27.3	186.9
5					40.1	31.5	36.3	35.8	283.4
6						19.3	23.1	26.8	186.9
7							25.2	28.3	220.0
8								27.3	236.2

For ease of calculation, all figures are placed in the same half of the table, although some crosses may, in fact, have been made reciprocally. Results for inbred lines are incorporated since these are used in the calculations. The 'general combining ability' of one parent plant with all others may be provisionally assessed by totalling all F_1 figures (viz. seven) which have the common parent either as male or female. Thus, without detailed analysis, parent 5 appears to be most successful in hybrid combination and is, incidentally, also the highest yielding inbred parent, although these two factors are not necessarily correlated.

Steps in the analysis are now as follows:

1. Calculate the corrected sum of squares for each array, (the parent and its F_1 hybrids) according to the formula

$$\Sigma 1^2 - \frac{(\Sigma 1)^2}{n}, \text{ where } 1 = \text{ number of array,}$$

and n = number of individuals within the array.
So, for array 1, the calculation is:
$$24.2^2 + 19.3^2 + 26.1^2 + 22.0^2 + 37.7^2 + 23.1^2 + 26.5^2 + 30.3^2 - \frac{(233.4)^2}{8}$$

For array 5:
$$37.7^2 + 34.6^2 + 43.7^2 + 23.7^2 + 40.1^2 + 31.5^2 + 36.3^2 + 35.8^2 - \frac{(323.5)^2}{8}$$

2. Calculate the covariance of each array – by squaring the parental value and then multiplying each member of the particular array by the *non-recurrent parent* on the lower diagonal.

Formula: $$\Sigma xy - \frac{\Sigma x \Sigma y}{n}$$

For array 1:
$$24.2^2 + (19.3 \text{x} 15.6) + (26.1 \text{x} 30.6) + (22.0 \text{x} 21.9) + (37.7 \text{x} 40.1) + (23.1 \text{x} 19.3)$$
$$+ (26.5 \text{x} 25.2) + (30.3 \text{x} 27.3) - \frac{(233.4 \text{x} 204.2)}{8}$$

For array 5:

$$(37.7 \times 24.2) + (34.6 \times 15.6) + (43.7 \times 30.6) + (23.7 \times 21.9) + 40.1^2 + (31.5 \times 19.3)$$
$$+ (36.3 \times 25.2) + (35.8 \times 27.3) - \frac{(323.5 \times 204.2)}{8}$$

The eight variances and covariances are next plotted on a graph to allow visual interpretation of genetic effects. The genetic reasoning may be broken down into further detail by continuing the analysis, but the position of the points on the graph should indicate where to place the emphasis in the current and future breeding programmes.

Calculated array values which, when plotted, lie near the lower left end of the regression line show those parents which possess most dominant polygenes for the character under study.Arrays furthest from the zero point contain most recessive polygenes. If points are clustered together, no dominance has been identified.

The graph plotted from the variances and covariances in the present example indicates that array 4 exhibits the greatest dominance effects while array 3 possesses most recessives. Other arrays are spread fairly evenly along the diagonal although array 5 indicates a tendency towards a 'general combining ability' with other arrays and therefore has a special value for F_1 hybrid production.

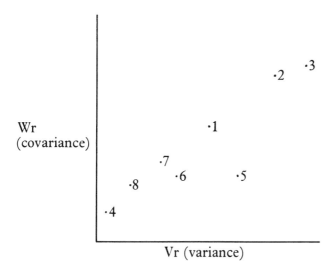

Wr (covariance) / Vr (variance)

The Layout and Analysis of Field Variety Trials

Randomised Block Trials
The most widely used statistical method of assessing horticultural cultivars in the field is through the use of *randomised blocks*. While it is possible to obtain a reasonable comparison of cultivars by growing them adjacent to one another, there is a danger that results will be distorted because minor soil and environmental differences may affect some cultivars more than others. For example, cultivars at each end of the row will either benefit from the extra space available on one side, or may suffer because of their exposure to adverse weather conditions. Similarly, another cultivar may be sited upon a highly fertile patch of ground, or may suffer from waterlogging, because it has been planted in a hollow.

In order to overcome these diverse effects, the group of cultivars under test should be grown in separate *replications* of a *randomised block trial* so that each cultivar is represented more than once (usually three or four times), in a 151 different position in each *replicate*. Each cultivar must consist of the same number of plants (or length of row in the case of row-crops like onions) and all must be planted under identical conditions of row space, planting or sowing method, equivalent seed and pest control, etc. The whole trial area should be roughly square, but each block of cultivars should be rectangular in order to cover all the soil variability in that area. Numbers of plants per cultivar must be decided by:

a) Availability of seed – the smallest seed quantity dictating the *maximum* plot size.

b) The homogeneity of individual lines (F_5 and F_6 lettuce will be very uniform and good assessments could be made with 10 plants per plot, while F_5 and F_6 carrots will be variable and up to 100 plants per plot should be grown).

c) The practical consideration of sowing, cultivating, harvesting and recording.

Within each replication (or block) cultivars should be planted in randomised order. Each cultivar should be given a number (referable to its name on the master plan) which is used throughout the trial and, by shuffling the order of numbers in each block, a field plan should be prepared from which to label and mark out the ground area.

A randomised trial of eight lettuce cultivars in four replications with twenty plants per plot should, on the field plan, look like the following:

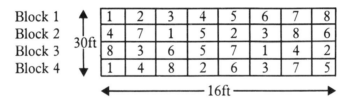

Block 1, Block 2, Block 3, Block 4 — 30ft high, 16ft wide. Grid:
1 2 3 4 5 6 7 8
4 7 1 5 2 3 8 6
8 3 6 5 7 1 4 2
1 4 8 2 6 3 7 5

2 Rows of plants at 9in between plants, 2ft between rows.

Randomisation is just as marked for the first block as for the other three although cultivars are in numerical order. The choice of numbers for each cultivar is normally quite arbitrary since it is unlikely that alphabetical and numerical coincidence will have any hidden significance, and there are advantages from the observation and demonstration points of view in having a recognisable sequence in the first block.

Around each complete experiment should be grown a double 'guard' row of the same species to provide all experimental plants with the same environmental limitations. Recording of data is usually carried out over as short a period as possible, according to the characters under study. The date when 50 per cent of a line or cultivar reaches market maturity would thus be recorded only once for each plot within each block but plant weights would be recorded on a number of occasions (and finally totalled) since not all plants would reach maturity at the same time. For recording plant weights, record sheets would be drawn up similar to that shown in Table 19. For ease of recording and subsequent analysis, separate sheets would be used for each replication. Cultivars should be listed in numerical order in spite of the fact that they would be randomised in the field.

It will be appreciated from the table that data over and above what was originally intended may also be derived. Thus, the dates of 50 per cent maturity need not have been recorded as a separate operation, since they can be obtained from the records. Similarly, the comparative rates of maturity for each cultivar also provide useful information of overall performance.

TABLE 19   APPENDIX 3
SAMPLE RECORD SHEET FOR RECORDING PLANT WEIGHTS OF
LETTUCE AT MARKET MATURITY. 4 RANDOMISED BLOCKS. 8 PLOTS
(CULTIVARS)

EACH OF 10 PLANTS

REPLICATION 1

CULTIVARS

	1	2	3	4	5	6	7	8
Date								
No. of Plants								
Weight								
Date								
No. of Plants								
Weight								
Date								
No. of Plants								
Weight								
Mean weight								

The Analysis of Variance

When all data have been collected, the value of each cultivar can be assessed
correctly by subjecting the information to an analysis of variance. This
measures the reliability of the data for each cultivar and indicates which of them
is most likely to produce consistently better or worse performances than the
others. The following example indicates the various steps in the analysis.

		A	B	C	D	E	F	G	H	*Block Totals*
					Cultivars					
Blocks	I	20.2	15.2	23.0	15.6	21.2	15.8	8.2	23.0	142.2
	II	16.3	15.3	26.1	18.3	19.0	19.6	10.3	26.2	151.1
	III	14.1	14.0	18.3	15.1	15.3	17.0	9.1	23.3	126.2
	IV	21.3	16.2	21.4	19.1	15.4	21.3	9.2	25.8	149.7
Var. Totals:		71.9	60.7	88.8	68.1	70.9	73.7	36.8	98.3	569.2
Var. Means:		18.0	15.2	22.2	17.0	17.7	18.4	9.2	24.6	

1. Assemble data in a table similar to above (totals for cultivars and blocks are
    calculated as analysis proceeds).

2. Calculate the sum of squares (S.S.) for all individuals. e.g. $20.2^2 + 16.3^2 +
    14.1^2 + 21.3^2 + 15.2^2 +----------23.3^2 + 25.8^2$

3. Calculate the correction factor (CF). This will be used throughout the
    analysis and is calculated by squaring the grand total and dividing this by n
    (n = number cf individuals comprising the grand total).
    e.g. $\frac{569.2^2}{32} = 10124.64 = C.F.$

4. Total SS is now obtained by subtracting CF from the previous SS for
    individuals as calculated in 2 above, and is entered as the first figure in a
    summarising table as shown below (i.e. 722.22)

	SS	DF	MS	VR	P	SE
Varieties	588.56	7	84.0800	20.8	<0.001	
Blocks	48.93	3	16.3100	4.0		
Error	84.73	21	4.0348			±2.0087
Total	722.22	31				

5. Obtain SS for cultivars (viz. $71.9^2 + 60.7^2$ --------- $+ 98.3^2$) *and divide this total by the number of blocks* – in this instance, four. Subtract correction factor from this figure and the varieties SS is then entered as above (i.e. 588.56)

6. Obtain SS for blocks by squaring block totals ($142.2^2 +$----- 149.7^2) *and divide this figure by the number of cultivars* (8) before subtracting CF.

7. SS for error is obtained as the difference between the Total SS and the cultivars + blocks SS.

8. Degrees of freedom (D.F.) are one less than the number of individuals concerned, e.g. total degrees of freedom = {8 cultivars x 4 (blocks)} – 1 = 31. Degrees of freedom for cultivars = 8 – 1, etc.

9. Mean square (or *variance*) is obtained by dividing the appropriate sums of squares by their respective degrees of freedom.

10. Variance ratio (VR) is a measure of the accuracy of the experiment since it is related to the error mean square. Each VR is obtained as a result of division of the appropriate mean square by the error mean square.

11. Probability (P) is calculated from tables of Variance ratio (Appendix 5) and indicates whether or not there are significant differences between cultivars and/or blocks. In this example, using DF's 7 (cultivars) and 21 (error) in the table of variance ratios, P = <0.001 for cultivars. This means that there is less than one chance in 1,000 that the result is not representative for the cultivars under test as the variance ratio of 20.8 is considerably higher than that necessary for this significance level.

12. Standard Error (SE) shown in the example is the overall estimate of error for individual plots, and is the square root of the error mean square.

13. The normal method of assessing whether differences between varieties are significant is to use the LSD or least significant difference. If the difference between *the means* (in this case) of two cultivars exceeds the LSD, the cultivars are significantly different from one another. From our example, the LSD between means of two cultivars

$$= + \sqrt{\frac{4.0348 \times 2}{4}} \text{ x t (at P = 0.05)}$$

$$\text{or} \sqrt{\frac{\text{E.m.s. x 2}}{\text{no of blocks}}} \text{ x t}$$

The value of 't' is found by consulting 't' tables (Appendix 5) deciding beforehand which significance level is to be used (normally P = 0.05). Degrees of freedom in t tables are those for *error*. LSD between means of two cultivars therefore becomes: 2.442.

From this it follows that the significant differences between cultivars are as follows:

Cultivar H is not significantly better than C because there is less than 2.442 difference between their mean values, but both are better than any other cultivar in this experiment.

Many other field designs are used to test the attributes of cultivars with or without special treatment but, in general, they are more complicated both for field planting and recording, as well as in their mathematical treatments. The analysis of variance for randomised block experiments should be adequate for wide comparisons between new and existing cultivars, but further information can be obtained by using split plots, latin squares, lattices, balanced-incomplete blocks, or other more sophisticated techniques, which are referred to in the bibliography.

SPLIT PLOT experiments are designed to superimpose another factor upon cultivars under test. If, for example, eight cultivars were being treated for comparative yields in a randomised block experiment, the test could be more informative if half of each plot was heavily fertilised while the remaining half received the normal dressing of fertiliser. Depending upon plot size, it could be of value to 'split' each plot into even more parts as long as each part still remained large enough to give meaningful results. The statistical analysis would then assess each cultivar under a larger range of conditions and would probably extract enough information to allow recommendation of cultivars for well-defined cultural conditions.

LATIN SQUARES are most useful when the number of cultivars under test is fairly limited – usually between five and eight. Under these circumstances, a two-dimensional arrangement (see below) may be used to give the same number of replications as there are cultivars. All cultivars should be present *once only* in each row and each column.

Both split-plot experiments and Latin squares are analysed by slight modification of the analysis of variance.

FIELD LAYOUT OF a) SPLIT PLOT EXPERIMENT b) LATIN SQUARES
c) BALANCED INCOMPLETE BLOCKS and d) LATTICE

a) Split Plot Experiments with 6 cultivars and 3 replications.
    Split for 0, 1 and 2 dressings of fertiliser.

Rep 1

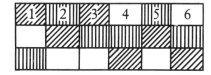

Rep 2

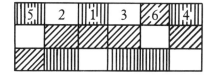

Similar for Rep 3

Fig 16. Field layout of (a) split block experiments, (b) Latin squares, (c) balanced incomplete blocks and (d) lattice.

b) Latin squares with 6 cultivars.

1	2	3	4	5	6
2	3	4	5	6	1
3	4	5	6	1	2
4	5	6	1	2	3
5	6	1	2	3	4
6	1	2	3	4	5

c) Balanced Incomplete Block, 25 cultivars, 4 replications in 20 groups of 5

Groups

A	B	C	D	E	B	A	C	B	C	D	E	A	E	D	C	B	A	D	E
1	6	11	16	21	10	5	13												
2	7	12	17	22	6	3	15												
3	8	13	18	23	8	1	11	etc_ _ _ etc_ _			_ _ _ _ _ _ _ _ _			_ _ _ _ _			_ _ _ _ _ _	
4	9	14	19	24	7	4	12												
5	10	15	20	25	9	2	14												

d) Lattice design of 25 cultivars.

1	10	11	20	21
2	9	12	19	22
3	8	13	18	23
4	7	14	17	24
5	6	15	16	25

BALANCED INCOMPLETE BLOCKS are a valuable means of obtaining meaningful data when a very large number of cultivars is to be studied. Since direct comparisons are impossible because the field trial would become unwieldy and very subject to experimental error, cultivars are associated with one another in groups of sets. The 'balanced incomplete block' is finalised when all possible groups of sets are made and every cultivar is replicated the same number of times. Because cultivars are not represented in each set, direct comparisons are not always possible, but by ensuring that specified cultivars are paired, direct comparison between these can be made while other cultivars can be compared indirectly by using the average of associated cultivars. The example in Figure 16 illustrates 25 cultivars in sets of five, so that four replications of each cultivar are possible with one set missing from each group. Each set is paired with every other set three times.

LATTICE DESIGNS bear some similarity to balanced incomplete blocks, but whereas the latter requires a high number of replications in order to attain the balanced layout (a great disadvantage when a large number of cultivars already create planning difficulties) the lattice allows indirect comparisons through intermediate cultivars and so reduces the seed for true replication.

In figure 16 the 25 cultivars are tested in blocks of five, using rows and also columns separately. Thus, cultivar 1 will be tested against 2, 3, 4 and 5 in one block, and against 10, 11, 20 and 21 in the other. It will not, however be tested directly against the remaining 16 cultivars, although cross-reference will be possible through cultivars which it has in common with other cultivars in the test. This system allows two replications – so for greater accuracy of statistical interpretation, a further identical set of 25 can be planted and recorded. In spite of the lack of direct comparison between all cultivars, the design is effective, since it allows good statistical conclusions to be made while economising on land area, seed and numbers of records.

Statistically designed field trials provide the plant breeder with the opportunity to compare his various lines with other commercially available material in an environment which is unlikely to favour one more than the other. In these circumstances, an advantage shown by any one cultivar is most unlikely to be due to chance positioning in the experimental layout and, if the Probability (P) indicates significance, the cultivar should be expected to repeat its performance and could be recommended with confidence.

In any form of randomised, replicated layout, varietal comparisons are based upon variances which take account of deviations around the mean value. Thus, a cultivar with a mean value of 160 could in four replications, have produced results of 225, 140, 105 and 170 while another cultivar gave the same mean through readings of 150, 165, 170 and 155. Under the conditions of the experiment, it would be assumed that the two cultivars were similar – based upon mean values – but the latter was obviously more stable (with a lower variance). While much can be interpreted from mean values, these alone are not reliable and should be related to variances – calculated with the use of the Student 't' test.

For the above results, therefore, cultivar A =

$$\frac{\{(225^2 + 140^2 + 105^2 + 170^2) - \dfrac{(225 + 140 + 105 + 170)^2}{4}\}}{4 - 1}$$

$$= \frac{110150 - 102400}{3} = 2583.3$$

$$\text{Cultivar B} = \frac{\{(150^2 + 165^2 + 170^2 + 155^2) - \dfrac{(150 + 165 + 170 + 155)^2}{4}\}}{4 - 1}$$

$$= \frac{102650 - 102400}{3} = 83.3$$

The larger variance (that of cultivar A) is next divided by the smaller and the result

$$(\frac{2583.3}{83.3} = 31.0)$$

referred to the tables of variance ratio (Appendix 5). Using 3 degrees of freedom for N_1 (the larger variance) and the same number for N_2, since both variances were based upon four figures, the tables for 5%, 1% and 0.1% levels of significance are consulted. If the calculated variance ratio exceeds that given for the appropriate number of degrees of freedom, the result is more significant than the level of significance in the particular table under scrutiny. So, for 3d.f. x 3d.f. in the Table of Variance ratio with a 0.01 significance level, the appropriate figure is 29.5. Since our figure is higher than this, the variance ratio table for the next level of significance must be studied, this gives the figure 141. The significance of our figure therefore, lies between 0.01 and 0.001, though much closer to the former. It is now deduced that there is a highly significant difference in the variability of the two cultivars since $P = >0.01$, i.e. the probability that the differences are real is greater than 100:1.

Because we are testing both cultivars to find which is most variable however, and are not comparing one with a known variability against an unknown, a more cautious statistical assessment must be made. The significance levels are doubled so that the table for 5%, 1% and 0.1% become 10%, 2% and 0.2% respectively and our figure 31.0 is significant at $P = 0.02$. The probability that the differences between cultivars are real now drops to a 100:2 (or 50:1) chance.

Appendix 4

Practical Hints

Pollination and Fertilisation

One pollen grain is able to fertilise a single ovule only. Flowers which normally produce many seeds therefore need to have numerous pollen-grains on their stigmas to achieve complete fertilisation. Flowers which form few seeds may still require a liberal application of pollen to the stigma since pollen grains often germinate better 'in company'.

Flowers and pollen must be thoroughly dry and overhead watering should be avoided if successful fertilisation is to be achieved. Pollination of cucumbers is most successful in high humidity, however.

When pollen is to be used in crosses in which the 'female' flowers are still immature, it may be stored in a sealed container in a domestic refrigerator (at approximately 1°C) without a dramatic loss of viability until such time as it can be used. The pollen of different species naturally varies in its capacity for storage, but in an emergency it is better to attempt to store than to lose the chance of making a valuable cross-pollination.

Self-incompatibility of *Brassica* flowers may be overcome by pollinating them with 'self' pollen upon a brush composed of wire bristles which help to rupture the stigmatic surface (Roggen and van Dyk).

Mass-pollination of a group of plants is normally achieved by isolating the selections from others of the same species and allowing natural pollination by bees or other insects. Bees may also be used as pollinators in an enclosed area although they tend to cluster on the glass or netting – particularly if the number of flowers is limited. In enclosed conditions the blow-fly is a useful alternative pollinator although it does its work by crawling over flower heads rather than actively collecting nectar. Blowfly larvae may be obtained from local angling shops and should be kept in bran or sawdust until they pupate. Blowflies emerge from pupae approximately 12 days later but this period may be extended by storing pupae (in a container with a porous lid) in a domestic-type refrigerator if not all pupae are required at once. Pupae should be placed in the isolation area with the selected plants; pollination starts when the flies emerge. Blowflies will live approximately a week under those conditions and, as most plants flower over a considerably longer period, their replacements should be introduced to the compartment at appropriate intervals.

Seed Collection, Cleaning and Multiplication

For most families such as *Liliaceae, Leguminosae, Cruciferae,* and *Papa-* 159 *veraceae,* seedpod collection should be started when the ovary wall starts to change colour from green to yellow. As long as the pod is kept dry *and not packed closely together with others in storage* the contents will mature evenly and threshing-out of the seed should be an easy task. With other families such as *Compositae, Labiatae,* and *Umbelliferae,* shedding of the exposed seed is likely to occur if individual flower heads are allowed to become dead ripe. For these families (depending upon the size of population) each flower head should be harvested individually when seed is turning brown and when the main flower stalk appears to be almost dead. After three to four days storage under dry conditions (or less under glass), seeds should easily shake off or become detached from the main stalk.

Because *Labiateae* and families with similar flower heads produce their flowers up the same stalk over a period, it is almost impossible to save all seed unless handling only a small number of plants. Seed of the lower flowers can be allowed to ripen completely before the stalk is cut, then, if flower heads are stored loosely in trays or on paper, the seed forming in the upper flowers will be able to ripen as the flower head dies and will be additional to the already ripe seed of the lower flowers.

The method by which seed is harvested is dictated to a large extent by the amount to be produced. For large quantities, mechanical harvesting is obviously desirable but only if seed heads mature simultaneously or remain without deteriorating until all flower heads have produced seeds. Heads with light, exposed, seeds are best harvested by hand into a suitable container on four or five occasions until the crop has produced a maximum yield. Many *compositae* such as *arctosis,* daisy, *calendula* and lettuce, with *begoniaceae* and *papaveraceae* if grown on a small scale, repay the extra labour requirements through the value of seed retrieved.

Other crops such as wallflowers, *antirrhinums, brassicas,* runner and dwarf beans, retain their seeds so well in pods or capsules that harvesting can be delayed and carried out on a single occasion. Although garden and sweet peas also bear pods these must be harvested before they become too brittle when they easily shed their seeds.

The golden rule for seed collection is that seed samples should never be bulked in storage prior to threshing, but should be allowed to dry slowly and thoroughly by exposing them to currents of warm dry air. This should be possible either by spreading the samples on mesh trays, in loosely filled and well-spaced sacks hung in an air current, or even by spreading over plastic or canvas on the floor. Very rapid drying is likely to do more harm than good. If moist samples are crowded together, overheating and fungal infection will destroy or spoil the larger part – and a season's work could be wasted.

For large amounts of material, seed cleaning and threshing is a mechanical process but the plant breeder is most likely to handle small quantities from a great number of plants. Threshing and cleaning are usually combined in the same operation and use is made of sieves, rubbing boards and small winnowing machines. Rubbing boards are most useful for releasing seed from pods, particularly of *cruciferae,* and are designed as a one-ended trough. After breaking the pods, seed can be rolled into a suitable container from the open end of the trough.

The greatest requirement when cleaning small quantities of seed is a good pair of lungs, since the unwanted chaff must be continually blown away from the seed. This is most effectively carried out if seed and chaff are contained in a shallow oval dish with ends which may be used as pouring lips.

160   The need for scrupulous cleaning of all surfaces between successive samples

Plate 33. Small-scale threshing and cleaning equipment.

must also be emphasised *and seed which has been spilt should never be retained* because of the danger of contamination between samples.

If seed samples are impossible to clean satisfactorily, the seed may be stored in a 'dirty' condition as long as the accompanying residues are completely dry. It may also be sown in an uncleaned state since only the seeds will germinate! *Brassica*, wallflowers, etc. pods may be sown even though they still contain seed, since germination will take place normally and be only slightly retarded by the pod.

Seed of certain species must be threshed and cleaned by specialised methods. Tomato seed is surrounded by a slippery protective mucilage which must be removed to allow the seed to dry. The conventional technique is to harvest ripe fruits and to transfer the mucilagenous portion containing the seed into a beaker. The seed mass is then covered by an equivalent volume of hydrochloric acid (H.Cl.) at ten per cent concentration for a period of twenty to thirty minutes. Following this, the seed is cleaned by immersing it in running water in a fine-meshed sieve which allows the residue to disperse but retains the seed. After thorough air-drying the seed can be packeted. Throughout the whole process great care must be taken to keep each sample accurately labelled.

When cleaning large quantities of tomato seed it is often more economical of time and labour to squash whole fruits in a large plastic container. The 'soup' may be left undisturbed for up to two weeks. Even when fermentation occurs the seed should be unharmed and the eventual cleaning process is carried out with H.Cl. in a similar manner to that already described. For every 1lb of fruit one fluid ounce of ten per cent H.Cl. should be added. This should be thoroughly mixed with the squashed fruit for an hour, after which the seeds are strained off and washed clean in running water. This 'whole-fruit' method is liable to produce more residues, particularly fruit skin, but is a fairly rapid system for large quantities.

Cucumber seed is often cleaned by using H.Cl. or pectinase (a commercially   161 available enzyme) although here it is best to remove as much of the fruit flesh as possible. Cucumber, melon and marrow seed may also be removed cleanly if the fruit is stored under dry conditions for six months before being cut open.

Beetroot seed is produced in clusters of three or four true seeds which are held together in a 'utricle' consisting of fused flower bracts. They may be broken down into single seeds by rubbing dry utricles between two solid surfaces.

Identification of Seed Lots

The importance of keeping seed-lots separate and clearly identified has already been underlined. The nature of plant breeding is such that simple programmes rapidly become complicated because of the build-up in numbers of selected plants, special crosses, separate progenies from crosses etc. At as early a stage as possible a reliable classification system should be introduced, usually numerical, and should be fully recorded. Thus, initial plant selections would be given a simple number in a record book.

A common system is to use the last two numbers of the appropriate year followed by the seed number of the harvested sample e.g. 8004 (1980, seed lot 4). The use of the double digit after the year allows 99 entries. Each entry should apply only to seed harvested, since the recording of unsuccessful crosses or selections is unnecessary.

As long as each entry is sufficiently detailed, they can describe any form of cross or selection. 8004, for example, may be selfed seed (S_1) from a double pink rose cultivar while 8062 may be seed from an open-pollinated flower of a single yellow *Rosa foetida*. If these seeds were later sown and crosses made between plants derived from them, the labels on pollinated flowers would read either 8004 x 8062 or the converse if 8062 was the female parent. Seed from each successful cross would be harvested separately and would be given new numbers.

Descriptions of the type or method of pollination will probably be recorded in the plant breeder's own 'shorthand' and as long as it is genetically meaningful the programme should run smoothly. 'Shorthand' is often necessary because of the many selection situations which cause different behaviour between related lines. As an example, an S_1 line has obviously been derived from a single pollination, but selections within this line may be (a) selfed again = S_2, (b) open-pollinated but seed saved from separate plants, (c) inter-crossed between selected plants with some seed saved separately and other seed bulked together, (d) single plants crossed with single plants from another line etc.!

Whatever the situation it is a golden rule that seed lots, once separated, should never be bulked – except possibly towards the completion of a programme when a high level of uniformity exists.

Seed Multiplication

Once the early stages of a breeding programme have been completed and the potential of a new cultivar has been assessed by studying small numbers of plants, it becomes necessary to increase the seed quantities either for further testing or for commercialisation.

Each crop has a fairly well-defined 'seed multiplication rate' which measures the average amount of seed produced in each generation. Thus, one pea seed for example, should produce a plant which, grown under 'average conditions', should give approximately nine or ten pods which would mature sufficiently to give about 70 seeds (at eight per pod). However, these ideal conditions rarely occur and the multiplication rate of peas is generally considered to be ten or thereabouts.

This figure is derived by assuming that four seeds are necessary to produce one plant, which in turn should produce about eight pods with five seeds (allowing for diseased or parasitised seeds) or, conversely, five pods with eight seeds. If pods are healthy and full it is doubtful that an average plant could ripen more than five to eight successfully. The multiplication rate is, of course, based upon averages since very high yielding and very low yielding plants would contribute to the final result.

Typical multiplication rates under average field conditions would be:
Antirrhinum (30 capsules x 200 seeds per capsules) ÷ 4 seeds to raise one plant = 1500

It could be argued that antirrhinum sowings, in boxes under glass, are very economical so that a single plant may be raised from less than four seeds. In practice, however, many seedlings are discarded at the pricking-out stage, while field selection or roguing is also likely to remove further plants.

Cornflower	(25 capitulae x 25 seeds) ÷ 3 seeds to raise 1 plant (less wasteful at pricking out) = 208
Salvia	(120 flowers x 3 seeds) ÷ 2 seeds = 180
Wallflower	(250 pods x 30 seeds) ÷ 6 seeds (damage and planting losses because it is a biennial) = 1250
Lettuce	(500 capitulae x 14 seeds) ÷ 5 seeds = 1400
Onion	(6 umbels x 300 capsules, each of 3 seeds) ÷ 30 seeds (to raise one bulb which is selected from a harvested and graded crop) = 180

Isolation Requirements

Because seed of many crops is multiplied in the field, great care must be taken to avoid contamination by cross-pollination with other crops of the same species. The likelihood of unwanted cross-pollination is related first to the proximity of similar crops and second to the breeding system of the crop from which seed is to be obtained.

When cross-compatible crops are flowering closely together the likelihood of cross-pollination between them can be deduced from their breeding systems as given in Table 4. Thus, different cultivars of crops such as peas, dwarf beans, lettuce and tomatoes may be grown adjacent to one another with little fear of cross-contamination as can flower cultivars of sweet peas, salpiglossis and salvia. In practice, seeding crops would be separated from one another by at least twenty yards, or, if closer planting was necessary to reduce land requirements, a 'barrier' crop of a non-compatible species would be interplanted. This would ensure that physical admixture of seed or plants was avoided at planting and harvesting time.

Naturally out-crossing cultivars need to be isolated from one another by greater distances at flowering time – the degree of isolation being dictated by the strength and direction of the prevailing wind, the size of population of pollinating insects and the amount of overlap in the flowering period between crops. Because the environmental factors are so liable to sudden changes, actual isolation distances between crops must be arbitrary to some extent. Since the main insect activity takes place within crops rather than between them, however, separation by not less than 250 yards is probably sufficient for all   163 facultative outbreeders. For obligate (or nearly so) outbreeders, isolation distances should not be less than 600 yards.

Genetic Tricks of the Trade

Self-Fertility

To assess the normal level of self-fertilisation of a plant, it should first be isolated from chance pollination and then:

(a) cross-pollinate – by brush, mature unemasculated flowers with pollen from a plant bearing a marker gene. Pollen upon the brush will become 'contaminated' with self-pollen during the pollination process and the proportion of non-marker seedlings in the progeny will give the approximate level of selfing to be expected under natural conditions.

(b) Self-pollinate five flowers and use a brush covered with pollen from sister plants to mass-pollinate five others on the same plant. A count of the numbers of seeds for each type of pollination (possible after four weeks for most species) will indicate the degree of self-fertility. While equal numbers of seeds indicate complete self-fertility, higher numbers for the mass pollinations than for the selfs indicate low self-fertility.

(c) Emasculate flowers of the plants to be tested before pollen is shed. When the flowers are fully open, mix pollen (on a glass plate, tile or other smooth surface) from fresh anthers of untreated flowers on the same plant with pollen from an equivalent number of anthers from a 'marker' plant of the same cultivar or species and apply, by brush, to the stigmas. Percentage self-fertilisation will be found by comparing the numbers of self and 'marker' seedlings in the subsequent progenies.

(d) Albino seedlings in the progeny of a self-fertilised plant indicate that cross-pollination normally occurs in the species. If selfing was common, albino characters would have been removed generations earlier.

Time-Saving Techniques

To speed-up the breeding programme without losing valuable genotypes;

a) raise and produce seed from all F_1 plants under glass to produce F_2 seed. Unless breeding specifically for F_1 hybrid lines, no selection should be practised until the F_2 generation.

For selection of polygenically-controlled characters, the complete F_2 could also be seeded under glass, deferring selection until the F_3 generation in the field. It has been found in peas that the chances of picking up the more extreme character expressions have been increased by selecting within the larger F_3 population rather than making decisions in F_2.

b) When carrying out a backcrossing programme the first backcross should be made at the F_1 stage – do not wait to select in F_2 before making a backcross since further selections will be required in the next, heterozygous, generation.

c) Take advantage of the known breeding system of plants to produce new lines or cultivars quickly. Tomato cultivars, for example are either F_1 hybrids or pure lines as stated in catalogues. Since the pure lines have proved themselves commercially, it follows that F_1 hybrids between them should be even better.

Plate 34. Frost hardiness contrasts between two S_2 lines of wallflower.
The line in the background will be discarded due to its frost susceptibility.

Test crosses can be made between pure lines (3 lines will give 3 F_1 combinations) and the F_1 hybrid crop can be raised in less than two years. If the F_1 hybrid suits the breeder, it can be produced at will by maintaining both parents.

d)   Grow the crop out of season in order to emphasise the defects which are to be removed by selection. Spring cabbage sown earlier than usual (June or July instead of September, for example) will be more likely to 'bolt' or commence flowering the following spring. Those plants which resist the bolting tendency should be used as the basis for further selection.

Antirrhinums grown late in the year are more likely to become infected by rust – a fungus disease, and plants which show least infection should be dug up to overwinter in the glasshouse, after which they may be seeded to produce less-susceptible lines.

Frost hardiness in most species can be improved by exposing large populations to severe conditions through earlier sowing or planting. Most plants will succumb to the environment but the survivors will be invaluable as parents of future populations.

e)   Sow seed of breeding lines without waiting for it to mature fully. Seed of many species (e.g. lettuce and cyclamen) shows dormancy when newly harvested after ripening on the plant, while immature seed is often capable of immediate germination. As long as the seed contents are solid, not liquid, there is a very good chance that germination will take place in a normal sowing medium. Lettuce seeds have germinated when harvested only 11 days after pollination under glass. The dormancy of most seeds may be broken by placing them on damp filter paper in a domestic refrigerator at $36°F$ for 48 hours, after which they should be sown.

f)   A method (communicated by Dr. R. Knight of East Malling Research Station) can be used to produce the end results of a backcrossing programme without resorting to continual pollination of parental types and selected segregants.

In the cross of blackcurrant (BB) x gooseberry (GG) – F_1 = BG

The chromosome number is next doubled with colchicine to give BBGG. The   165 first backcross (to G. in this case) = BBGG x GG, to give BGG, the triploid genotype.

With *triploid* pairing, a number of fertile *diploid* seeds should be produced with GG constitution (since like chromosomes will pair more successfully than unlike). Because of crossing over between B and G in the F_1 generation the G chromosomes in the new diploids should successfully isolate the most suitable backcross types.

The Induction of Polyploids

The artificial induction of polyploids as recommended under (f) above can be practised in a number of ways, using colchicine at a concentration of 0.5 to 1.0 per cent. At these concentrations, the length and method of exposure to colchicine are critical and can only be satisfactorily decided by experimentation. Since actively growing plant tissue must be treated, the most common methods of using colchicine are;

(a)   by applying it to seed which has already imbibed enough water for germination – by transferring seed from a water-soaked to a colchicine-soaked filter paper for approximately 24 hours.

(b)   by applying droplets of solution to the growing points of seedlings.

(c)   by applying colchicine in lanolin paste to growing points of seedlings.

(d)   by applying droplets as in (b) or (c) to active buds on mature plants – but removing all untreated bud growth.

Mixed tissues (diploid as well as polyploid) may arise after treatment and for successful results it is important to remove all shoots of the original non-polyploid, *more vigorous* type.

Final Notes on Selection

Accurate and rapid selection techniques are essential to a successful breeding programme.

a)   For initial selections, more plants should be chosen (usually by placing a bamboo cane adjacent to the appropriate plant) than will eventually be allowed to flower. Defective characters will become evident on many of the plants during their growth and development, their canes will be removed, and only the better individuals will remain.

b)   In cross-pollinated crops, only a small amount of seed should be saved from each selected plant and then used for progeny testing. In the subsequent crop, further selections will be made from the best progenies. It is only at this stage that labelling or recording will become necessary.

c)   Good seeding plants and, by inference, good flower producers, will be selected when mass-pollinating a small population. The threshed seed should contain higher proportions of seed from the good seeders than from the poor seeders. When a small population is grown for seed in the next season, the good seeders should form a large, if not major, part. This 'passive' selection technique is, in effect, equivalent to natural selection.

d)   When selecting within lines in the field always keep your back to the sun (if appropriate!) otherwise impressions of other lines will be misleading.

Plate 35. The induction of polyploidy by watering seed with 0.5% Colchicine solution for 24 hours after an initial 24 hours with normal H_2O. Seedling on right received no colchicine.

Future Possibilities of Breeding Techniques

Possibly the greatest advances to date in altering genetic forms without direct application of the reproductive cycle, have been those causing the production of mutations through irradiation, heat, shock or chemical treatments. These genetic mutations are quite haphazard however, and the methods involved have only a limited value. On the other hand, if it were possible to direct irradiation to a particular point on a specific chromosome so that a known result would occur, the rate of breeding would be greatly accelerated – but this refinement is probably many years away.

Technical advances such as illumination (for increasing the number of generations grown per year), tissue culture (for clonal production from minute pieces of tissue grown in nutrient solution), embryo culture (for raising seedlings from sterile interspecific crosses) and the use of growth hormones (for encouraging root growth and seed development) together with other less obvious advances such as mist propagation and bud-pollination have all aided the basic process of raising new cultivars. The only sign of a real breakthrough in altering the need for new forms to be produced by fertilisation, however, appears to lie in two main lines of research.

Culture of Pollen Grains

The first is the production of plants from pollen grains – most successfully achieved with *Nicotiana* (tobacco). The importance of this innovation is that all plantlets derived from pollen grains will be either haploid (x), or half of the normal chromosome complement if the genotype of the cultivar is more than diploid (2x). With a successful technique, vast numbers of seedlings may be raised.

The advantage of haploid material is that chromosome doubling (by colchicine or other treatments) will produce an entirely homozygous diploid

167

which will, of course, breed true. Thus, from a number of anthers, many new, original, true-breeding forms should arise. It must be apparent, however, that the technique is only of value with originally heterozygous material, either outbreeders or F_1 hybrids between inbred lines. As will be appreciated, the possibilities which could open up are immense, and successful research would mark the greatest step forward in plant breeding since Mendel's genetic concepts.

The general technique involved in pollen culture is to dissect anthers from flower buds at a stage when the division of *pollen mother cells* into true pollen grains has just started. This point in time can be related to the observed condition of the bud and, will be when, or just before, the petals emerge from the calyx. If anthers are removed and studied at the critical period, their contents should appear rather glutinous although not too liquid.

The outside of buds as well as needle and forceps should be sterilised (rapid immersion in methylated spirits is sufficient) before dissection. Anthers are transferred either to solidified agar with nutrients or into a liquid medium with sterile flasks or tubes, as described for raising bacterial cultures. Flasks should be kept under natural daylength at $20°C$ for as long as possible unless bacterial contamination occurs – when they are discarded. Anthers should be left in nutrient medium – under a wide range of environments (which should be accurately recorded for future references) – because plantlet formation may not occur until a long period has elapsed.

When plantlets form they should be allowed to grow in their agar medium but, if in a liquid solution, should be transferred to nutrient agar. When there is a danger that plantlets are becoming massed together, the group should be transplanted into sterile compost – which should never be allowed to dry out.

Since all plantlets or cell masses derived from the anthers will contain haploid tissue they must be treated – probably with colchicine – to provide the necessary diploid plants. In tobacco this treatment has been applied at a very early stage in plantlet development by floating anthers on a culture medium containing colchicine for 34 to 48 hours. The material was then returned to the earlier culture medium and eventually transferred to compost where normal diploid (homozygous) plants were produced.

Culture of Protoplasts

The second new potential for cultivar improvement without fertilisation would qualify for acceptance as science fiction. This is the prospect of producing previously unknown plant forms by fusing cells from one species with those of another. Cultures of cells of each species would be grown separately and then mixed together in certain proportions. Following treatment with enzymes, cell walls would be expected to disappear, allowing the cell contents to merge unimpeded. After the fusion of nuclei, cell walls should reform and further growth would be possible in nutrient culture. It has been found that fusion is facilitated by the addition of sodium nitrate to the culture solution.

Experiments on this form of 'vegetative hybridisation' are at present in an early stage, one of the most notable results being the creation of a hybrid Petunia, from protoplasts of two parent inbreds, which closely resembled the sexual hybrid between the same parents. If the difficulty of separating 'hybrid' from 'self' protoplast fusions in culture can be overcome, species which are totally impossibly to hybridise by nomal genetic means may one day be
combined to give economic or aesthetic forms which will help to revolutionise

horticulture. Without doubt, these forms will be genetically sterile so that their main value would be as ornamental, vegetatively propagated plants.

Mention must be made of a third futuristic technique which, so far, has been used most effectively on animal cells. This comes under the general heading of Genetic Engineering or Genetic Manipulation and uses biochemical techniques to incorporate genes or groups of genes from bacteria or simple life forms into a higher organism. Ironically, one of the major possibilities is that these 'foreign' genes (from what is regarded as a group of infective organisms), when introduced into the nucleus of higher plants, will confer disease resistance which could not be transferred in any other way.

Regardless of whether the old-established, or new and hardly-tried techniques will be most effective, plant breeding is likely to remain an exciting and rewarding discipline for many years.

Appendix 5

tables

Abridged from 'Statistical tables for biological, agricultural and medical research' by R.A. Fisher and F. Yates : Oliver and Boyd.

Table of X^2

Degrees of Freedom	0.99	0.98	0.95	0.90	0.50	0.10	0.05	0.02	0.01	0.001
1	0.000	0.001	0.004	0.015	0.455	2.71	3.84	5.41	6.64	10.83
2	0.020	0.040	0.103	0.211	1.386	4.61	5.99	7.82	9.21	13.82
3	0.115	0.185	0.352	0.584	2.366	6.25	7.82	9.84	11.34	16.27
4	0.297	0.429	0.711	1.064	3.357	7.78	9.49	11.67	13.28	18.47
5	0.554	0.752	1.145	1.610	4.351	9.24	11.07	13.39	15.09	20.52
6	0.872	1.134	1.635	2.204	5.35	10.65	12.59	15.03	16.81	22.46
7	1.239	1.564	2.167	2.833	6.35	12.02	14.07	16.62	18.48	24.32
8	1.646	2.032	2.733	3.490	7.34	13.36	15.51	18.17	20.09	26.13
9	2.088	2.532	3.325	4.168	8.34	14.68	16.92	19.68	21.67	27.88
10	2.558	3.059	3.940	4.865	9.34	15.99	18.31	21.16	23.21	29.59
11	3.05	3.61	4.57	5.58	10.34	17.28	19.68	22.62	24.73	31.26
12	3.57	4.18	5.23	6.30	11.34	18.55	21.03	24.05	26.22	32.91
13	4.11	4.76	5.89	7.04	12.34	19.81	22.36	25.47	27.69	34.53
14	4.66	5.37	6.57	7.79	13.34	21.06	23.69	26.87	29.14	36.12
15	5.23	5.99	7.26	8.55	14.34	22.31	25.00	28.26	30.58	37.70
16	5.81	6.61	7.96	9.31	15.34	23.54	26.30	29.63	32.00	39.25
17	6.41	7.26	8.67	10.09	16.34	24.77	27.59	31.00	33.41	40.79
18	7.02	7.91	9.39	10.87	17.34	25.99	28.87	32.35	34.81	42.31
19	7.63	8.57	10.12	11.65	18.34	27.20	30.14	33.69	36.19	43.82
20	8.26	9.24	10.85	12.44	19.34	28.41	31.41	35.02	37.57	45.32
21	8.90	9.91	11.59	13.34	20.34	29.61	32.67	36.34	38.93	46.80
22	9.54	10.60	12.34	14.04	21.34	30.81	33.92	37.66	40.29	48.27
23	10.20	11.29	13.09	14.85	22.34	32.01	35.17	38.97	41.64	49.73
24	10.86	11.99	13.85	15.66	23.34	33.20	36.42	40.27	42.98	51.18
25	11.52	12.70	14.61	16.47	24.34	34.38	37.65	41.57	44.31	52.62
26	12.20	13.41	15.38	17.29	25.34	35.56	38.89	42.86	45.64	54.05
27	12.88	14.12	16.15	18.11	26.34	36.74	40.11	44.14	46.96	55.48
28	13.56	14.85	16.93	18.94	27.34	37.92	41.34	45.42	48.28	56.89
29	14.26	15.57	17.71	19.77	28.34	39.09	42.56	46.69	49.59	58.30
30	14.95	16.31	18.49	20.60	29.34	40.26	43.77	47.96	50.89	59.70

Table of 't'

Degrees of Freedom for error	t				
	0.10	0.05	0.02	0.01	0.001
1	6.31	12.71	31.82	63.66	636.62
2	2.92	4.30	6.97	9.93	31.60
3	2.35	3.18	4.54	5.84	12.94
4	2.13	2.78	3.75	4.60	8.61
5	2.02	2.57	3.37	4.03	6.86
6	1.94	2.45	3.14	3.71	5.96
7	1.90	2.37	3.00	3.50	5.41
8	1.86	2.31	2.90	3.36	5.04
9	1.83	2.26	2.82	3.25	4.78
10	1.81	2.23	2.76	3.17	4.59
11	1.80	2.20	2.72	3.11	4.44
12	1.78	2.18	2.68	3.06	4.32
13	1.77	2.16	2.65	3.01	4.22
14	1.76	2.15	2.62	2.98	4.14
15	1.75	2.13	2.60	2.95	4.07
16	1.75	2.12	2.58	2.92	4.02
17	1.74	2.11	2.57	2.90	3.97
18	1.73	2.10	2.55	2.88	3.92
19	1.73	2.09	2.54	2.86	3.88
20	1.73	2.09	2.53	2.85	3.85
21	1.72	2.08	2.52	2.83	3.82
22	1.72	2.07	2.51	2.82	3.79
23	1.71	2.07	2.50	2.81	3.77
24	1.71	2.06	2.49	2.80	3.75
25	1.71	2.06	2.48	2.79	3.73
26	1.71	2.06	2.48	2.78	3.71
27	1.70	2.05	2.47	2.77	3.69
28	1.70	2.05	2.47	2.76	3.67
29	1.70	2.04	2.46	2.76	3.66
30	1.70	2.04	2.46	2.75	3.65
40	1.68	2.02	2.42	2.70	3.55
60	1.67	2.00	2.39	2.66	3.46
120	1.66	1.98	2.36	2.62	3.37
	1.65	1.96	2.33	2.58	3.29

Table of Variance ratio

N_1 (Treatments)					0.05 Significance Level				
N_2 (error)	1	2	3	4	5	6	12	24	∞
1	164.4	199.5	215.7	224.6	230.2	234.0	234.9	249.0	254.3
2	18.5	19.2	19.2	19.3	19.3	19.3	19.4	19.5	19.5
3	10.1	9.6	9.3	9.1	9.0	8.9	8.7	8.6	8.5
4	7.7	6.9	6.6	6.4	6.3	6.2	5.9	5.8	5.6
5	6.6	5.8	5.4	5.2	5.1	5.0	4.7	4.5	4.4

Table of Variance ratio

N₁ (Treatments)							0.05 Significance Level		
N₂ (error)	1	2	3	4	5	6	12	24	∞
6	6.0	5.1	4.8	4.5	4.4	4.3	4.0	3.8	3.7
7	5.6	4.7	4.4	4.1	4.0	3.9	3.6	3.4	3.2
8	5.3	4.5	4.1	3.8	3.7	3.6	3.3	3.1	2.9
9	5.1	4.3	3.9	3.6	3.5	3.4	3.1	2.9	2.7
10	5.0	4.1	3.7	3.5	3.3	3.2	2.9	2.7	2.5
11	4.8	4.0	3.6	3.4	3.2	3.1	2.8	2.6	2.4
12	4.8	3.9	3.5	3.3	3.1	3.0	2.7	2.5	2.3
13	4.7	3.8	3.4	3.2	3.0	2.9	2.6	2.4	2.2
14	4.6	3.7	3.3	3.1	3.0	2.9	2.5	2.3	2.1
15	4.5	3.7	3.3	3.1	2.9	2.8	2.5	2.3	2.1
16	4.5	3.6	3.2	3.0	2.9	2.7	2.4	2.2	2.0
17	4.5	3.6	3.2	3.0	2.8	2.7	2.4	2.2	2.0
18	4.4	3.6	3.2	2.9	2.8	2.7	2.3	2.1	1.9
19	4.4	3.5	3.1	2.9	2.7	2.6	2.3	2.1	1.9
20	4.4	3.5	3.1	2.9	2.7	2.6	2.3	2.1	1.8
22	4.3	3.4	3.1	2.8	2.7	2.6	2.2	2.0	1.8
24	4.3	3.4	3.0	2.8	2.6	2.5	2.2	2.0	1.7
26	4.2	3.4	3.0	2.7	2.6	2.5	2.2	2.0	1.7
28	4.2	3.3	3.0	2.7	2.6	2.4	2.1	1.9	1.7
30	4.2	3.3	2.9	2.7	2.5	2.4	2.1	1.9	1.6
40	4.1	3.2	2.9	2.6	2.5	2.3	2.0	1.8	1.5
60	4.0	3.2	2.8	2.5	2.4	2.3	1.9	1.7	1.4
120	3.9	3.1	2.7	2.5	2.3	2.2	1.8	1.6	1.3
	3.8	3.0	2.6	2.4	2.2	2.1	1.8	1.5	1.0

Table of Variance ratio

					0.01 Significance Level					
	1	2	3	4	5	6	8	12	24	∞
1	4052	4999	5403	5625	5764	5859	5981	6106	6234	6366
2	98.5	99.0	99.2	99.3	99.3	99.4	99.3	99.4	99.5	99.5
3	34.1	30.8	29.5	28.7	28.2	27.9	27.5	27.1	26.6	26.1
4	21.2	18.0	16.7	16.0	15.5	15.2	14.8	14.4	13.9	13.5
5	16.3	13.3	12.1	11.4	11.0	10.7	10.3	9.9	9.5	9.0
6	13.7	10.9	9.8	9.2	8.8	8.5	8.1	7.7	7.3	6.9
7	12.3	9.6	8.5	7.9	7.5	7.2	6.8	6.5	6.1	5.7
8	11.3	8.7	7.6	7.0	6.6	6.4	6.0	5.7	5.3	4.9
9	10.6	8.0	7.0	6.4	6.1	5.8	5.5	5.1	4.7	4.3
10	10.0	7.6	6.6	6.0	5.6	5.4	5.1	4.7	4.3	3.9
11	9.7	7.2	6.2	5.7	5.3	5.1	4.7	4.4	4.0	3.6
12	9.3	6.9	6.0	5.4	5.1	4.8	4.5	4.2	3.8	3.4
13	9.1	6.7	5.7	5.2	4.9	4.6	4.3	4.0	3.6	3.2
14	8.9	6.5	5.6	5.0	4.7	4.5	4.1	3.8	3.4	3.0
15	8.7	6.4	5.4	4.9	4.6	4.3	4.0	3.7	3.3	2.9
16	8.5	6.2	5.3	4.8	4.4	4.2	3.9	3.6	3.2	2.8
17	8.4	6.1	5.2	4.7	4.3	4.1	3.8	3.5	3.1	2.7
18	8.3	6.0	5.1	4.6	4.3	4.0	3.7	3.4	3.0	2.6
19	8.2	5.9	5.0	4.5	4.2	3.9	3.6	3.3	2.9	2.5
20	8.1	5.9	4.9	4.4	4.1	3.9	3.6	3.2	2.9	2.4

Table of Variance ratio

	1	2	3	4	5	6	8	12	24	∞
					0.01 Significance Level					
22	7.9	5.7	4.8	4.3	4.0	3.8	3.5	3.1	2.8	2.3
24	7.8	5.6	4.7	4.2	3.9	3.7	3.3	3.0	2.7	2.2
26	7.7	5.5	4.6	4.1	3.8	3.6	3.3	3.0	2.6	2.1
28	7.6	5.5	4.6	4.1	3.8	3.5	3.2	2.9	2.5	2.1
30	7.6	5.4	4.5	4.0	3.7	3.5	3.2	2.8	2.5	2.0
40	7.3	5.2	4.3	3.8	3.5	3.3	3.0	2.7	2.3	1.8
60	7.1	5.0	4.1	3.7	3.3	3.1	2.8	2.5	2.1	1.6
120	6.9	4.8	4.0	3.5	3.2	3.0	2.7	2.3	2.0	1.4
	6.6	4.6	3.8	3.3	3.0	2.8	2.5	2.2	1.8	1.0

TABLE OF THE CORRELATION COEFFICIENT (r)

Degrees of Freedom	0.10	0.05	0.02	0.01	0.001
1	.988	.997	.999	1.000	1.000
2	.900	.950	.980	.990	.999
3	.805	.878	.934	.959	.992
4	.729	.811	.882	.917	.974
5	.669	.754	.833	.874	.951
6	.621	.707	.789	.834	.925
7	.582	.666	.750	.798	.898
8	.549	.632	.716	.765	.872
9	.521	.602	.685	.735	.847
10	.497	.576	.658	.708	.823
11	.476	.553	.634	.684	.801
12	.457	.532	.612	.661	.780
13	.441	.514	.592	.641	.760
14	.426	.497	.574	.623	.742
15	.412	.482	.558	.606	.725
16	.400	.468	.543	.590	.708
17	.389	.456	.528	.575	.693
18	.378	.444	.516	.561	.679
19	.369	.433	.503	.549	.665
20	.360	.423	.492	.537	.652
25	.323	.381	.445	.487	.597
30	.296	.349	.409	.449	.554
35	.275	.325	.381	.418	.519
40	.257	.304	.358	.393	.490
45	.243	.287	.338	.372	.465
50	.231	.273	.322	.354	.443
60	.211	.250	.295	.325	.408
70	.195	.232	.274	.302	.380
80	.183	.217	.256	.283	.357
90	.173	.205	.242	.267	.337
100	.164	.195	.230	.254	.321

Glossary of Genetic Terms

Adaptation. The relationship of a plant to its environment – such as the positioning of male and female organs in flowers which are pollinated by insects.

Adventitious growth. The 'eruption' of new growth from surface areas where natural buds are absent – as from the base of *Brassica* stems or the cut surfaces of tomato plants.

Alleles. Components of a single gene which are present in at least two forms (dominant and recessive), and which are responsible for determining heritable characteristics.

Allopolyploids (Amphidiploids). Plants which bear chromosome sets from at least two parents of different species and which owe their fertility to the doubling of the basic chromosome complement. e.g. swede (4x), from a cross between turnip and rape (both 2x).

Anthers. The pollen-bearing structures which, supported by the filaments, form the *stamens* within every flower.

Anthesis. The release of pollen from the anthers.

Apomixis. Seed formation without fertilisation, often stimulated by the presence of foreign pollen. In heterozygous plants, limited gene recombination may occur, thus allowing segregation within the apomictic progeny.

Asexual reproduction. Production of the next generation by vegetative tissue (e.g. Dahlia tubers) instead of by seed.

Autopolyploids. Plants in which the basic chromosome number (x) has been increased in complete sets over and above the diploid chromosome number. e.g. autotetraploids (4x).

Axillary buds. Buds of new tissue which arise in the axils (the junction between leaf and main stem) of the leaves – most clearly exemplified by the 'buttons' of Brussels sprout.

Backcrossing. The cross of a hybrid plant to one of its parents. Recurrent backcrossing continues the back-cross programme to the same parental type for a number of generations with the object of transferring a desirable character into a standard genotype.

Bifurcate. Splitting open at the tip (as applied to stigmas).

Bracts. Leafy growths below the true flower, often highly coloured as for Poinsettia. In cauliflower, protruding through the edible 'curd'.

Bud pollination. The application of pollen to the stigma of an immature flower by splitting the bud to expose the reproductive organs. This technique is most commonly adopted when producing selfed seed from self-incompatible (in the mature-flower stage) plants.

Calyx. The ring of flower segments surrounding the true petals of a flower.

Usually similar in colour to the vegetative plants but can be coloured as in Salvia.

Capsule. Mature ovary containing numerous loose seeds as for poppy or Lychnis.

Cell. Small unit containing nucleus and cytoplasm which, in combination with numerous others, comprises the complete organism. Certain cells of limited function lack a nucleus.

Centromere. An 'inert' portion of chromosome which appears to control the movement of chromosomes and chromatids during cell division.

Chiasma. The point of exchange of paired chromatids at the first meiotic division.

Chimaera. A mixture of cellular tissues within the plant, often exhibited as patches of white or yellow against the normal green due to absence of chloroplasts.

Chloroplast. Cellular plastid containing chlorophyll which converts sunlight into usable energy.

Chromatid. One part of a longitudinally dividing chromosome.

Chromosomes. The structures within a nucleus (being characteristic in number for each species) which carry the genes in linear order.

Cleistogamy. Fertilisation of the flower by self-pollination before it has opened.

Clone. A group of organisms derived by vegetative, rather than sexual means.

Convergent improvement. A breeding technique whereby a number of genotypes contribute to the eventual cultivar.

Cotyledons. The protective 'seed-leaves' surrounding the embryo which nourish it during germination.

Crossing over. The exchange of paired chromatid segments in meiosis.

Cytoplasm. Extra-nuclear substance which fills each cell and comprises a minute amount of genetic material.

Diallel cross. A crossing programme in which each parent or a group is crossed with every other member of that group.

Dioecious. Separation of the sexes to give only male or only female plants.

Diploid. A plant having twice the basic number of chromosomes, commonly shown as 2x.

Dominant allele. That part of a gene which exhibits its characteristics when paired with its recessive allele in a heterozygote.

Double cross. A technique most commonly used in maize breeding whereby the commercial F_1 hybrid is produced by crossing together two other F_1 hybrids.

Emasculation. Removal of the anthers, usually from the flower bud.

Embryo. Fertilised ovule.

Environment. The normal growing conditions to which a plant must respond.

Epistasis. Orders of dominance of multiple alleles or, interaction between alleles where expression of a character is affected by the strengths of alleles at different loci.

F_1. The first generation of a cross.

F_1 hybrid. Commonly accepted as being the commercial seed resulting from a cross between two highly selected inbred lines.

F_2. The progeny from selfed or inter-pollinated F_1 plants.

Fecundity. The reproductive ability of a plant compared with its potential for seed production.

Fertility. The ability to produce functional seeds.

Fertilisation. The fusion of nuclei from male and female gametes.

Filament. Stalk on which the anther is attached.

Gamete. Egg cell or pollen grain, formed after meiotic division.

175

Gene. The unit of inheritance, borne (with others) upon the chromosome.

Genotype. The genetic constitution of an individual.

Haploid. The basic chromosome number for the species (x) as in gametes of a diploid (2x) plant.

Hermaphrodite. Both sexes present within the same flower.

Heterosis. Extreme vigour as shown by F₁ hybrids.

Heterozygote. A plant bearing both dominant and ressive alleles for a particular character. As for cross-pollinated species or cultivars.

Homozygote. A plant having the same alleles at each locus so that there can be no genetic segregation. As applied to self-pollinated species or cultivars.

Hybrid. The product of a cross between genetically dissimilar parents.

Immunity. The highest level of resistance to disease.

Inbred. Plant resulting from self-fertilisation of previous generations.

Inbreeding. The act of fertilising a plant with its own pollen.

Isolation. Separation of plants from one another in order to avoid cross-contamination.

Line. A group of closely related plants which have been derived from pollination of a single plant or from pollination of a small number of plants, usually having genetic or morphological relationships.

Linkage. Association of characters due to the proximity of their controlling genes upon the chromosome.

Locus. The position of a gene upon its chromosome.

Male-sterility. Lack of or non-release of pollen in normally hermaphrodite plants.

Mass-pollination. Random cross-pollination amongst a group of selected individuals.

Mass-selection. Selection of a number of individuals with the intention of producing progeny by mass-pollination.

Meiosis. Process of cell division in anthers and ovary during which there is an exchange of genetic material, and after which the pollen grains and ovules form, bearing half the chromosome number of the mother-plant.

Mitosis. Division of the cell nucleus to form two identical nuclei.

Modifiers. Genes which modify the expression of other (usually major) genes.

Monoecious. Male and female flowers formed separately on the same plant.

Mutation. An unexpected, heritable, change in the function of a gene.

Outbreeder. Plant, cultivar or species which is normally cross-pollinated (outcrossed).

Parthenogenesis. Development of a fruit without fertilisation of its ovules (e.g. cucumber).

Phenotype. External appearance of an individual which may or may not reflect its genotype.

Polygene. A gene having very limited effects but segregating in a Mendelian manner.

Progeny. Offspring of (usually) a single plant.

Progeny-test. Assessment of the value of a parent through the performance of its progeny.

Protandry. Maturation of the anthers before the stigma becomes receptive.

Protogyny. Stigma in a receptive state before the anthers have matured.

Pure-line. A completely homozygous line, normally maintained by self-fertilisation.

Qualitative characters. Characters showing discontinuous variation.

Quantitative characters. Characters showing continuous variation, being additive in effect.

Recessive allele. That part of a gene which expresses itself only when homozygous, being masked by its dominant allele in a heterozygote.

Reciprocal cross. A cross-pollination made in the opposite direction from the initial cross.

Recombination. New combinations of genes expressed in the segregating progenies from crosses between different genotypes.

Recurrent backcross. Further crosses of successive generations to the common, or backcross, parent.

Rogue. An unwanted or atypical plant which is removed from a breeding line. Usually more evident when the breeding line has almost achieved homozygosity or is being multiplied for seed.

Selection. Retention of desirable individuals in a plant population. Usually practised in the early stages of a breeding programme.

Self-fertilisation (Selfing). Fusion of male and female gametes after pollination between flowers of the same plant.

Self-incompatibility. The inability of the mature flower to set selfed seed.

Self-incompatibility (gametophytic). Non-formation of selfed seed due to the presence of similar S alleles in pollen and style.

Self-incompatibility (sporophytic). Non-formation of selfed seed due to antagonistic reactions between self-pollen (which has the genetic constitution of the parent plant) and the stigmatic region.

Sporophyte. The genetic form resulting from fusion of gametes.

Synthetic cultivar. A cultivar which has been produced by allowing inter-pollination of a known number of genotypes which have been shown to combine well with one another.

Tetraploid. An organism with four sets of chromosomes (4x) Hexaploid = 6 sets, octoploid = 8 sets.

Triploid. An organism with three sets of chromosomes (3x), usually highly infertile.

Bibliography

Text books

Allard, R.W. 1966. Principles of Plant Breeding. Wiley, N. York and London.
Brownlee, K.A. 1949. Industrial Experimentation. H.M.S.O.
Darlington, C.D. and Wylie, A.P. 1955. Chromosome Atlas of cultivated plants. George Allen and Unwin.
Kempthorne, G. 1957. An introduction to genetic statistics. Wiley, N. York and London.
Lerner, I.M. 1954. Genetic Homeostasis. Wiley, N. York and London.
Mather, K. 1949. Biometrical genetics. Methuen, London.
Russell, G.E. 1978. Plant Breeding for pest and disease resistance. Butterworth, London.
Williams, W. 1964. Genetical Principles and Plant Breeding. Blackwell, Oxford.
Wishart, J. 1940. Field trials: Their layout and statistical analysis. C.A.B. Cambridge.

References in text

Aziz Al-Yasiri, S.A. and Coyne, D.P. 1966. Interspecific hybridisation in the genus *Phaseolus*. Crop Sci. 6: 59-61.

Bemis, W.P. and Kedar, N. 1961. J. Hered 171-178.

Buishand, T.J. 1956. The crossing of beans (*Phaseolus* spp). Euphytica 5: 41-50.

Carlton, B.C. and Paterson, C.E. 1963. Breeding carrots for sugar and dry matter content. Proc. Amer. Soc. Hort. Sci. 82: 332-40.

Chedd, G. 1971. The new botanists. New Scientist. 50: 262-264.

Coffin, J.L. and Harney, P.M. 1978. Intersubgeneric crosses within the genus Pelargonium. Euphytica 27: 567-576.

Coyne, D.P. 1964. Species hybridisation in Phaseolus. J. Hered. 55: 5-6.

Coyne, D.P. and Schuster, M.L. 1979. Bacterial diseases of legumes. Ann. Rept. Bean. Improv. Coop. 22: 21-22.

Daker, M.G. 1969. Pelargonium 'Kleine Liebling' – a most unusual cultivar. Jour R.H.S. 94: 353-354.

East, E.M. and Park, J.B. 1917. Studies on self-sterility I. The behaviour of self-sterile plants. Genetics 2: 505-609.

Ellison, J.H. and Schermerhorn, L.G. 1958. Selecting superior asparagus plants on the basis of earliness. Proc. Amer. Soc. Hort. Sci. 72: 353-359.

Emsweller, S.L., Asen, S. and Uhring, J. 1962. Lilium speciosum x Lilium auratum. Lily YB N. Am. Lily Soc. 15: 7-15.

Hayase, O. 1961. Utilisation of bud pollination in obtaining interspecific hybrids of Cucurbita pepo x C. maxima. Jap. J. Breeding 11: 277-284.

Hayase, O. 1963. Flower ages and reciprocal cross-compatibility in C. pepo, C. moschata and C. maxima. Jap. J. Breeding 13: 159-167.

Honma, S. 1956.A bean interspecific hybrid. J. Hered. 47: 217-220.

Honma, S. and Heeckt, O. 1958. Bean interspecific hybrid involving Phaseolus coccineus x Ph. lunatus. Proc. Amer. Soc. Hort. Sci. 72: 360-364.

Honma, S. 1959. A method for celery hybridisation. Proc. Amer. Soc. Hort. Sci. 73: 345-348.

Jinks, J.L. 1954. The analysis of continuous variation in a diallel cross of Nicotiana rustica varieties. Genetics 39: 767-788.

Johnson, A.G., Brenda Adams and Janet Cotton. 1970. Practical studies on bud-pollination of Brussels sprouts. Hort. Res. 10: 34-39.

Jones, H.A. and Clarke, A.E. 1943. Inheritance of male-sterility in the onion and the production of hybrid seed. Proc. Amer. Soc. Hort. Sci. 43: 189-194.

Kho, Y.O. and Baer, J. 1971. An investigation into the cause of sterility in double flowered freesia varieties and the possibility of restoring fertility Euphytica 20: 493-497.

Kooistra, E. 1967. Femaleness in breeding glasshouse cucumbers Mededeling 269. I.V.T. Wageningen 1-17.

Kroh, M. 1962. Vergleichende untersuchungen an Phaseolus coccineus – Selbstungen und Kreuzungen zwischen Ph. vulgaris und Ph. coccineus. Z. Pflanzenz 201-216.

Mainlane, G.B. 1951. J. Heredity p.237.

McNaughton, I.H. 1963. The scope and problems involved in synthesising new amphidiploid and autotetraploid fodder brassicas in the group B. Napus. L., B. campestris L. and B. oleracea L. Ann. Rep. Scot. Pl. Br. Sta. 1-21.

Mَer, Q.P. van der and Bennekom, J.L. van. 1971. Frequencies of genetical factors determining male sterility in Onion (Allium cepa L.) and their significance for the breeding of hybrids. Euphytica 20: 51-56.

Murabaa, A.I.M. el. 1957. Factors affecting seed set in Brussels sprout, radish and cyclamen. Mededelingen 168. L.V.T. Wageningen.

Nakanishii, T. Esashi, Y. and Hinata, K. 1969. Control of self-incompatibility by CO_2 gas in Brassica. Pl. and Cell Phys. 10: 925-927.

Power, J.B., Cummins, S.E. and Cocking, E.C. 1970. Fusion of isolated plant protoplasts Nature 225: 1016-1018.

Roggen, H.P.J.R. and van Dijk, A.J. 1972. Breaking incompatibility of Brassica oleracea L. by steel brush pollination. Euphytica 21: 424-425.

Roggen, H.P.J.R. and van Dijk, A.J. 1976. 'Thermally aided pollination' – a new method of breaking self-incompatibility in B. oleracea. L. Euphytica 25: 643-646.

Rudorf, W. 1954. Neue Beobachtungen an Bastarden von Phaseolus vulgaris L x Phaseolus multiflorus Lam. und Ph. multiflorus x Ph. vulgaris. Proc. 9th Int. Congr. Genet. 844-845.

Sampson, D.R. 1956. The genetics of self- and cross-incompatibility in Brassica oleracea. Genetics 42: 253-263.

Smartt, J. 1970. Interspecific hybridisation between cultivated American species of the genus Phaseolus. Euphytica 19: 480-489.

Smith, P.G. and Heiser, C.B. 1957. Breeding behaviour of cultivated peppers. Proc. Amer. Hort. Sci. 70: 286-290.

Sparnaaij, L.D., Kho, Y.O. and Baer, J. 1968. Investigations on seed production in tetraploid Freesias. Euphytica 17: 289-297.

Stebbins, G.L. 1957. Self-fertilisation and population variability in the higher plants. Amer. Nat. 91: 337-354.

Thomas, H. 1964. Investigations into the inter-relationships of Phaseolus vulgaris L. and P. coccineus Lan. Genetics 35: 59-74.

Verkerk, K. 1954. The influence of low temperature on flower initiation and stem elongation in Brussels sprouts. Korinkl. Nederl. Akad. Wesenschappen. Amsterdam.

Vries, D.P. de and Lidwein A.M. Dubois. 1978. On the transmission of the yellow flower colour from Rosa foetida to recurrent flowering hybrid tea roses. Euphytica 27: 205-210.